THE FORMS OF MUSIC

Other books by the same author

THE FORMS OF MUSIC

By
DONALD FRANCIS TOVEY
SOMETIME REID PROFESSOR OF MUSIC IN THE
UNIVERSITY OF EDINBURGH

With an Editorial Preface by
HUBERT J. FOSS

LONDON
OXFORD UNIVERSITY PRESS

Oxford University Press, Ely House, London W.1

GLASGOW NEW YORK TORONTO MELBOURNE WELLINGTON
CAPE TOWN SALISBURY IBADAN NAIROBI LUSAKA ADDIS ABABA
BOMBAY CALCUTTA MADRAS KARACHI LAHORE DACCA
KUALA LUMPUR HONG KONG TOKYO

First published as
'Musical Articles from the Encyclopaedia Britannica'
1944
Reprinted 1945 and 1947
Reprinted under the present title 1957 and 1967

PRINTED IN GREAT BRITAIN

EDITORIAL PREFACE

THE desire to set down upon paper a comprehensive system of musical education was present in the mind of Donald Tovey for the greater part of his life. In 1896, when he was 21, he wrote in a letter to a friend that he had 'begun a great work "on the means of Expression in Music". . . . If ever I finish the thing, into print it shall go.' Thirty years later, he was talking about a series of four text-books on music. But into print neither the one scheme nor the other went: the final expression of his ideas on music was never written. It never could be written, because it was never final in the mind of that incessant discoverer in music. Nor was his method of writing that of finality.

The nearest point to finality which Tovey ever reached in his expression of a formal philosophy in music is to be found in the articles on 'technique and aesthetics of music' (as he called them himself in the list of his writings supplied to *Who's Who*) which he contributed to the *Encyclopaedia Britannica*. Those articles, written from 1906 onwards for the eleventh edition of the *Encyclopaedia*, and revised again, almost rewritten, for the fourteenth edition in 1929, were necessarily cast in the imposed form of treatises under word-headings. Yet they coalesce very firmly into a clear and coherent testament, almost into a text-book of the art of music in its widest meaning. Like the Glossary to the *Essays in Musical Analysis*, the entries are unconnected, the whole comprehensive, and while not attempting completeness, afford the reader a wider range of musical thought and a fuller discussion of technical problems than most of the exhaustive and laborious theses now available.

Tovey himself set great store by these articles. They formed for him the basis of his teaching at the University of Edinburgh. They are the background to those fuller considerations of musical compositions which are his *Essays in Musical Analysis*. It was his own proposal that these articles should be gathered together into one volume, an idea expressed to me as long ago as 1926. Means were then taken towards the end of publishing, and it was agreed that Tovey should in his own time make any alterations or corrections necessary for the new method of presentation. But many other fresh and no doubt more important ideas and schemes came bubbling up into that wonderfully fertile brain, and nothing was done about the book of musical articles. I say more important because, though he was in life so fully occupied, it has now been found possible to publish these articles after the author's death.

This book contains all the articles which Tovey wrote for the

Encyclopaedia Britannica, as they now appear there, with the exception of one on ' Modern Music ' and the biographies. The book was set up from printed slips, and thus follows the text finally approved and corrected by the author. The very long musical examples are printed in full. In book form, a few minor alterations have been necessary, mostly in the excising of references, and the bringing of the 'printer's style' into line with that of Tovey's other books. An occasional slip in the musical examples has been corrected. We do not know what Tovey, an inveterate improver of his own works, might have done to these articles to-day, had he been alive to read them again in corrected proofs: we do know that they stand as he passed them for publication.

The alphabetical order of the key-words has, after much consideration, been retained. Those who argue that the general article ' Music ' should be printed first can, as many people will, read it out of order before the others. An index has been added.

Permission to reprint these articles as they stand has been kindly granted by the publishers of the *Encyclopaedia Britannica*, to whom also thanks are due for the facilities given towards the preparation of the book. The proofs have been read by Dr. Ernest Walker and Mr. R. C. Trevelyan, whose skilful assistance I gratefully acknowledge.

HUBERT J. FOSS

1943

CONTENTS

ARIA

ARIA, a term, equivalent to the English 'air', signifying a melody apart from the harmony, but especially a musical composition for a single voice or instrument, with an accompaniment of other voices or instruments.

The classical aria developed from the expansion of a single vocal melody, generally on the lines of what is known as binary form (*see* SONATA and SONATA FORMS). Accordingly, while the germs of aria form may be traceable in advanced examples of folk-song, the aria as a definite art-form could not exist before the middle of the seventeenth century, because the polyphony of the sixteenth century left no room for the development of melody for melody's sake. When at the beginning of the seventeenth century the Monodists (*see* HARMONY) dimly conceived the enormous possibilities latent in their new art of accompanying single voices by instruments, it was natural that for many years the mere suggestiveness and variety of their experiments should suffice, without coherent forms, to retain the attention of contemporary listeners. But, even at the outset, the most novel harmonies used with the most poignant rhetoric were not enough in themselves to satisfy the pioneers. Accordingly, Monteverdi's famous lament of the deserted Ariadne is one of many early examples that appeal to a rudimentary sense of form by making the last phrase identical with the first.

As instrumental music grew, and the classical sense of key became strong and consistent (in the hands of Alessandro Scarlatti), composers were driven to appeal to that sense of harmonically-solid melody which had asserted itself in folk-music before the history of harmonic music may be said to have begun.

By Scarlatti's time it was thoroughly established that an extended melody should normally modulate to the dominant after establishing its own key, and that the subsequent modulations should work through other related keys back to the tonic. Introduce the voice by an instrumental 'ritornello', containing the gist of the melody and recurring, in part or in whole, at every full close; and you have a form which can expand a melody so as to give ample scope both to the singer and to the accompanying players. The aria became the prototype of the CONCERTO (q.v.).

The addition of a middle section with a da capo results in the universal eighteenth-century da capo form of aria. The possibilities of variety are greater than the description might suggest. The voice may enter with a different theme from that of the ritornello; the ritornello may be stated in separate portions; the

ritornello may have its own contrast between solo and tutti instruments; the vocal material may combine with it contrapuntally,
and so on. All the arias and duets in Bach's B minor Mass and
Christmas Oratorio differ in these matters, and the differences
well repay analysis, being often subtly suggested by the sense of
the words. The middle section generally contributes no new
element, except that it avoids the tonic. Gluck, who swept away
the whole method as inherently anti-dramatic, points out, in the
preface to *Alceste*, that the middle section is generally perfunctory,
and that the sole object of the da capo is to enable the singer to
display new ornaments. Nevertheless, the classical (or Neapolitan) aria is a composition of considerable length, in a form which
cannot fail to be effective and coherent; and there is little cause
for wonder in the extent to which it dominated eighteenth-
century music.

The aria forms are profoundly influenced by the difference
between the sonata style and the style of Bach and Handel. But
the scale of the form is inevitably small, and in any opera an aria
is hardly possible except in a situation which is a tableau rather
than an action. Consequently there is no such difference between
the form of the classical operatic aria of Mozart and that of the
Handelian type as there is between sonata and suite music. The
scale, however, has become too large for the da capo, which was
in any case too rigid to survive in music designed to intensify a
dramatic situation instead of to distract attention from it. The
necessary change of style was so successfully achieved that, until
Wagner succeeded in devising music that moved absolutely *pari
passu* with his drama, the aria remained as the central formal
principle in dramatic music; and few things in artistic evolution
are more interesting than the extent to which Mozart's predeces-
sor, the great dramatic reformer Gluck, profited by the essential
resources of his pet aversion the aria style, when he had not only
purged it of what had become the stereotyped ideas of ritornellos and vocal flourishes, but animated it by the new sense of
dramatic climax to which the sonata style appealed.

In modern opera the aria is almost always out of place, and the
forms in which definite melodies nowadays appear are rather
those of the song in its limited sense as that of a poem in formal
stanzas all set to the same music. In other words, a song in a
modern opera tends to be something that would be sung even if
the drama had to be performed as a play without music, whereas
a classical aria would in non-musical drama be a soliloquy.

In the later works of Wagner those passages in which we can
successfully detach complete melodies from their context have,
one and all, dramatically the aspect of songs and not of solilo-
quies. Siegmund sings the song of Spring to his sister-bride;

Mime teaches Siegfried lessons of gratitude in nursery rhymes; and the whole story of the *Meistersinger* is a series of opportunities for song-singing. The distinctions and gradations between aria and song are of great aesthetic importance, but their history would carry us too far. The main distinction is obviously of the same importance as that between dramatic and lyric poetry.

The term 'aria form' is applied, generally most inaccurately, to all kinds of slow cantabile instrumental music of which the general design can be traced to the operatic aria. Mozart, for example, is very fond of slow movements in large binary form without development, and this is constantly called aria form, though the term ought certainly to be restricted to such examples as have some traits of the aria style, such as the first slow movement in the great Serenade in B flat. At all events, until writers on music have agreed to give the term some more accurate use, it is as well to avoid it and its cognate version, Lied form, altogether in speaking of instrumental music.

The air or aria in Bach's suites is a short binary movement in a flowing rhythm in not very slow common or duple time.

CANTATA

CANTATA (Italian for a song or story set to music), a vocal composition accompanied by instruments and generally containing more than one movement. In the sixteenth century, when all serious music was vocal, the term had no reason to exist, but with the rise of instrumental music in the seventeenth century cantatas began to exist under that name as soon as the instrumental art was definite enough to be embodied in sonatas. From the middle of the seventeenth till late in the eighteenth century a favourite form of Italian chamber music was the cantata for one or two solo voices, with accompaniment of harpsichord and perhaps a few other solo instruments. It consisted at first of a declamatory narrative or scene in recitative, held together by a primitive aria repeated at intervals. Fine examples may be found in the church music of Carissimi; and the English vocal solos of Purcell (such as 'Mad Tom' and 'Mad Bess') show the utmost that can be made of this archaic form. With the rise of the da capo aria the cantata became a group of two or three arias joined by recitative. Handel's numerous Italian duets and trios are examples on a rather large scale. His Latin motet *Silete Venti*, for soprano solo, shows the use of this form in Church music.

The Italian solo cantata soon became indistinguishable from a scene in an opera. In the same way the Church cantata, solo or choral, is indistinguishable from a small oratorio. This is equally evident in the two hundred Church cantatas of Bach or in the Chandos Anthems of Handel. Many of Bach's larger cantatas are actually called oratorios; and the *Christmas Oratorio* is a collection of six Church cantatas originally intended for performance on six different days, though together forming as complete an artistic whole as any classical oratorio.

Bach's Church cantatas formed part of a Church service, well-organized for a coherent musical scheme. Many of Bach's greatest cantatas begin with an elaborate chorus followed by a couple of arias and recitatives, and end with a plain chorale. Such a scheme is pointless in the concert-room, but it is magnificently appropriate to the Lutheran Church service. The text was based upon the gospel or lessons for the day; unless the cantata was short, the sermon probably took place after the first chorus or one of the arias, and the congregation joined in the final chorale. Thus the unity of the service was the unity of the music; and, in the cases where all the movements of the cantata were founded on one and the same chorale tune, this unity has never been equalled, except by those sixteenth-century masses and motets which are

4

founded upon the Gregorian tones of the festival to. which they are written. In modern times the term cantata is applied almost exclusively to choral, as distinguished from solo, vocal music. It is also used as equivalent to 'secular oratorio'.

It is possible to recognize as a distinct artistic type that kind of early nineteenth-century cantata in which the chorus is the vehicle for music more lyric and song-like than the oratorio style, though at the same time not excluding the possibility of a brilliant climax in the shape of a light order of fugue. Beethoven's *Glorreiche Augenblick* is a brilliant 'pot-boiler' in this style; Weber's *Jubel-Cantate* is a typical specimen, and Mendelssohn's *Walpurgisnacht* is the *locus classicus*. Mendelssohn's 'symphony cantata', the *Lobgesang* (Hymn of Praise), is a hybrid work, partly in the oratorio style. It is preceded by three symphonic movements, a device avowedly suggested by Beethoven's Ninth Symphony; but the analogy is not accurate, as Beethoven's work is a symphony of which the fourth movement is a choral finale of essentially single design, whereas Mendelssohn's 'symphony cantata' is a cantata with a triple symphonic prelude.

The full lyric possibilities of a string of choral songs were realized at last by Brahms in his *Rinaldo*, set to a text which Goethe wrote at the same time as he wrote that of the *Walpurgisnacht*. The point of Brahms's only experiment in this *genre* has been missed by critics who expected so voluminous a work to be on more elaborate lines. But it represents a definite art-form. The remaining types of cantata (beginning with Beethoven's *Meeresstille*, and including most of Brahms's and many notable English small choral works) are merely so many different ways of setting to choral music a poem which is just too long to be comprised in one movement.

CHAMBER MUSIC

CHAMBER MUSIC, a term obviously denoting music for performance in a room of a private house, has acquired the special meaning of large works in the sonata style for a group of individual instruments; although it may be borne in mind that in the early eighteenth-century vocal cantatas for solo voices were at least as important as purely instrumental compositions.

One feature of immaturity is common to all the chamber music, vocal and instrumental, between and including Corelli and Bach; namely, that the harmonic background is left to the harpsichord player to extemporize from the indications given by a figured bass (q.v.). Even works with elaborate obbligato harpsichord parts have passages which presuppose this extempore element. Only the concerted music of the French clavecinists Couperin and Rameau consistently leaves nothing undetermined.

Works with Continuo.—The forms of chamber music are those of music at large, and it has no independent history. But it is very definite in the principles which determine its texture; and the element of the figured bass or continuo puts the earlier chamber music into an altogether different category from the art which arose with Haydn. As is shown in the articles INSTRUMENTATION, MUSIC, and SONATA FORMS, the sonata style of Haydn and Mozart irrevocably brought the dramatic element into music; but in addition to this, it brought alike into chamber music and orchestral music a fundamental principle that all players in an instrumental combination should between them provide their own harmonic background without the aid of a continuo part.

The disappearance of the continuo in later chamber music marks the realization of the central classical idea of the style, according to which there is no part in the ensemble left either indeterminate or in permanent subordination.

With its disappearance must also disappear the conception of the ensemble as a group of treble instruments over a firm bass, requiring a middle mass of harmony on an altogether remoter plane to hold them together. The middle part must be on the same plane as the others, and all must be as ready to provide the background as to carry on the main lines. There were no string quartets in the continuo period; and, what is more significant, the viola parts in the orchestra of Bach and Handel are, except when accompanying a choral fugue, neither interesting in themselves nor sufficient to fill up the gap between violins and bass. Their function is to reinforce the continuo without going a step out of their way to make the harmony always complete.

6

Haydn's first Quartets.—Rightly understood and performed, the result is perfectly mature; but it is worlds away from the crudest of Haydn's first Quartets, which, written before the death of Handel, show the criterion of self-sufficiency firmly established so that there is no room for a continuo. The first string quartets are not clearly distinguished from orchestral music; wind parts have been discovered for Haydn's op. 1, no. 5 and op. 2, no. 3, and Haydn throughout his life remained capable of occasionally forgetting that his quartet-violoncello was not supported by a double-bass. But it is fascinating to watch the steady emergence of Haydn's quartet-style from the matrix of orchestral habit. In the Quartets of op. 9 which he afterwards wished to regard as the beginning of his work, the four string parts are equally necessary and equally alive. They are not equally prominent; because the criterion is not polyphony but self-sufficiency for the purposes of this kind of music; and in this kind of music the normal place for melody is on the top.

In the very important six Quartets, op. 20, Haydn discovers the character of the violoncello as something more than a bass to the violins—you can hear him discover it in the fourth bar of op. 20, no. 1; and with this discovery all possibility of the use of a double-bass vanishes, though miscalculations occur in the latest quartets. Had Haydn been a great violoncellist his first quartets might have been as luxurious as the quintets of Boccherini, and he might have dallied longer in the bypaths of a style which tries to give each instrument in turn its display of solo-work. But Haydn's line of progress is steady and direct, and no document in the history of music is more important than his op. 20, with its three fugues (which secure autonomy and equality of parts by a return to the old polyphony), its passages of turn-about solo, its experiments in rich and special effects, and, most important of all, its achievements in quite normal quartet-writing such as pervades the remaining forty-odd quartets which end with his pathetic last fragment, op. 103.

Haydn's Pianoforte Trios also cover his whole career but they show, from first to last, no effort to achieve more than pianoforte sonatas with string accompaniment.

Mozart.—Mozart was an inveterate polyphonist by the time he was 12 years old, and the character of the viola, unnoticed by Haydn in his ripest quartets, is imaginatively realized in quartets written by Mozart at the age of 17. The point is not that the viola takes part in a more polyphonic style (though Mozart's early quartets are full of contrapuntal and canonic forms) but that the composer's imagination is attentive to the tone of the instrument in every note he writes for it.

Mozart's Pianoforte Trios, which are very insufficiently appreciated by historians and players, are perfect examples of independence of parts, no less than the two great Pianoforte Quartets (which should have been six but that the publisher cried off his bargain because of their difficulty) and the Quintet for pianoforte and wind instruments. The set of six great String Quartets (avowedly inspired by and affectionately dedicated to Haydn) contains some of the profoundest music outside Beethoven; and of the four remaining quartets, the last three, written for the King of Prussia, who was a good violoncellist, gave his majesty a grateful and prominent part and showed that Mozart's wit was able to maintain the full greatness of his style even when he was restricted to a lighter vein of sentiment.

His String Quintets are as great as the quartets. Mozart prefers a second viola as the fifth member; and the only case where he suggested a second violoncello was by way of substitute for the horn in a little quintet for the curious combination of one violin, two violas, violoncello, and horn. The combination of wind instruments with strings is a special problem the mention of which brings us back to reconsider the central idea of chamber music as now realized by Haydn and Mozart.

Vocal music has here dropped below the horizon. The human voice inevitably thrusts all instruments into the background; and we are now at the stage where the forces engaged in chamber music must be on planes sufficiently near to combine in one mental focus. A slight divergence of plane will give the mind pleasures analogous to those of stereoscopic vision. For example, the greatest masters of chamber music with pianoforte take pleasure in supporting heavy but incomplete pianoforte chords by the low notes of the violoncello: a procedure puzzling to self-centred pianoforte virtuosos, and never risked by composers who have not attained a pure style. Again, the clarinet, in the wonderful Quintets by Mozart (A major) and Brahms (B minor) does not and is not intended to blend with the strings, but it nowhere gives a more intense pleasure than where it behaves as an inner part exactly like the others. These works belong to the highest regions of the art.

Wind and Other Combinations.—The flute blends with nothing; even among other wind instruments it is like water-colour among oils. It accordingly plays a part in witty little works, such as Beethoven's Serenade for flute, violin, and viola (twice imitated by Reger), and Mozart's two Quartets with strings. The oboe, once not much less important in continuo chamber music than the flute (Handel confessed to 'writing like a devil for it' when he was a boy) requires other wind instruments to relieve the ear of its plaintive tone, though Mozart wrote a pretty little Quartet for it with strings, and Beethoven achieved a remarkable *tour de force* in an early Trio for two oboes and cor anglais. But the further consideration of wind instruments brings us again to the borderland regions of chamber music. What are the smallest forces that can make a coherent combination for chamber music; and at what point do the forces become too large to cohere?

The pianoforte, even when treated in Mozart's hard-pencil line-drawing style, provides a central mass of complete harmony that can absorb shocks and combine (*pace* the virtuoso player) with anything. The question begins to be interesting when we deal with the strings alone. Duets for two violins are obviously a *tour de force*, since their bass can never go below a contralto G. This *tour de force* is executed on a large scale with a mastery and euphony beyond praise by Spohr. Mozart, coming to the rescue of Michael Haydn, who was prevented by illness from completing a set of six commissioned by the Archbishop of Salzburg, wrote two for violin and viola, which profit greatly by the extra lower fifth, and which are written with great zest and a reckless disregard (justified by personal knowledge) of the chance that the Archbishop might detect their difference from the dutiful efforts of brother Michael.

Trios for two violins and any kind of bass but the viola are ominously suggestive of a return to, or non-emergence from, the continuo method; and indeed it may be doubted whether any Italian composer before Cherubini ever did quite emerge therefrom. Trios for violin, viola, and violoncello are a very different matter. They represent the problem of the string quartet intensified into a *tour de force*. Mozart's great example, the Divertimento in E flat, is in all its six movements on a scale and a plane of thought that its title vainly belies. It inspired Beethoven to one of his biggest early works, the Trio, op. 3; and the success of this encouraged Beethoven to write the three String Trios, op. 9, of which the first, in G major, and the third, in C minor, are bolder in conception and execution than even the largest of the six String Quartets, op. 18, and not less sonorous than any string quartet written before or since.

The string quartet represents the normal apparatus for a chamber music work of homogeneous tone. String quintets are usually produced in Mozart's way by doubling the viola. Doubling the violoncello, as in Schubert's great C major Quintet, produces a very rich tone and sets the first violoncello free to soar into the cantabile region without (as in other quintets and in quartets) depriving the ensemble of a deep bass. Sextets, for two violins, two violas, and two violoncellos, are represented in the two great works of Brahms. Octets for strings show signs of clotting into an orchestral style. Spohr hit upon the device of dividing the eight into antiphonal quartets; and his four double quartets are much nearer to the true style of chamber music than his string quartets, where his lower parts have the simplicity of early Haydn while the first violin plays a concerto above them. Mendelssohn in the wonderful Octet which he wrote at the age of 16, does not find Spohr's simple antiphonal scheme worth the trouble of specially grouping the players when he can use 255 different combinations of the eight without inquiring how they are seated.

As for the semi-orchestral borderland of septets and octets in which several wind instruments join and a double-bass adds depth without any normal capacity to rise into cantabile or solo work, this borderland (inhabited by Beethoven's Septet, Schubert's Octet, and many glorious serenades and divertimenti of Mozart) has a fascinating aesthetic of its own. Wind instruments by themselves are happiest in pairs, as their tones contrast too sharply otherwise to blend at all, though Reicha, who composed regularly for two hours before breakfast every morning, ground out over 100 quintets for flute, oboe, clarinet, horn, and bassoon, all admirably euphonious, if they are up to the sample passages quoted by him in his treatise on composition. It is unreasonable to blame Mozart's glorious Serenade for thirteen wind instruments for sounding like a military band; we ought rather to wish that a military band could sound like a Mozart serenade.

Modern Tendencies.—Nothing remains to be said about chamber music, classical or modern, apart from the general tendencies of the art. The exclusive prevalence of sonata form in the classics is a result of the fact that when several persons assemble to play together they prefer to make the most of their opportunity. Smaller works are liable to be overlooked; how otherwise can we account for the fact that most musicians do not realize the existence of three quiet minutes of the most delicate writing in Beethoven's third manner, the Quintet-Fugue, op. 137? A spirited Capriccio and a pretty Fugue by Mendelssohn have dropped out of sight for no other reason, while the Andante and Scherzo published with them and Schubert's Allegro in C minor have roused interest as fragments of full-sized works.

In modern times the sonata form no longer obstructs the view of other possibilities. The late Mr. W. W. Cobbett's prize competitions stimulated English composers to the production of fantasies in terse continuous-movement forms. Less important are the numerous experiments in the use of the human voice without words in an otherwise instrumental scheme. Nature responds cattishly to the pitchfork. Saint-Saëns has a charming manner which puts the trumpet on its best behaviour in his amusing Septet. The trombone and side-drums in the chamber music of Stravinsky will do well enough in a very smart house-party where all the conversation is carried on in an esoteric family slang and

the guests are expected to enjoy booby-traps. Very different is
the outlook of some of our younger masters such as Hindemith,
Jarnach, and others, whose renunciation of beauty was in itself
a youthfully romantic gesture, and was accompanied by endless
pains in securing adequate performance. The work of masterly
performers can indeed alone save the new ideas from being
swamped in a universal dullness which no external smartness can
long distinguish from that commemorated in the Dunciad.

CHORALE

CHORALE, a term used by English writers to indicate the hymn-tunes composed or adopted for use in church by the German reformers (Lat. *Choralis*). German writers, however, apply the terms 'Choral' and 'Choral-gesang', as Luther himself would have applied them, to any solemn melody used in the church. It is thus the equivalent of canto fermo; and the German rhymed versions of the biblical and other ancient canticles, such as the Magnificat and the Te Deum, are set to curious corruptions of the corresponding Gregorian tunes, which adaptations the composers of classical German music called chorales with no more scruple than they applied the name to tunes of secular origin, German or foreign. The peculiarity of German chorale-music, however, is not only that its use, and consequently much of its invention, arose in connexion with the Reformation, by which the liturgy of the church became 'understanded of the people', but also that it belongs to a musical epoch in which symmetry of melody and rhythm was beginning to assume artistic importance. The growing sense of form shown by some of Luther's own tunes (e.g. "Vom Himmel hoch, da komm' ich her) soon advanced, especially in the tunes of Crüger, beyond any that was shown by folk-music; and it provided a massive bulwark against the chaos that was threatening to swamp music on all sides at the beginning of the seventeenth century.

By Bach's time all the polyphonic instrumental and vocal art-forms of the eighteenth century were mature; and though he loved to derive the design as well as the details of a large movement from the shape of the chorale-tune on which it was based, he became quite independent of any aid from symmetry in the tune as raw material. The chorus of his Cantata *Jesus nun sei gepreiset* is one of the most perfectly designed and quite the longest of movements ever based upon a chorale-tune treated phrase by phrase. Yet the tune is one of the most intractable in the world, though its most unpromising portion is the basis of the most impressive feature in Bach's design (the slow middle section in triple time).

In recent times the great development of interest in folk-music, and the discovery of the unique importance of Bach's work, have combined to tempt writers on music to overestimate the distinctness of the art-forms based upon the German chorale. There is really nothing in these art-forms which is not continuous with the universal practice of writing counterpoint on a canto fermo. Thus Handel in his Italian and English works wrote no entire chorale movements, yet what is the passage in the 'Hallelujah' Chorus from 'the kingdom of this world' to the end, but a treatment of the second part of the chorale 'Wachet auf'? Again, to return to the sixteenth century, what are the hymns of Palestrina but figured chorales? In what way, except in the lack of symmetry in the Gregorian phrasing, do they differ from the contemporary setting by Orlando di Lasso, also a Roman Catholic, of the German chorale 'Vater unser im Himmelreich'? In later times the use of German chorales, as in Mendelssohn's oratorios and organ sonatas, has had rather the aspect of a revival than of a development; though the technique and spirit of Brahms's posthumous Organ Chorale-preludes is thoroughly modern and vital.

One of the most important, and practically the earliest, collection of chorales is that made by Luther and Johann Walther (1496–1570), the 'Enchiridion', published in 1524. Next in importance we may place the Genevan Psalter (1st edition, Strasbourg, 1542; final edition, 1562), which is now conclusively proved to be the work of Bourgeois. From this Sternhold and Hopkins borrowed extensively (1562). The Psalter of C. Goudimel (Paris, 1565) is another among many prominent collections showing the steps towards congregational singing, i.e. the restriction to 'note-against-note' counterpoint (sc. plain harmony), and, in twelve cases, the assigning of the melody to the treble instead of to the tenor. The first hymn-book in which this latter step was acted on throughout is Osiander's 'Geistliche Lieder . . . also gesetzt, das ein christliche Gemein durchaus mitsingen kann' (1586). But many of the finest and most famous tunes are of much later origin than any such collections. Several (e.g., 'Ich freue mich in dir') cannot be traced before Bach, and were very probably composed by him.

CONCERTO

CONCERTO, a term which appears as early as the beginning of the seventeenth century, at first with vague meanings, but soon acquiring a sense justified by its etymology (Lat. *concertus*, from *certare*, to strive; also confused with *concentus*), being applied chiefly to compositions in which unequal instrumental or vocal forces are brought into opposition.

Although by Bach's time the concerto as a purely instrumental form was thoroughly established, the term frequently appears in the autograph title-pages of his Church cantatas, even when the cantata contains no instrumental prelude. Indeed, so entirely does the actual concerto form, as Bach understands it, depend upon the opposition of masses of tone unequal in volume, with a compensating inequality in power of commanding attention, that Bach is able to rewrite an instrumental movement as a chorus without the least incongruity of style. The very title of his secular cantata, *Vereinigte Zwietracht der wechselnden Saiten* ('united contest of turn-about strings'), is a perfect definition of the earlier form of concerto grosso, in which the chief mass of the orchestra was opposed, not to a mere solo instrument, but to a small group called the concertino; unless, indeed, the whole work was for a large orchestral mass in which tutti passages alternate with passages in which the whole orchestra is dispersed in every possible kind of grouping.

But the special significance of this cantata is that its first chorus is arranged from the second movement of the first Brandenburg Concerto, and that, while the orchestral material is merely transposed and arranged for larger forces, the whole four-part chorus has been evolved from the solo part for a kit-violin (violino piccolo). This shows that the true relation between the opposed factors in a concerto depends not on volume of sound, but on power to command attention.

A conveniently isolated individual will command more attention than the crowd, whether in real life, drama, or instrumental music. But in music the human voice, with human words, will thrust any orchestral force into the background, whether the voice be individual or choral. The full chorus is the equivalent of the kit-violin and the kit-violin is the equivalent of the full chorus because both assert personality against the orchestra.

Hence the polyphonic concerto is fundamentally identical with the vocal aria, as matured by Alessandro Scarlatti. The orchestra is entrusted with a short pregnant summary or ritornello of the main contents of the movement, and the solo, or the groups corre-

sponding thereto, will either take up this material or first introduce new themes to be combined with it, and, in short, enter
into relations with the orchestra very like those between the
actor and the chorus in Greek drama. The polyphonic concerto,
the vocal aria, and the forms of many of Bach's choruses, even
including some that contain fugues, ought to be classed under
the head of ritornello forms. (*See* ARIA.) Many of Bach's larger
movements for solo instruments without orchestra will at once
reveal the proper lines of their interpretation in the light of
ritornello form. The harpsichord, no less than the organ, can
obviously imitate contrasts between solos and tuttis with excellent
effect.

In slow movements of concertos Bach uses the ground bass
(*see* VARIATIONS), diversified by changes of key (Clavier Concerto
in D minor); the more melodic types of binary form, sometimes
with the repeats ornamentally varied or inverted (Concerto for
three claviers in D minor, Concerto for clavier, flute, and violin
in A minor), are found besides aria-form on the aria scale. In
finales the rondo form (Violin Concerto in E major, Clavier
Concerto in F minor) and the binary form (third Brandenburg
Concerto) may be found.

When musical forms changed to those of the dramatic sonata
style, the problems of the concerto proved ridiculously easy to
ordinary musicians and became tasks of the highest interest to the
greatest composers. Bach's sons took important new steps.
Philipp Emanuel Bach developed a romantic rhetoric. Johann
Christian, the 'London' Bach, initiated the all-important method
of emphasizing a change of key so that it became a dramatic event
irreversible except by other dramatic developments. Mozart, as
a boy, modelled himself closely on Johann Christian Bach, and
by the time he was twenty was able to write concerto ritornellos
that gave the orchestra admirable opportunity for asserting itself
by the statement, in charmingly epigrammatic style, of some five
or six sharply contrasted themes, afterwards to be worked out
with additions by the solo, with the orchestra's cooperation and
intervention.

The problem changes rapidly as the scale of the composition
grows. On a large scale a too facile alternation between solo and
tutti produces forms too sectional for the high organization required in first movements; yet frequent alternation is evidently
necessary, as the solo is audible only above a very subdued
orchestral accompaniment, and it would be inartistic to confine
the orchestra to that function. Hence in the classical concerto the
ritornello is never abandoned, in spite of the enormous dimensions
to which the sonata style expanded it. Mendelssohn and most
later composers evidently see in it only a conventional impedi-

ment easily abandoned. Yet its absence reduces the whole style to a more theatrical and lighter art-form. Hence it is restored to its place, not only by Brahms in his four magnificent examples, but by Joachim in his Hungarian Concerto and by Elgar in his Violin Concerto. The danger in so long an orchestral prelude is that the work may for some minutes be indistinguishable from a symphony, and thus the entry of the solo may be unexpected without being inevitable. This will happen if the composer treats his tutti so like the exposition of a sonata movement as to make a deliberate transition from his first group of themes to a second group in a complementary key, even if the transition be only temporary—as in Beethoven's C minor Concerto. But Beethoven's C minor Concerto is the one which Spohr and Hummel and even Joachim took as their model, and thus the true solution of the problem remained for Brahms to rediscover.

Mozart keeps his whole tutti in the tonic, relieved only by his mastery of sudden subsidiary modulation. Beethoven, in turn, after the C minor Concerto, grasped the true function of the opening tutti and enlarged it to his new purposes. With an interesting experiment of Mozart's before him, he, in his G major Concerto, op. 58, allowed the solo player to state the opening theme, making the orchestra enter pianissimo in a foreign key. In this concerto he also gave variety of key to the opening tutti by means of an important theme which modulates widely, an entirely different thing from a deliberate modulation from material in one key to material in another. His fifth and last Pianoforte Concerto in E flat begins with a rhapsodical introduction for the solo player, followed by a long tutti confined to the tonic major and minor with a strictness explained by the gorgeous modulations with which the solo subsequently treats the second subject. In this concerto Beethoven also organizes the only undigested convention of the form, namely, the cadenza, a custom elaborated from the operatic aria, in which the singer was allowed to extemporize a flourish on a pause near the end. A similar pause was made in the final ritornello of a concerto, and the soloist was supposed to extemporize what should be equivalent to a symphonic coda. Cadenzas are, to this day, a form of musical appendicitis, since the player (or cadenza-writer) cannot be the composer himself and is rarely so capable of entering into his intentions as Joachim, whose written cadenzas for classical violin concertos are unsurpassable.

Brahms's First Concerto in D minor, op. 15, was the outcome of many changes, and, though on a mass of material originally intended for a symphony, was nevertheless so perfectly assimilated into concerto form that in his next essay, the Violin Concerto, op. 77, he had no more to learn and was free to continue making true innovations. He found out how to include wide key-contrasts in the opening tutti, thus giving the form a wider range in definitely functional key than any other instrumental music. Further, it may be noted that in this work Brahms develops a counter-plot in the opposition between solo and orchestra; giving not only the development by the solo of material stated by the orchestra, but also a counter-development by the orchestra of material stated by the solo. This concerto is, on the other hand, remarkable as being the last in which a blank space is left for a cadenza; a testimony of confidence in Joachim. In the Piano-forte Concerto in B flat, and in the Double Concerto, op. 102, the idea of an introductory statement in which the solo takes part before the opening tutti is carried out on a large scale, and in the Double Concerto both first and second subjects are thus suggested.

The forms of slow movements and finales in classical concer-tos, though often treated in special ways, present no general principles peculiar to the concerto; for a sectional opposition between solo and tutti is not of great disadvantage to slow move-ments and finales. The scherzo, on the other hand, is normally too sectional for successful adaptation to classical concerto style, and the solitary great example of its use is the second movement of Brahms's B flat Pianoforte Concerto, a movement in a very special form.

The post-classical concertos, in which the first movement dis-penses with the opening tutti, began with Mendelssohn, whose Violin Concerto dominates the whole subsequent history of the form. The happy idea of putting a cadenza at the dramatic crisis of the return after development instead of in the coda has almost become a convention. The other movements of concertos have not been affected by Mendelssohn's changes, nor does the linking of all three movements uninterruptedly together make any essen-tial difference to the scheme. But there is no limit to the expan-sion or reduction of the first movement. Spohr reduces it to an accompanied recitative in his *Gesangs-scene*, a work in which he discovered that a concerto could be an aria, which astonished him as the swimming of ducklings astonishes the fostering hen. Bruch's famous G minor Concerto (not his only interesting ex-periment in new concerto forms) also reduced the first movement to dramatic gestures without dramatic action. On the other hand, the huge first movement of Schumann's Pianoforte Concerto was originally intended to stand alone under the title of Fantasia. This example would cover the case of most first movements of this size in modern concertos, whether like Schumann's they have second subjects and recapitulations or not.

The case where the concerto as a whole is a fantasia (as with

Liszt) needs no discussion. Another line has been struck out by Saint-Saëns, most neatly in his first Violoncello Concerto; namely, that the whole work is one movement, but that after an exposition comprising a 'first' and 'second' subject the development drifts into a slow movement (or scherzo), and that this is followed by a finale of which the matter is partly independent and partly a recapitulation completing the first movement. In his C minor Pianoforte Concerto Saint-Saëns begins with a theme with variations and proceeds with a slow second theme, followed by a scherzo and finale which transform their own and the previous materials in various effective ways. But really the term Fantasia would adequately cover all post-classical forms of concerto. The only modern meaning of the word is 'composition for one or more solo players with orchestra'; and no special aesthetic or formal questions remain to be considered within the limits of this article.

CONTRAPUNTAL FORMS

THE forms of music may be considered in two aspects, the texture of the music from moment to moment, and the shape of the musical design as a whole. Historically the texture of music became definitely organized long before the shape could be determined by any but external or mechanical conceptions. The laws of musical texture were known as the laws of 'counterpoint' (*see* COUNTERPOINT and HARMONY). The 'contrapuntal' forms, then, are historically the earliest and aesthetically the simplest in music; the simplest, that is to say, in principle, but not necessarily the easiest to appreciate or to execute. Their simplicity is like that of mathematics, the simplicity of the elements involved; it develops into results more subtle and intricate than popular; whereas much of the art that is popular contains many and various elements combined in ways which, though familiar in appearance, are often not recognized for the complex conventions of civilization that they really are.

I. CANONIC FORMS AND DEVICES

In the canonic forms, the earliest known in music as an independent art, the laws of texture also determine the shape of the whole, so that it is impossible, except in the light of historical knowledge, to say which is prior to the other. The principle of canon being that one voice shall reproduce note for note the material of another, it follows that in a composition where all parts are canonic and where the material of the leading part consists of a predetermined melody, such as a Gregorian chant or a popular song, the composer has nothing to do but to adjust minute detail till the harmonies fit. The whole composition is the predetermined melody plus the harmonic fitness. The art does not teach composition, but it does teach fluency under difficulties, and thus the canonic forms play an important part in the music of the fifteenth and sixteenth centuries; nor indeed have they since fallen into neglect without grave injury to the art. But strict canon is inadequate, and may become a nuisance, as the sole regulating principle in music; nor is its rival and cognate principle of counterpoint on a canto fermo (*see* p. 30) more trustworthy in primitive stages. These are rigid mechanical principles; but even mechanical principles may force artistic thought to leave the facile grooves of custom and explore the real nature of things. Even to-day the canonic forms are great liberators if studied with intelligence.

19

The earliest canonic form is the rondel or rota as practised in
the twelfth century. It is, however, canonic by accident rather
than in its original intention. It consists of a combination of
short melodies in several voices, each melody being sung by each
voice in turn. Now it is obvious that if one voice began alone,
instead of all together, and if when it went on to the second
melody the second voice entered with the first, and so on, the
result would be a canon in the unison. Thus the difference
between the crude counterpoint of the rondel and a strict canon
in the unison is a mere question of the point at which the composition begins, and a twelfth-century rondel is simply a canon
in the unison begun at the point where all the voices have already
entered. There is some reason to believe that one kind of rondeau practised by Adam de la Hale was intended to be sung in
the true canonic manner of the modern round; and the wonderful
English rota, 'Sumer is icumen in', shows in the upper four
parts the true canonic method, and in its two-part *pes* the method
in which the parts began together. In these archaic works the
canonic form gives the whole a stability contrasting oddly with
its cacophonous warfare between nascent harmonic principles
and ancient antiharmonic criteria. As soon as harmony became
established on the true contrapuntal basis, the unaccompanied
round attained the position of an elegant trifle, with hardly more
expressive possibilities than the triolet in poetry, a form to which
its brevity and lightness render it fairly comparable. Orlando
di Lasso's *Célébrons sans cesse* is a beautiful example of the sixteenth-century round with a delightful climax in its fourth line.
In classical times the possibilities of the round enormously

Ex. 1 *Round (originally for male voices) When the first voice reaches
the 2nd line, the 2nd voice begins the 1st line, and so on.*

ORLANDO DI LASSO

increased; and with the aid of elaborate instrumental accompaniments it plays an important feature at points where a tableau is possible in an operatic ensemble. In such a round the first voice can execute a long and complete melody before the second voice joins in. Even if this melody be not instrumentally accompanied, it will imply a certain harmony, or at all events arouse curiosity as to what the harmony is to be. And the sequel may shed a new light upon the harmony, and thus by degrees the whole character of the melody may be transformed. The humorous and subtle possibilities of this form were first fully revealed by Mozart, whose astounding unaccompanied canons would be better known but for his habit of extemporizing unprintable texts for them.

The round or the catch (which is simply a specially jocose round) is a favourite English art-form, and the English specimens of it are almost as numerous and sometimes as anonymous as folk-songs. But they are apt to achieve only the easy task comprised in a good piece of free and fairly contrapuntal harmony in three or more parts, so arranged that it remains correct when the parts are brought in one by one. Even Cherubini gives hardly more than a valuable hint that the round may rise to higher things; and, unless he be an adequate exception, the unaccompanied rounds of Mozart and Brahms stand alone as works that raise the round to the dignity of a serious art-form.

With the addition of an orchestral accompaniment the round obviously becomes a larger thing; and in such specimens as that in the finale of Mozart's *Cosi fan tutte*, the quartet in the last act of Cherubini's *Faniska*, the wonderfully subtle quartet 'Mir ist so wunderbar' in Beethoven's *Fidelio*, and the very beautiful numbers in Schubert's Masses where Schubert finds expression for his genuine contrapuntal feeling in lyric style, we find that the length of the initial melody, the growing variety of the orchestral accompaniment, and the finality and climax of the free coda combine to give the whole a character closely analogous to that of a set of contrapuntal variations, such as the slow movement of Haydn's 'Emperor' String Quartet, or the opening of the finale of Beethoven's Ninth Symphony. Berlioz is fond of beginning his largest movements like a kind of round; e.g. his *Dies Irae* and the 'Scène aux Champs' in the *Symphonie Fantastique*, and the opening of his *Damnation de Faust*.

Three conditions are necessary if a canon is to be a round. First, the voices must imitate each other in the unison; secondly, they must enter at equal intervals of time; and thirdly, the whole melodic material must be as many times longer than the interval of time as the number of voices; otherwise, when the last voice has finished the first phrase, the first voice will not be ready to return to the beginning. Strict canon is, however, possible under innumerable other conditions, and even a round is possible with some of the voices at the interval of an octave, as is of course inevitable in writing for unequal voices. And in a round for unequal voices there is obviously a new means of effect in the fact that, as the melody rotates, its different parts change their pitch in relation to each other.

The art by which this is possible without incorrectness is that of double, triple, and multiple counterpoint (*see* COUNTERPOINT). Its difficulty is variable, and with an instrumental accompaniment there is none. In fugues, multiple counterpoint is one of the normal resources of music; and few devices are more self-explanatory to the ear than the process by which the subject and countersubjects of a fugue change their positions, revealing fresh melodic and acoustic aspects of identical harmonic structure at every turn. This, however, is rendered possible and interesting by the fact that the passages in such counterpoint are often separated by episodes and are free to appear in different keys. Many fugues of Bach are written throughout in multiple counterpoint; but the possibility of this depends upon the freedom of the musical design, which allows the composer to select the most effective permutations and combinations of his counterpoint, and also to put them into whatever key he chooses. Some of Bach's choruses might be called Round-Fugues, so regular is the course by which each voice proceeds to a new countersubject as the next voice enters. See the 'Et in terra pax' of the B minor Mass, and the great double chorus, *Nun ist das Heil.*

The resources of canon, when emancipated from the principles of the round, are considerable when the canonic form is strictly maintained, and are inexhaustible when it is treated freely. A canon need not be in the unison; and when it is in some other interval the imitating voice alters the expression of the melody by transferring it to another part of the scale. Again, the imitating voice may follow the leader at any distance of time; and thus we have obviously a definite means of expression in the difference of closeness with which various canonic parts may enter; as, for instance, in the stretto of a fugue. Again, if the answering part enters on an unaccented beat where the leader began on the accent (*per arsin et thesin*), there will be artistic value in the resulting difference of rhythmic expression. All these devices ought to be quite definite in their effect upon the ear, and their expressive power is undoubtedly due to their special canonic nature. The beauty of the pleading, rising sequences in crossing parts in the canon at the second at the opening of the 'Recordare' in Mozart's *Requiem* is attainable by no other technical means. The close canon in the sixth at the distance of one minim in reversed accent in the eighteenth of Bach's 'Goldberg' Variations owes its smooth harmonic expression to the fact that the two canonic parts move in sixths which would be simultaneous but for the pause of the minim, which reverses the accents of the upper part while it creates the suspended discords which give harmonic character.

Two other canonic devices have important artistic value, viz., augmentation and diminution (two different aspects of the same thing), and inversion. In augmentation the imitating part sings twice as slow as the leader, or sometimes still slower. This obviously should impart a new dignity to the melody, and in diminution the usual result is an accession of liveliness. Beethoven, in the fugues in his Sonatas, opp. 106 and 110, adapted augmentation and diminution to sonata-like varieties of thematic expression, by employing them in triple time, so that, by doubling the length of the original notes across this triple rhythm, they produce an entirely new rhythmic expression.

Ex. 2

Theme of Fugue in Beethoven. Sonata, Op. 106

(a)

(b) Inverted

inexact

(c) Augmented, producing new rhythmic sense.

etc.

(d) Cancrizans, or backwards; producing new rhythms.

* ♭ 7 is equivalent to a crotchet. Trills are not inverted.

The device of inversion consists in the imitating part reversing every interval of the leader, ascending where the leader descends and vice versa. Its expressive power depends upon so fine a sense of the harmonic expression of melody that its artistic use is one of the surest signs of the difference between classical and merely scholastic music. There are many melodies of which the inversion is as natural as the original form, and does not strikingly alter its character. Such are, for instance, the theme of Bach's *Kunst der Fuge*, most of Purcell's contrapuntal themes, the theme in the fugue of Beethoven's Sonata, op. 110, and the eighth of Brahms's Variations on a Theme by Haydn. But even in such cases inversion may produce harmonic variety as well as a sense of melodic identity in difference. Where a melody has marked features of rise and fall, such as long scale passages or bold skips, the inversion, if productive of good harmonic structure and expression, will be a powerful method of transformation. This is admirably shown in the twelfth of Bach's 'Goldberg' Variations, in the fifteenth fugue of the first book of his Forty-eight Preludes and Fugues, in the finale of Beethoven's Sonata, op. 106, and in the second subjects of the first and last movements of Brahms's Clarinet Trio. The only remaining canonic device which figures in classical music is that known as cancrizans, in which the imitating part reproduces the leader backwards. It is of extreme rarity in serious music; and though it sometimes happens that a melody or figure of uniform rhythm will produce something equally natural when read backwards (as in Ex. 3), there is only one example of its use that appeals to the ear as well as the eye.

EX. 3 *Harmless cancrizans devices for the eye, depending on the clefs used.*
(*a*) *Mozart*, 'Jupiter' Symphony (recapitulation in finale).

(*b*) *Brahms*, Quartet in A minor, Op. 51 No. 2

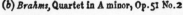

This is to be found in the finale of Beethoven's Sonata, op. 106, where it is applied to a theme with such sharply contrasted rhythmic and melodic features that with long familiarity a listener would probably feel not only the wayward humour of the passage in itself, but also its connexion with the main theme. All these devices are also independent of the canonic idea, since they are so many methods of transforming themes in themselves, and need not always be used in contrapuntal combination.

II. FUGUE

In the polyphonic sixteenth-century motets the essentials of canonic effect are embodied in the entry of one voice after another with a definite theme stated by each voice, often at its own convenient pitch, thus producing a free canon for as many parts as there are voices, in alternate intervals of the fourth, fifth, and octave, and at artistically proportionate distances of time. It is not necessary for the later voices to imitate more than the opening phrase of the earlier, or, if they do imitate its continuation, to keep to the same interval.

Such a texture differs in no way from that of the fugue of more modern times. But the form is not what is now understood as fugue, inasmuch as sixteenth-century composers did not normally think of writing long movements on one theme or of making a point of the return of a theme after episodes. With the appearance of new words in the text, the sixteenth-century composer naturally took up a new theme without troubling to design it for contrapuntal combination with the opening; and the form resulting from this treatment of words was faithfully reproduced in the instrumental *ricercari* of the time. Occasionally, however, breadth of treatment and terseness of design combined to produce a short movement on one idea indistinguishable in form from a fughetta of Bach; as in the Kyrie of Palestrina's *Missa Salve Regina*. But in Bach's art the preservation of a main theme is more necessary the longer the composition; and Bach has an incalculable number of methods of giving his fugues a symmetry of form and balance of climax so subtle and perfect that we are apt to forget that the only technical rules of a fugue are those which refer to its texture.

In *Die Kunst der Fuge* Bach has shown with the utmost clearness how in his opinion the various types of fugue may be classified. That extraordinary work is a series of fugues, all on the same subject. The earlier fugues show how an artistic design may be made by simply passing the subject from one voice to another in orderly succession (in the first example without any change of key except from tonic to dominant). The next stage of organization is that in which the subject is combined with inversions, augmentations, and diminutions of itself. Fugues of this kind can be conveniently called stretto-fugues.[1] The third and highest stage is that in which the fugue combines its subject with contrasted countersubjects, and thus depends upon the resources of double, triple, and quadruple counterpoint. But of the art by which the episodes are contrasted, connected climaxes attained, and keys and subtle rhythmic proportions so balanced as to give the true fugue forms a beauty and stability second only to those of the true sonata forms, Bach's classification gives us no direct hint.

A comparison of the fugues in *Die Kunst der Fuge* with those elsewhere in his works reveals a necessary relation between the nature of the fugue-subject and the type of fugue. In *Die Kunst der Fuge* Bach has obvious didactic reasons for taking the same subject throughout; and, as he wishes to show the extremes of technical possibility, that subject must necessarily be plastic rather than characteristic. Elsewhere Bach prefers very lively or highly characteristic themes as subjects for the simplest kind of instrumental fugue. On the other hand, there comes a point when the mechanical strictness of treatment crowds out the rhetorical development of musical ideas; and the seventh fugue (which is one solid mass of stretto in augmentation, diminution, and inversion) and the twelfth and thirteenth (which are inverted bodily) are academic exercises outside the range of free artistic work. On the other hand, the fugues with well-developed episodes and the fugues in double and triple counterpoint are perfect works of art and as beautiful as any that Bach wrote without didactic purpose. The last fugue Bach worked out up to the point where three subjects, including the notes B, A, C, H, were combined. It has been found that the theme of the rest of *Die Kunst der Fuge* makes a fourth member of the combination and that the combination inverts. This accounts for the laborious exercises shown in the twelfth and thirteenth fugues. It is high time that teachers of counterpoint took *Die Kunst der Fuge* seriously.

Fugue is still, as in the sixteenth century, a texture rather than a form; and the formal rules given in most technical treatises are based, not on the practice of the world's great composers, but on the necessities of beginners, whom it would be as absurd to ask to write a fugue without giving them a form as to ask a schoolboy to write so many pages of Latin verses without a subject. But this standard form, whatever its merits may be in combining progressive technique with musical sense, has no connexion with the true classical types of fugue, though it played an interesting part in the renascence of polyphony during the growth

[1] For technical terms *see* articles COUNTERPOINT and FUGUE.

of the sonata-style, and even gave rise to valuable works of art (e.g. the fugues in Haydn's Quartets, op. 20).

One of its rules was that every fugue should have a stretto. This rule, like most of the others, is absolutely without classical warrant; for in Bach the ideas of stretto and of countersubject almost exclude one another except in the very largest fugues, such as the twenty-second in the second book of the Forty-eight; while Handel's fugue-writing is a masterly method, adapted as occasion requires, and with a lordly disdain for recognized devices. But the pedagogic rule proved to be not without artistic point in later music; for fugue became, since the rise of the sonata-styles, a contrast with the normal means of expression instead of being itself normal. And while this was so, there was considerable point in using every possible means to enhance the rhetorical force of its peculiar devices, as is shown by the astonishing dramatic fugues in Beethoven's last works. Nowadays, however, polyphony is universally recognized as a permanent type of musical texture, and there is no longer any reason why if it crystallizes into the fugue-form at all it should not adopt the classical rather than the pedagogic type. It is still an unsatisfied wish of accurate musicians that the term fugue should be used to imply rather a certain type of polyphonic texture than the whole form of a composition. We ought to describe as 'written in fugue' such passages as the first subjects in Mozart's *Zauberflöte* Overture, the andantes of Beethoven's First Symphony and C minor Quartet, the first and second subjects of the finale of Mozart's G major Quartet, the second subject of the finale of his D major Quintet, and the exposition of quintuple counterpoint in the coda of the finale of the 'Jupiter' Symphony, and countless other passages in the developments and main subjects of classical and modern works in sonata form.

III. COUNTERPOINT ON A CANTO FERMO

The early practice of building polyphonic designs on a voice-part confined to a given plainsong or popular melody furnishes the origin for every contrapuntal principle that is not canonic, and soon develops into a canonic principle in itself. When the canto fermo is in notes of equal length and is sung without intermission, it is of course as rigid a mechanical device as an acrostic. Yet it may have artistic value in furnishing a steady rhythm in contrast to suitable free motion in the other parts. When it is in the bass, as in Orlando di Lasso's six-part *Regina Coeli*, it is apt to cramp the harmony; but when it is in the tenor (its normal place in sixteenth-century music) or any other part, it determines little but the length of the composition. It may or may not appeal to the ear; if not, it at least does no harm, for its restricting influence on the harmony is small if its pace is slower than that of its surroundings. If, on the other hand, its melody is characteristic, or can be enforced by repetition, it may become a powerful means of effect.

When the rhythm of the canto fermo is not uniform, or when pauses intervene between its phrases, whether these are different figures or repetitions of one figure in different parts of the scale, the device passes into the region of free art. An early example of its simplest use, as it appears in Josquin's wonderful 'Miserere' and in a motet by Lasso, is described in the article MUSIC. A sixteenth-century mass, when it is not derived from those secular melodies to which the Council of Trent objected, is often so closely connected with the Gregorian tones, or at least with the themes of some motet appropriate to the holy day for which it was written, that in a Roman Catholic cathedral service the polyphonic music of the best period co-operates with the Gregorian intonations to produce a consistent musical whole with a thematic coherence oddly suggestive of Wagnerian leitmotive. In later times the Protestant music of Germany attained a similar consistency, under more popular and complex musical conditions, by the use of chorale tunes; and in Bach's hands the fugal and other treatment of chorale melody is one of the most varied and expressive of artistic resources. The chorale is not unknown in Handel's English works (*see* CHORALE, p. 12).

From the use of an old canto fermo to the invention of an original one is a small step; and it merges into the free development of counterpoint on a canto fermo, the general art of combining melodies which gives harmony its deepest expression and musical texture its liveliest action. Nor is there any line to separate polyphonic from non-polyphonic methods of accompanying melody; and Bach's *Orgelbüchlein* and Brahms's posthumous Organ Chorales show every conceivable gradation between plain harmony or arpeggio and the most elaborate canon.

In Wagnerian polyphony canonic devices are rare except in such simple moments of anticipation or of communion with nature as we have before the rise of the curtain in the *Rheingold* and at daybreak in the second act of the *Götterdämmerung*. On the other hand, the art of combining contrasted themes crowds almost every other kind of musical texture (except tremolos and similar emotional symptoms) into the background, and is itself so transformed by new harmonic resources, many of which are Wagner's own discovery, that it may almost be said to constitute a new form of art. The influence of this upon instrumental music is as yet helpful only in forms which break away from the limits of the sonata style. Styles which break farther away than the omnivorous art of Richard Strauss generally revolt against polyphony altogether. That revolt is suicidal, and polyphony returns every time a brand-new theory of harmony has pitch-forked it out. All that is certain is that the two elements by which the music of the future will solve its problem are not those of instrumentation and external expression, but phrase-movement (or musical paragraphing) and counterpoint. These have always been the elements which suffered from neglect or anarchy in earlier transition periods, and they have always been the elements that gave rationality to the new art to which the transitions led.

COUNTERPOINT

COUNTERPOINT, the art defined by Sir Frederick Gore Ouseley as that of 'combining melodies' (Lat. *contrapunctus*, 'point counter point', 'note against note'). This neat definition is not quite complete. Classical counterpoint is the conveying of a mass of harmony by means of a combination of melodies. Thus the three melodies combined by Wagner in the *Meistersinger* Prelude do not make classical counterpoint, for they require a mass of accompanying harmony to explain them. That accompaniment explains them perfectly and thereby proves itself to be classical counterpoint, for its virtue lies in its own good melodic lines, both where these coincide with the main melodies and where they diverge from them. From this it will be seen that current criticism is always at fault when it worries as to whether the melodies are individually audible in a good piece of counterpoint.

What is always important is the peculiar life breathed into harmony by contrapuntal organization. Both historically and aesthetically 'counterpoint' and 'harmony' are inextricably blended; for nearly every harmonic fact is in its origin a phenomenon of counterpoint. Instrumental music develops harmony in unanalysed lumps, as painting obliterates draughtsmanship in masses of colour; but the underlying concepts of counterpoint and draughtsmanship remain.

In so far as the laws of counterpoint are derived from harmonic principles—that is to say, derived from the properties of concord and discord—their origin and development are discussed in the article HARMONY. In so far as they depend entirely on melody they are too minute and changeable to admit of general discussion; and in so far as they show the interaction of melodic and harmonic principles it is more convenient to discuss them under the head of harmony. All that remains, then, for the present article is the explanation of certain technical terms. The musical examples are printed at the end of the article.

1. *Canto Fermo* (i.e. plainchant) is a melody in long notes given to one voice while others accompany it with quicker counterpoints (the term 'counterpoint' in this connexion meaning accompanying melodies). In the simplest cases the canto fermo has notes of equal length and is unbroken in flow. When it is broken up and its rhythm diversified, the gradations between counterpoint on a canto fermo and ordinary forms of polyphony, or indeed any kind of melody with an elaborate accompaniment, are infinite and insensible.

2. *Double Counterpoint* is a combination of melodies so de-

signed that either can be taken above or below the other. When this change of position is effected by merely altering the octave of either or both melodies (with or without transposition of the whole combination to another key), the artistic value of the device is simply that of the raising of the lower melody to the surface. The harmonic scheme remains the same, except in so far as some of the chords are not in their fundamental positions, while others, not originally fundamental, have become so. But double counterpoint may be in other intervals than the octave; that is to say, while one of the parts remains stationary, the other may be transposed above or below it by some other interval, thus producing an entirely different set of harmonies.

Double Counterpoint in the twelfth has thus been made a powerful means of expression and variety. The artistic value of this device depends not only on the beauty and novelty of the second scheme of harmony obtained, but also on the change of melodic expression produced by transferring one of the melodies to another position in the scale. Two of the most striking illustrations of this effect are to be found in the last chorus of Brahms's *Triumphlied* and in the fourth of his Variations on a Theme of Haydn. Inversion in the twelfth also changes the concord of the sixth into the discord of the seventh; a property used with powerful effect by Bach in Fugue 16 of Book II of *Das Wohltemperirte Klavier*.

Double Counterpoint in the tenth has the property that the inverted melody can be given in the new and in the original positions simultaneously.

Double counterpoint in other intervals than the octave, tenth, and twelfth is rare, but the general principle and motives for it remain the same under all conditions. The two subjects of the 'Confiteor' in Bach's B minor Mass are in double counterpoint in the octave, eleventh, and thirteenth. And Beethoven's Mass in D is full of pieces of double counterpoint, in the inversions of which a few notes are displaced so as to produce momentary double counterpoint in unusual intervals, obviously with the intention of varying the harmony.

3. *Triple, Quadruple, and Multiple Counterpoint.*—When more than two melodies are designed so as to combine in interchangeable positions, it becomes increasingly difficult to avoid chords and progressions of which some inversions are incorrect. Triple counterpoint is normally possible only at the octave; for it will be found that if three parts are designed to invert in some other interval, this will involve two of them inverting in a third interval which will give rise to incalculable difficulty. This makes the fourth of Brahms's Variations on a Theme of Haydn appear almost miraculous. The whole variation beautifully illustrates

the melodic expression of inversion at the twelfth; and during eight bars of the second section a third contrapuntal voice appears, which is afterwards inverted in the twelfth, with natural and smooth effect. But this involves the inversion of two of the counterpoints with each other in the almost impracticable double counterpoint in the ninth. Brahms probably did not figure this out at all but profited by the luck which goes with genius.

Quadruple Counterpoint is not rare with Bach; and the melodically invertible combination intended by him in the unfinished fugue at the end of *Die Kunst der Fuge* requires one of its themes to invert in the twelfth as against the others. (*See* my edition published by the Oxford University Press.)

Quintuple Counterpoint is admirably illustrated in the finale of Mozart's 'Jupiter' Symphony, in which everything in the successive statement and gradual development of the five themes conspires to give the utmost effect to their combination in the coda. Of course Mozart has not room for more than five of the one hundred and twenty possible combinations, and from these he, like all the great contrapuntists, selects such as bring fresh themes into the outside parts, which are the most clearly audible.

Sextuple Counterpoint may be found in Bach's great double chorus, *Nun ist das Heil*, in the finale of his Concerto for three claviers in C, and probably in other places.

4. *Added Thirds and Sixths.* This is merely the full working out of the sole purpose of double counterpoint in the tenth, namely, the possibility of performing it in its original and inverted positions simultaneously. The 'Pleni sunt coeli' of Bach's B minor Mass is written in this kind of transformation of double into quadruple counterpoint; and the artistic value of the device is perhaps never so magnificently realized as in the place, at bar 84, where the trumpet doubles the bass three octaves and a third above while the alto and second tenor have the counter-subjects in close thirds in the middle.

Almost all other contrapuntal devices are derived from the principle of the canon and are fully discussed in the article CONTRAPUNTAL FORMS.

As a training in musical grammar and style, the rhythms of sixteenth-century polyphony were early codified into 'the five species of counterpoint' (with various other species now forgotten) and practised by students of composition. The exercise should not claim to teach rhythm, but it does teach measurement.

The classical treatise on which Haydn and Beethoven were trained was Fux's *Gradus ad Parnassum* (1725). This was superseded in the nineteenth century by Cherubini's, the first of a long series of attempts to bring up to date as a dead language

what should be studied in its original and living form. Dr. R. O.
Morris has thoroughly exposed the humbug and illustrated the
true severe scholarship in *Contrapuntal Technique in the Sixteenth
Century* (Oxford University Press).

Ex. I.   *Double Counterpoint in the 8ve, 10th, and 12th*

(b) Combination of all inversions; 8ve between 2 & 3;   10th between 1 & 3   and 2 &
4; 12th between 1 & 4.

Ex. II. *Triple Counterpoint in the 12th and incidentally the 9th*

BRAHMS, Op. 56

(b) III in 12th with I, and 9th with II

Ex. III. *Quintuple Counterpoint; capable of* **120** *permutations*

MOZART, Finale of 'Jupiter' Symphony

Ex. IV. *Scholastic Exercise in the Five Species of Counterpoint*

(The combination of all five species, here used to save space, does not allow the 2nd species to move conjunctly as is desirable. The use of two chords in a bar, forbidden by some teachers, is good if the words are clearly expressed. The suspension in the 7th bar (4–3 over a $\frac{6}{3}$ chord), though frequent in sixteenth century music, is considered licentious in an exercise of less than 6 parts.)

5th species (florid)
2nd species (2 notes to 1)

3rd species (4 notes to 1)

4th species (syncopated)
CANTO FERMO
1st species (note against
note)

FUGUE, the mutual 'pursuit' of voices or parts. It was, up to the end of the sixteenth century, if not later, the name applied to two art-forms. (A) *Fuga ligata* was the exact reproduction by one or more voices of the statement of a leading part. The reproducing voice (*comes*) was seldom if ever written out, for all differences between it and the *dux* were rigidly systematic; e.g., it was an exact inversion, or exactly twice as slow, or to be sung backwards, &c., &c. Hence a rule or canon was given, often in enigmatic form, by which the *comes* was deduced from the *dux*; and so the term canon became the name for the form itself and is still retained. (B) A composition in which the canonic style was cultivated without canonic restriction was, in the sixteenth century, called *fuga ricercata* or simply *ricercare*, a term which is still used by Bach as a title for the fugues in *Das musikalische Opfer*.

Fugue is a texture the rules of which do not suffice to determine the shape of the composition as a whole. Schemes such as that laid down in Cherubini's treatise, which legislate for the shape, are pedagogic fictions; and such classical tradition as they represent is too exclusively Italian to include Bach. Yet, strange to say, the Italian tradition in fugue style is represented by hardly any strict works at all. Under the general heading of CONTRAPUNTAL FORMS many facts concerning fugues are discussed; and only a few technical terms remain to be defined here. The musical examples are printed at the end of the article.

1. If during the first entries or 'exposition' of the fugue, the counterpoint with which the opening voice accompanies the answer is faithfully reproduced as the accompaniment to subsequent entries of the subject, it is called a 'countersubject'. Obviously the first countersubject may continue with a second when the subject enters in the third part and so on. The term is also applied to new subjects appearing later in the fugue in combination (immediate or destined) with the original subject. Cherubini, holding the arbitrary dogma that a fugue cannot have more than one subject, applies the term to the less prominent of the subjects of what are commonly called double fugues, i.e., fugues which begin with two parts and two subjects simultaneously, and so also with triple and quadruple fugues. It is remarkable that Bach (with only three known exceptions) never writes this kind of double fugue, but always introduces his new subjects later.

2. Episodes are passages separating the entries of the subject. There is no reason for distinguishing episodes that occur during the exposition from later episodes. Episodes are usually

developed from the material of the subject and countersubjects;
they are, when independent, conspicuously so.

3. Stretto is the overlapping of subject and answer. A 'stretto
maestrale' is one in which the subject survives the overlapping.
The makers of musical terminology have no answer to the question of what a non-magistral stretto may be.

4. The distinction between real and tonal fugue is a matter
of detail concerning the answer. A fugal exposition is not intended to emphasize a key-contrast between tonic and dominant.
Accordingly the answer is (especially in its first notes and in
points that tend to shift the key) not so much a transposition
of the subject to the key of the dominant as an adaptation of it
from the tonic part to the dominant part of the scale or vice
versa; in short, the answer is as far as possible *on* the dominant,
not *in* the dominant. This is effected by a kind of melodic fore-
shortening on principles of great aesthetic interest but difficult
to reduce to rules of thumb. The rules as often as not produce
answers that are exact transpositions of the subject; and so the
only kind of 'real' fugue (i.e., fugue with an exact answer) which
could rightly be contrasted with the tonal fugue would be that
in which the answer ought to be tonal but is not.

The term answer is usually reserved for those entries of the
subject that are placed in what may be called the 'complementary' position of the scale, whether they are tonal or not. Thus
the order of entries in the exposition of the first fugue of *Das
Wohltemperirte Klavier* is subject, answer, answer, subject, a
departure from the usual rule, according to which subject and
answer are regularly alternated in the exposition.

The nature of fugue and of polyphony as building harmony in
'horizontal' melodic threads instead of in 'vertical' chordal
lumps is all summarized by Milton, during no classical period of
polyphony, but in the chaotic time half-way between the death
of Frescobaldi and the birth of Bach.

> His volant touch
> Instinct through all proportions low and high
> Fled and pursued transverse the resonant fugue.

Paradise Lost, Book XI, ll. 561-3

Ex. I. *Stretto-Fugue in 4 parts*

Λ = Subject. C.S = Counter Subject. ▯ = Diminution. V = Inversion. Λ̃ = Variation.

BACH. *Das Wohltemperirte Klavier.* II 9

End of exposition

Stretto I

Canonic Episode
suggested by C.S(a)

Stretto II: chromatic, with two new countersubjects

New C.S 1

New C.S 2

New C.S 1 (combined at different point)

New C.S 2 (ditto)

New C.S 1

New C.S 2

Stretto III on a variation of the subject

Stretto IV by diminution (Note new position in scale, with first two entries)

Stretto V combining normal subject with diminution freely inverted and direct

Stretto VI, reviving C.S as a result of

** These two notes would have been an 8ve higher if 10ths could be stretched on Bach's instruments

Ex. II. *Fugue in 3 parts, with 2 countersubjects and highly organized episodes*

BACH. *Das Wohltemperirte Klavier,* I, 2

HARMONY

IN its earliest English sense the term harmony is applied to any pleasing arrangement of musical sounds; but technically it is confined to the science of the simultaneous combination of sounds of different pitch, without regard to their quality of tone or timbre, a matter which belongs to the province of INSTRUMEN-TATION (q.v.). The sense of the word harmony is further restricted to the study of combinations rather as blocks of sound than as textures. The fundamental aesthetic texture of harmony is counterpoint (q.v.).

But while the abstraction of harmony from instrumentation is as legitimate and necessary as the abstraction of draughtsmanship from colour, the abstraction of harmony from counterpoint cuts music adrift from its foundations and leads to no better results than the abstraction of sound from sense. Harmony is to classical music what perspective is to pictorial art. But visual perspective is a science, whereas this musical perspective is wholly an art. The present article aims at showing that its laws are true to the nature of art and are no mere rules of a game. But we must not impute the meaning of its laws to any music earlier than the four-teenth century, and even in the spacious days of Elizabeth and Palestrina there are many things in harmony which do not mean what we would mean by them to-day.

I. ORIGIN OF CONCORD AND DISCORD

The diatonic major scale (or something very like it) may be found by playing eight successive white notes from C to C on the pianoforte. It would be better to accept this as a scientific defini-tion than to begin the study of harmony with questions like that whether the first hen preceded or followed the first egg. The interesting fact is that the ancient Greeks showed a latent har-monic sense by developing the diatonic scale, which has proved itself capable of bearing our classical system of harmony. In the article MUSIC the origin of scales is touched upon; in the mean-time we may assume that eggs are eggs without waiting for the latest researches of bio-chemistry.

The one ostensible effort the Greeks made at organizing simul-taneous notes of different pitch was the practice of 'magadizing'. The magadis was a stringed instrument with a bridge that divided the strings at two-thirds of their length. The shorter portion of the string then sounded an octave higher than the longer. To magadize, therefore, was to get the voices of children or women to sing in octaves above the voices of men.

44

Now we may begin our survey of harmonic combinations with two propositions. First, any two notes an octave apart are harmonically identical. From this we may draw two useful inferences—first, that doubling in octaves never was and never will be a process of harmonization; and, secondly, that a combination does not change its meaning by the addition or subtraction of an octave.

The second fundamental proposition is that harmonies are built upwards from the bass. This will be denied by some theorists; but the present line of thought is not an *a priori* theory, but the observation of facts. By 'low' notes we mean sounds produced by slow vibrations, and by 'high' notes sounds produced by rapid vibrations.

The harmonic identity of notes an octave apart was a matter of physical sensation before the dawn of history. In 1862 Helmholtz explained it and a great many other facts in musical aesthetics. He solemnly warned musical theorists against hastily applying his scientific results to the art of music, and warned them in vain. But we may safely draw some inferences from his discovery that the timbre of a note depends upon the selection and proportion of a series of overtones in the vibration-ratios of aliquot parts of the fundamental note. Thus, a note adds nothing to a lower note if it is at the distance of an overtone; except in that if the distance is not exactly one or more octaves, the combination will assume the harmonic sense of its difference from an octave; thus, a twelfth is equivalent to a fifth.

Distances of pitch are called intervals. They are reckoned (numerically and inclusive of both notes) up a diatonic scale. From the fundamental (or tonic) note of a major scale (as from C on the white notes of the pianoforte) all intervals within that scale are major, and the fourth, fifth, and octave are called perfect. Intervals a semitone less than major are called minor, except in the case of perfect intervals, which become imperfect or diminished when reduced by a semitone. Otherwise a diminished interval is a semitone less than minor. An augmented interval is a semitone greater than major. The terms 'augmented' and 'diminished' should be applied only to chromatic intervals, that is to say, to intervals of which one note is foreign to the scale of reference. There is in every scale one fourth that is greater than perfect (F to B in the scale of C) and one imperfect fifth (B to F). This diatonic enlarged fourth is called the tritone. Intervals are 'inverted' by raising the lower note to a higher octave; thus the imperfect fifth is the inversion of the tritone fourth.

Helmholtz's discovery of the nature of timbre proves that certain aspects of harmony are latent in nature. Conversely, the art of harmony constantly produces effects of timbre apart from those of the particular instruments in use. But musical elements interact in ways that quickly carry musical aesthetics into regions far removed from any simple relation between harmony and timbre. What acoustics can tell us of concord and discord is not only inadequate for our musical experience, but contrary to it. Acoustics tell us that the rapid 'beats' that distress the ear in harsh combinations are due to the periodic reinforcements and weaknesses that occur as the waves get in and out of phase with each other. When these beats are so rapid as to produce a note of their own, this resultant tone may or may not be pleasant; the painful stage of beats is that in which they are noticeable, as a flickering light is noticeable. Combinations that are out of beating distance may set up beats between the upper note and the octave harmonic of the other. On this criterion, thirds and sixths, especially the minor sixth, are rougher than many combinations that rank as discords, or than some that have never been digested in classical harmony, such as the seventh overtone.

The art of music had not attained to the simplest scheme for dealing with discords before it traversed the acoustic criterion in every direction. It became a language in which sense dictated what should be accepted in sound. The minor sixth, as the inversion of the major third, occurs in many positions of what has come to be the most fixed chord in music, the major triad. On the other hand, a discord beyond beating-distance will have no beats if it is produced in a timbre that has no octave overtones; but if its sense has come to be that of a discord, its timbre will not make it a concord.

The theorists of the sixteenth century shrewdly regarded the major triad as really a chord of six notes, in the ratios of 1,2,3,4,5,6, which they called the Sestina:

Ex. 1

Long before this natural phenomenon had been recognized, music had organized many other elements into its language, and harmony had become (what it has ever since remained, apart from experiments) counterpoint. This arose, slowly and painfully, out of devices diametrically opposed to it. The organum or diaphonia of the tenth century amounted to a magadizing in all the perfect concords, i.e., in fourths or fifths doubled by octaves, thus—

Ex. 2

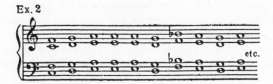

etc.

Its intention was that of a glorified unison and it survives, unheard except as artificial timbre, in the guise of a shrill aura above the notes of the full organ when that instrument is using the most ancient of its registers, the mixture stops. (Some observers have reported the present practice of something like diaphonia in remote parts of Japan.)

The problem of counterpoint was attacked in two ways. First there was a slow evolution through experiments in ornamenting one or more voices of an organum. This gradually took shape as the art of discant, and was slow to move far from the foundation of parallel perfect concords. On the other hand, a violent frontal attack was made by the motets of the thirteenth and fourteenth centuries, which had no connexion with the sublime motet-form of sixteenth-century Church music, but consisted in the simultaneous singing of several melodies, independent and perhaps pre-existing; the combination being rough-hewn into a harmony justified by the rule of *marche, ou je t'assomme*. The rough-hewing consisted in contriving that the perfect concords should be conspicuous at the strong accents, on which condition the rest of the harmony could take care of itself. We are apt to misread our documents by forgetting that the note which is now double the length of the longest note in normal use originally deserved its name of 'breve'. A Hungarian band produces a general harmonic effect more like that of Brahms's Hungarian Dances than like any less classical music; but if the details of the Hungarian ornamentation and part-writing were written in breves, semibreves, and minims we should find them remarkably like medieval counterpoint.

II. PURE POLYPHONY

The first matter of principle that emerged from the chaos was that if the parallel movement of perfect concords was right, everything else was wrong. A few compositions show an evenly-balanced conflict of opposing principles. Our wonderful English rota 'Sumer is icumen in' sounds to us like a tuneful six-part double canon spoilt (or rendered quaint) by numerous consecutive fifths. Its contemporaries were more likely to have regarded it as a beautiful scheme of perfect concords spoilt or illuminated

by dangerous licences. There was no room for prolonged doubt
as to where the path of progress and freedom lay. And if the
basis of harmony was to be independent melody, then one of the
main cares of the composer was to prevent his independent
melodies from lapsing into duplications. Fifths and octaves will
still form (as they do at the present day) cardinal points in every
chord that is dwelt upon; but no two voices can double each
other for two consecutive octaves or fifths without dissolving
their integrity in a false resonance.

As to discords the criterion ceased to be acoustical. After
centuries of trial and error, musicians accepted thirds and sixths
as concords; and all discords became equal to one another in
mildness when they occurred as unaccented passing-notes pro-
ceeding by diatonic conjunct notes between one concord and the
next. Polyphony made musical accents far stronger than those
of speech; and so the behaviour of accented discords was more
restricted. The accented discord must be 'prepared' by first
appearing as a concord. It then becomes a discord by being
held or 'suspended' while the other voices move against it; after
which it must 'resolve' by a step downwards. Upward resolutions are harsh and of complex import, intelligible only in a later
system, and so are discords that skip.

Ex. 3 shows passing-notes (marked *) moving up and down
between concords:

In Ex. 4 the tied C is a suspension, prepared by having begun
as an octave, becoming a discord by colliding as a fourth against
a fifth, and resolving by stepping down to a third.

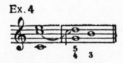

Four three-note chords attained the rank of concords. (Two
of them were only inversions of the other two.) First, of course,
there was the major triad, the upper three notes (4, 5, 6) of the
sestina (Ex. 1). All doublings and differences of octave are
negligible in the distribution of a chord so long as they do not
bring its middle or upper notes into the bass. All the following
examples are concords identical with the sestina and with each
other, though the positions that leave two parts low at a distance

from the upper parts, or that double the third, are acoustically as rough as many a discord. Positions (*d*) and (*e*) could be justified only in circumstances of great polyphonic or instrumental interest.

The essential intervals are those of position (*a*) and comprise a perfect fifth (G–D), a major third from the bass (G–B), and a minor third above (B–D).

Now in listening to polyphony the mind can appreciate the parts two at a time; and the sixteenth-century theorists avoid reasoning as if the mind could do more. They were probably right as well as cautious; nor is it necessary that the mind should attempt more. For any fault in the aggregate of the richest polyphony must be a fault between two parts. If it concerns more, then it is more than a single fault; and if there are no faults, the ear enjoys the faultless aggregate whether it can distinguish the parts or not. Accordingly the question arises: will the ear resent an aggregate which corresponds as such to nothing in nature, but which contains no intervals that have not already been accepted in the sestina? In other words, can we treat as a concord a triad which puts the minor third below the major?

The history of harmony not only answers this in the affirmative, but shows that the contrast between this artificial concord and the major triad is essential to the formation of a flexible musical language. Some theorists, fascinated by the ways in which minor harmonies behave like major harmonies reversed, have invented schemes according to which the 'roots' of minor chords are their top notes. The way in which minor chords happen in music does not support any theory which makes Ex. 6 anything other than an artificial alteration of Ex. 5, with the same entirely fundamental behaviour of the same bass-note in every relevant musical context. The artificiality of the chord is not arbitrary or conventional; it is of the very nature of art and is far more self-explanatory than most of the phenomena of spoken language.

Both the major and the minor triad are found in inverted positions. An inversion is not a reversal, but a position in which one of the upper notes of the normal chord has become the bass-note. When the third of a triad is in the bass we have the chord of the sixth, thus:

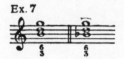

Ex. 7

And now arises a phenomenon wholly unintelligible to acoustics and unpredictable by theory. The once perfect concord of the fourth becomes a discord when taken from the bass. Between any higher parts it is a concord; but from the bass it will never do except as a passing-note or a properly prepared and duly resolved suspension. The reason for this is purely contingent. It so happens that practically every context in which an accented fourth occurs from the bass implies a fifth above it, as in Ex. 4. If instead of the fifth you substitute a sixth you will obtain a chord which is theoretically a second inversion of a triad.

Ex. 8

But no amount of logic will persuade the ear that this sixth is more than another appoggiatura or 'leaning-note' demanding as urgently to resolve on the fifth as the fourth demands to resolve on the third. The fact is an accident of far-reaching importance, but as unamenable to grammatical logic as the reason why a modern English poet should not apply the epithet 'blooming' to his lady's cheek. Find a context for a fourth from the bass which does not imply the $\frac{6}{4}$ $_3$ of Ex. 4, and that fourth will cease to be a discord. But it will be some strange and pregnant language, not to be taken in vain; like the cry at the beginning and end of the Allegretto of Beethoven's Seventh Symphony. And even there the ear is, at the outset, expecting the true bass and remembering it at the end.

The harmonic materials of sixteenth-century polyphony are, then, the major and minor triads, their inversions as chords of $\frac{6}{3}$, and the discords of the second and seventh and (from the bass) the fourth, treated either as suspensions or as passing-notes. The scale in which the flux of polyphony moved through transient

discord from concord to concord was the diatonic scale preserved
from ancient Greece and handed down directly from the Greco-
Roman or Ptolemaic system to the Church music of the Middle
Ages, doubtless with conflation from Jewish sources.

III. MODAL TONALITY

Tonality is the element which groups a succession of musical
sounds intelligibly round some centre. With the development of
polyphony, tonality becomes as important as the concord-discord
system itself; and, indeed, that system could not have existed
without tonal guidance at every point. Discord is transition;
concord is finality. The task of tonality is to organize various
degrees of finality among concords. The first decision made by
pure polyphony (but revoked in a later age) was that the minor
triad, though it might be a concord, could never be final. A bare
fifth or even a bare octave would be more acceptable, as being
a potential major triad. The final chord, whether complete or
not, requires to be approached by chords in a well-defined relation to it. Two types of full close, or cadence, thus came into
existence—the authentic, in which the final chord is preceded by
a major chord whose bass is a fourth below or a fifth above the
final bass, and the plagal, in which the penultimate chord is
based a fourth above or a fifth below the final, and is major or
minor according to the mode:

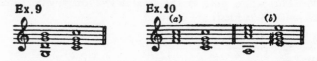

The modes were named after those of ancient Greece, wrongly
identified in particular; and theory clung to terms derived from
non-harmonic notions long after the practice of composers had
become inveterately harmonic. An aesthetically correct account
of Palestrina's tonality is much more easily achieved by a description in terms of Beethoven's key-system than by any attempt to
refer it to the orthodox modal theory.

According to the finally prevalent statement of that theory
there were ideally fourteen modes, two based on each degree of
the diatonic scale. Practically the modes based on B were impossible, as the diatonic fifth from B is imperfect. The numbers of
these imaginary modes, XI and XII, were piously retained for
them, together with the name of Locrian. The 'authentic' modes
ran from the 'final' or fundamental note to its octave. Each
authentic mode was allied to a 'plagal' mode, having the same
final, but lying a fourth lower. This is an important distinction

in purely melodic music and can be clearly recognized in folk-
songs. Thus, 'The Bluebell of Scotland' is authentic, while
'Auld Lang Syne' is, except for an isolated top note, typically
plagal. In polyphonic music the difference between an authentic
mode and its plagal companion is a vague matter settled by the
position of the tenor voice.

The word 'modulation' was used in the theory of modal music
to denote the formation of full closes on other notes than the
final. The sixteenth-century composer developed a perfect sense
of key around his cadences, and he knew very well what he was
doing when he avoided stimulating that sense elsewhere. He
selected his subordinate cadences on no more cogent principle
than the avoidance of monotony. He was like a painter whose
draughtsmanship is faultless in faces and figures, but who sees
no objection to implying a different horizon for each detail in his
picture. And harmony has no such relation to external nature as
can justify critics in calling modal tonality archaic. Palestrina's
tonality is one of the most mature and subtle things in music, and
later developments cannot lessen its truth to the nature of art.

Here are the twelve modes which theoretically underlie the
tonality of the sixteenth century. Every composition was written
in one of these modes, and its incidental modulations were not
regarded as visits to another mode, though that is aesthetically
what they really were. The diagram gives the name of the authentic position above each scale, and the plagal name and position
below. The white note is the final. The imaginary Locrian
modes (with B as final) are omitted.

Ex. 11

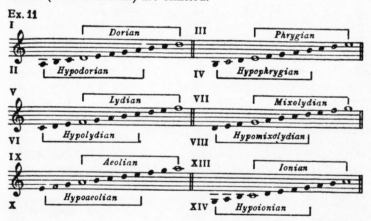

In practice these modes are not always easy to ascertain. The
B natural in Lydian tonality is so difficult to handle that the
great masters almost always flattened it permanently and put the

flat as a key-signature, thus producing an Ionian mode transposed, or plain modern F major. (All modes could be thus written a fourth higher; and apart from this, the actual pitch of performance was determined by convenience and was bound by no fixed standard.) The Phrygian mode cannot form an authentic cadence; and its plagal cadence (shown in Ex. 10b) sounds to our ears like a half-close on the dominant of A minor. This is quite final enough for modal harmony; but a very slight impulse may make Palestrina reverse the cadence and so end with a chord of A. This does not make the mode Aeolian, and, though the Aeolian mode looks as if it was the origin of our minor scale, true Aeolian polyphony is of all harmonic styles the most remote from modern music. The Dorian and Phrygian modes are much nearer to our notions of a well-grounded minor key. The Ionian mode is identical with our major key; and Mixolydian tonality is like a major key with either an excessive emphasis on the subdominant or a top-heavy and finally prevalent dominant.

Extraneous sharps constantly come into modal music through the necessity of providing major penultimate chords in authentic cadences, as well as final major thirds for minor modes. Flats were no less often necessary to correct the tritone fourth between F and B (hence the shape of the flat, and Morley's naming of it as the B clef). The rules governing these accidentals were so well known that singers resented the providing of the signs where the need of such *musica ficta* was self-evident. On the other hand, many of the most mystical harmonies, such as the opening of Palestrina's *Stabat Mater*, were the gifts of creative imagination equally remote from modal theory and modern tonality. Brahms understood modal harmony much better than the critics who blame him for violating the modes of folk-songs by not setting them in a kind of musical Wardour Street. If you want to set old tunes without using leading-notes and changes of key you should not harmonize them at all.

IV. ESSENTIAL DISCORDS AND RIGID TONALITY

The strict theory of suspensions and passing-notes was diversified by many idioms which grew up charmingly and illogically. Logic itself admitted harshnesses which the pure taste of Victoria and Palestrina rejected without waiting for the judgement of theorists. For instance, our glorious Tudor masters shared with many other composers outside the Hispano-Roman orbit a keen intellectual pleasure in violent collisions between a major and a minor third over the same bass; *some* third being essential to the harmony and each of the conflicting voices having unanswerable reasons for its own version. But these 'false rela-

tions', as we now call them, are both archaic and provincial, for
all their logic. The overlapping of harmonic ideas produced
many results both more pleasant and more fruitful.

Here is an extreme case in which the ordinary rules of *musica
ficta* give results which strain the nineteenth-century theorist
and compel him to discover 'double roots' and other cabalistic
secrets.

Ex. 12

The bass singer, knowing his rules of *musica ficta*, would be
insulted at such a 'donkey's mark' as a flat to the B for the purpose of correcting the inadmissible tritone, comprised between
F and B. The treble singer would automatically sharpen his G,
under the impression that he was making a close on A; and so
the augmented sixth, one of the most complex discords known
to Bach and Mozart, did frequently occur in sixteenth-century
performances and was not always regarded as a blunder. In
Ex. 12 the treble singer would happen to be mistaken in sharpening the G, for it is not really part of a close on to A. The close
is on to D, and the middle singer would recognize its leading-
note without the aid of 'donkey's marks'. For our Boeotian age
we require a flat to the B in the bass and sharps for the penultimate Cs in the middle part. If the sixteenth-century composer
intended to produce an augmented sixth, he would provide
the soprano with a sharp to the G in order to reassure the
singer.

But the beginning of the seventeenth century saw a musical
revolution far beyond the scope of any accumulation of licences
on the polyphonic basis. The feeble efforts of the first Monodists,
Jacopo Peri, Emilio Cavalieri, and other pioneers of opera and
solo vocal declamation with lute or keyboard accompaniment had
already drawn attention to the value of any and every chord as
a thing in itself, apart from its position in a polyphonic flux, when
the masterful spirit of Monteverdi gave to the new movement all
the power of his intellect and rhetorical instinct. Only a polyphonist can appreciate the real aesthetic values of monody, and
Monteverdi was a vigorous though decadent polyphonist, both
before and after he took up monody. But not even his mastery
could organize the chaos that overwhelmed the art of music when
the limitations of the golden age had been broken down. For one

thing, pure polyphony dealt only with unaccompanied voices. When instruments were treated as important elements in serious music the polyphonic hypothesis became inadequate and several new sets of laws had to be found by experiment. A century was no long time for such a task.

Monteverdi's chief innovation is popularly said to be the 'invention' of the dominant seventh and of other so-called 'essential' discords. An essential discord is merely a discord which through custom has ceased to require preparation; and to attribute its invention to any particular author is like naming the first writer who used a metaphor instead of a full-blown simile. Most, if not all, of the discords that have become essential are based on that part of the key which we call the dominant; for the reason that all harmonic phenomena gravitate towards the full close as inevitably as all verbal statements gravitate round the subject-predicate-copula group. The dominant of a key is the bass of the penultimate chord of an authentic cadence. Opposed to the dominant there is another centre, the subdominant, which supports the penultimate chord of a plagal cadence. A key has, then, three cardinal points: the key-note, or tonic; the dominant, the chief means of orientation in modulations; and the subdominant, whose function we should understand much more readily if we called it the anti-dominant.

The chief and not wholly unconscious aim of the successors of Monteverdi (that is to say, of the composers of the mid-seventeenth century) was to establish the tonic-dominant-subdominant orientation of major and minor keys in a system which could digest essential discords. A modal composition visited other modes than its own whenever it made a cadence other than on its own final; but it did not establish itself in the visited modes; and still less did it go into regions that produced its own mode at a different pitch.

Throughout the seventeenth century the various streams of music were trickling gently towards a mighty lake, from which all later music takes its origin. Alessandro Scarlatti is now less known to us than his wayward son, Domenico, whose harpsichord music is in a *genre* by itself. But Alessandro, more than any other composer in history, deserves to be considered the founder of a great classical tradition. He is called the founder of the Neapolitan school. And classical tonality is primarily Neapolitan. It recognizes only two modes—the major and the minor. The loss of modal subtleties is more than compensated by the powerful dramatic and architectonic values of clearly-established keys with a capacity for modulation to similar keys in relations of clear harmonic significance.

The following eight bars from the end of the first recitative in Handel's *Messiah*, epitomize several normal features of the system:

Ex. 13   'The voice of one that crieth in the wilderness'

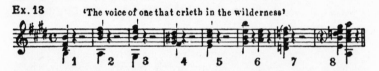

Before discussing this example, we must further explain the system of major and minor keys. Here are the first six degrees of the scale of C major (which, being without sharps and flats, is taken as the standard key) with a triad, or common chord, on each. The notes of these triads are all within the key. The functional names of each degree are given below, and the number above in Roman figures. Capital figures indicate major chords; and small figures minor.

Ex. 14

The seventh degree, or leading note, bears no common chord within the key, for its triad has an imperfect fifth. The submediant is so called because the subdominant is not conceived as the note below the dominant, but as an anti-dominant, a fifth below the tonic, so that there is a submediant as a third between it and the tonic, just as there is a mediant as a third between the tonic and dominant.

Another most important gain of the new tonality as against the modal system is that the minor mode can now so firmly support its tonic by its other chords that a minor tonic chord becomes convincing as a final. The contrast between major and minor keys acquires a high emotional value. We must clearly understand that the minor mode, like the minor triad, is identified with the major mode on the same tonic. The so-called 'relative major' is one of five equally direct relations to a minor tonic and the 'relative minor' is one of five to a major tonic. The minor mode of C is not (as the Tonic Sol-fa system will have it) A minor, but C minor.

In the minor mode a strict confinement to cardinal harmonies produces a melodically awkward augmented second between the flat sixth and the necessarily sharp leading note. Accordingly the external form of the scale varies and the variations have harmonic results. Ex. 15 shows the so-called harmonic and melodic minor scales.

Ex 15

Harmonic   *Melodic.*

The melodic form avoids the augmented second by sharpening
the sixth in ascent and flattening both sixth and seventh in
descent.

V. CLASSICAL KEY-RELATIONSHIPS

A fundamental proposition in the aesthetics of tonality is that
key-relationship subsists between two tonics only and has nothing
to do with the intervention of a third tonic. Observe the word
tonic; the proposition commits us to no specified mode on either
side of the relation.

Direct relationship exists between two keys when the tonic
chord of one is among the common chords of the other. If our
first key is major, we simply identify its related keys with its
common-chords other than its tonic; thus Ex. 14 shows that
C major is directly related to five keys, D minor the supertonic,
E minor the mediant, F major the subdominant, G major the
dominant, and A minor the submediant.

The relatives of a minor tonic have to be discovered by a converse process, for the minor scale is so unstable that the evidence
of its common chords is conflicting and misleading. For instance,
the dominant chord of a minor key is major. But you will receive
a shock if you try answering the subject of Bach's G minor Fugue,
Book I, No. 16, of *Das Wohltemperirte Klavier* in D major instead of D minor! Evidently the only directly related dominant
key to a minor tonic is also minor. This being so, the subdominant must be minor also, for it is the converse of the
dominant, the key to which the tonic is dominant. In order to
reach it the tonic chord must become major, a pathetic effect
constantly to be found near the end of classical slow movements
in minor keys.

The other relations of a minor tonic are converse to the relations of a major tonic. Thus, if D minor be the supertonic of
C major, we must find a name for the relation of C major to D
minor. We run up the scale of D minor and find that C is its flat
seventh. Similarly, if E minor is the mediant of C major, then
C major is the flat sixth or submediant of E minor; and, lastly,
if A minor is the submediant or relative minor of C major, then
C major is the mediant or relative major of A minor. And so the
relations of a minor tonic may be obtained by reading Ex. 14
backwards, with A minor as the key of reference. Transposing

Ex. 14 so that vi becomes C minor, we obtain the following five relations: B flat major the flat seventh, A flat major the submediant, G minor the dominant, F minor the subdominant, E flat the mediant (or relative major).

It is now easy to describe the drift of the Handelian chords of Ex. 13. The key-signature is that of E major, a key that differs only in pitch and in minute instrumental technicalities from all other major keys. (Ideas as to the characters of keys in themselves are entirely subjective, and no agreement is to be expected about them.) The first chord is a common chord of B major, the dominant of E. In its present context it represents not only the dominant chord, but the dominant key, for it happens to be the close of a passage in B major. The next chord is still a dominant chord, but effects a return to E, being the last inversion of the dominant seventh thereof. The seventh is in the bass, and duly resolves on G sharp in the next chord, a first inversion of E (bar 3). Handel would have had less scruple than many later writers in letting the bass skip down to E, so long as the G sharp was somewhere in the chord, but here he is making his bass regularly descend the scale. The next step, F sharp, supports another dominant chord, that of C sharp minor (vi from our tonic) in its last inversion, like that in bar 2. It also resolves in bar 5. Bar 6 passes to the subdominant (A major) and bar 7 establishes that key in a manner to remove all doubt by striking its subdominant chord, which is wholly outside the range of E major. The natural result is the full close in A major in bar 8. Such is the normal way of using key-relations in the essentially Neapolitan art of Handel; and all the intensity of Bach's thought adds nothing to its essential elements. When Bach modulates more widely his purpose is, like that of Handel in 'Thy rebuke hath broken his heart', not to explain, but to astound.

Another great change had to enlarge the art of music before key-relationships could attain their full meaning; but this time the change was accomplished without a period of chaos. It was like Kant's 'Copernican revolution' in philosophy; and its more general aspects are discussed in the articles INSTRUMENTATION, MUSIC, OPERA, and SONATA FORMS.

Its first effect on harmony was shown in a drastic simplification of style; for music had now become dramatic, and there was no musical resource of more cardinal dramatic importance than changes of key. Consequently the baldest facts of key-relation became dramatically significant, out of all proportion to their direct intellectual import. A musical historian can make no graver blunder than to mistake Mozart's and Haydn's harmonic simplicity for an intellectual simplicity. To prolong a preparatory harping on the dominant of a new key is equivalent to working up the entry of an important person in a drama.

A hundred years before, the problem which Alessandro Scarlatti solved in his youth might be described as that of finding the dominant. The simple-seeming Mozart is, as often as not, mocking us with the riddle 'When is a dominant not a dominant?' Musical perspective has gained another new depth in its command of planes. A modulation may establish a new key firmly enough for an incident in the course of a melody, but not nearly firmly enough for a new stage in the whole scheme. Conversely, a passage which at first sounded like vehement emphasis on the local dominant may, long afterwards, when the dominant key has been firmly established, be given note for note at the same pitch with a triumphantly tonic effect. And the dimensions over which Mozart's tonality maintains its coherence are enormous; sometimes almost on Beethoven's largest scale.

Music, which in Palestrina's age was 'a linked sweetness long drawn out', with the links extending only from one accent to the next, had by the beginning of the eighteenth century trained the mind to measure harmonic relations over melodic periods of eight or more bars; and the mighty polyphony of Bach and Handel broke down the melodic regularity, but did not greatly enlarge the range over which the listener must depend on his memory. These masters can visit the same key several times in a composition without inciting the listener to notice the fact either as a purpose or as a tautology. But Mozart, Haydn, and Beethoven build confidently on a knowledge of the exact effect that a modulation in one passage will have on a passage five or even ten minutes later. Beethoven's enormous architectural and dramatic power enabled him to discover and command the whole range of key-relationship theoretically possible within any definite meaning of the term. There is no limit to the possible range of modulation, as Bach took pains to show; but 'the unity of the chromatic scale' is a feeble dogma on which to base the notion that Beethoven ought to have treated all keys as equally related, instead of drawing the line where he did. Great artists discover facts and resources, not licences and vagaries.

Haydn, Mozart, Beethoven, Schubert, Brahms, and Wagner all agree in one simple and cogent method of extending the direct or natural series of key-relations. They merely changed the modes of either or both numbers of a directly related pair. Certain reservations were necessary; the supertonic of a major key which is quite happy as a minor neighbour completely fails to sound like a major key in its own right and behaves merely like 'dominant preparation' for the ordinary dominant. An analyst who imputes the key of A major to bars 19–24 of the first move-

ment of Beethoven's G major Sonata, op. 14, no. 2, *when he
hears them in their context*, should not attempt to discuss key-
relationship until he can discriminate between a passage *on* the
dominant and a passage *in* the dominant.

What is true of one key-relationship will be true of its converse: the key of the flat seventh refuses to assert itself as a real
key in relation to a major tonic. A dozen accessory chords in D
major would not make the seventh bar of Ex. 13 amount to more
than the subdominant chord in A major until they included a
chord of G. The testimony of such openings as those of Beethoven's Sonatas, opp. 31, no. 1, and 53, is emphatic.

In the rare cases where such keys do not thus explain themselves away, their effect is startling. (Ineptitudes may be
neglected.) The passage that follows the return of the main
theme in the first movement of Beethoven's 'Eroica' Symphony
is one of the supreme dramatic strokes in music. The hard-won
tonic of E flat gives way first to F major and then to the opposite
extreme, a third lower, D flat. Another third down brings us
safely to our own dominant chord.

One other type of key-relation is derived from a special form
of the minor scale, in which the lower tetrachord is made to
correspond with the upper:

Ex. 16

The first inversion of its flat supertonic chord is known as the
Neapolitan sixth; and the Neapolitan key-relations are the flat
supertonic major, equally related (as the E natural in Ex. 16
shows) to a major and a minor tonic, and the converse relation
of the sharp seventh. A minor tonic has no direct converse relation, for the Neapolitan chord is major. But, as Schubert shows
at the end of the first movement of his D minor Quartet and in
the slow movement of his String Quintet in C, an indirect relation may be established by making the Neapolitan chord minor.

We must beware of imputing relationship to keys separated
by discursive modulation unless we have strong collateral evidence from the key-functions of a musical design. Tonality and
form are inseparable; and great composers do not even expect
the tonic to be recognized after long wanderings without some
such conclusive evidence as the return of the opening theme.

On pages 62–64 are two tables, indicating by Roman figures
the whole scheme of key-relationships, first from a major tonic,
secondly from a minor tonic. Flats indicate degrees flattened in
comparison with those of the major scale of reference; and in

Table B sharps are used to distinguish cases where the key is a semitone above the corresponding degree of a minor scale. Thus, if C be the tonic, E major will be represented by III in Table A, and by III♯ in Table B. In either table, the figure iii♭ would, reckoned from C, be E flat minor.

The characters of key-relationships are solid facts, and they probably have some bearing on the various subjective ideas which many music-lovers entertain of the character of keys in themselves; for nobody can name a key without being aware of its distance from C major. Be this as it may, it is an undisputed fact that modulations in a dominant direction have an effect of action, while modulations towards the subdominant have an effect of retirement. With a major tonic the three remaining directly-related keys are minor, a contrast which outweighs their other distinctive characters. To move from a major tonic to the relations of its tonic minor, such III♭ and VI♭, is to pass into deep and warm shadow. Such modulations form characteristic purple patches in the course of Mozart's second subjects.

Changes from a major tonic to the major mode of its mediant or submediant are extremely bright. Haydn, who explored all the range of tonality in contrasts between whole movements, or between a minuet and its trio, is very fond of using them in this way in his later works. Beethoven incorporates them in the most highly-organized functions of his sonata-movements. The Neapolitan relations appearing once as a paradox in Haydn's last Pianoforte Sonata, are completely rationalized by Beethoven, Schubert, and Brahms. The flat supertonic casts a deep warm shadow over the tonal scheme, and becomes sheer blackness in the rare cases where it is changed to minor. Conversely, the move a semitone downwards from the tonic (to VII♯ or vii♯) is a move into mysterious brightness. Other extreme depths are sounded in the double changes from a major tonic to iii♭ or vi♭; which (with convenient change of notation) may be found in Beethoven's Sonata, op. 106, and Schubert's last Pianoforte Sonata. The converse relations III♯ and VI♯ from a minor tonic are very bright; the only really bright contrasts that the minor key-relations possess. Beethoven's C minor Concerto shows III♯, and his F minor Quartet shows VI♯.

VI. THOROUGH-BASS

The great classical tradition cares little for the study of chords as things in themselves; and the art of harmony perishes under a discipline that separates its details from counterpoint and its larger issues from form. An excellent means of mastering a good harmonic vocabulary is to practise the filling-out of classical figured basses at the keyboard; in other words, to exercise the function of the continuo-player who, from the time of Monteverdi to that of Beethoven's organ-teachers, used to supply accompaniments from a bass with figures indicating the gist of the chords required. Fluency in such a practice does not of itself

TABLE OF KEY-RELATIONSHIPS
A. From Major Tonic.

I	Direct Relationships	ii	iii	IV	V	vi
	Indirect through both i and the second key			iv	v	
Indirect through i IIIb VIb	Indirect through the second key		III			VI
Doubly indirect through the former indirect keys iiib vib						
Neapolitan direct	IIb		VII and vii			
Neapolitan, indirect	iib					
Unconnected	IV♯ and iv♯ = Vb and vb and all enharmonic synonymns of other keys					
Ambiguous	II VIIb and viib.					

confer the ability to produce original harmony, but it means that music can be read with understanding. It is an empiric craft. But it had the misfortune to become a science, when, early in the eighteenth century, Rameau discovered the theory of the fundamental bass. This is an imaginary bass (best when most imaginary) that gives 'roots' to all the essential chords of the music above it. The conception is true only of the most obvious harmonic facts; beyond them it is as vain as the attempt to ascertain your neighbour's dinner from a spectrograph of the smoke from his chimney. The augmented sixth which arose so innocently in Ex. 12 requires a double root. The first chord of Beethoven's Sonata in E flat, op. 31, no. 3, is an 'eleventh' with its root on the dominant in flat defiance of the fact that the dominant is the most inconceivable bass-note in the whole passage until it arrives as a climax in the sixth bar. But musical fundamentalists refuse to look six bars ahead.

Philipp Emanuel Bach, in conversation with Dr. Burney (*The*

TABLE OF KEY-RELATIONSHIPS
B. *From Minor Tonic.*

	i	Direct Relationships	IIIb	iv	v	VIb VIIb
		Indirect through both I and the second key		IV	V	
Indirect through I iii♯ vi♯		Indirect through the second key	iib			vib
Doubly indirect through the former indirect keys III♯—VI♯						
Neapolitan, direct		IIb				
Neapolitan, indirect		iib				VII♯ and vii♯
Unconnected		IV♯ and iv♯ =		Vb and vb and all enharmonic synonyms of other keys		
Ambiguous	ii	II viib				

Present State of Music in Germany, &c.), said that Rameau's theory was 'childish, for it reduces all music to full closes'. This is perfectly true, and the theory did no harm to eighteenth-century French music, which eschewed long sentences and seldom strayed far from the regions of the full close. But in England Rameau's doctrine raged unchecked by taste or common sense, and culminated in Dr. Day's famous application of homœopathy to the art of music. This would have mattered less if Dr. Day had not gained the ear of the greatest English academic musicians of mid-Victorian times. As Sir Charles Stanford aptly says (*Musical Composition*), Day's theory 'irrigated a wide area of low-lying ground, and we are still suffering from the

effects of its miasma'. The remedy lies in cultivating vivid
impressions of the actual relations between counterpoint and
harmony in detail, between tonality and form in general, and
between key-relations and chromatic chords. To this end,
thorough-bass should be cultivated not on paper but at the keyboard, with passages (graded according to difficulty) from the
continuos of Bach's Cantatas and Mozart's Church music.

VII. TEMPERAMENT AND JUST INTONATION

Even in pure sixteenth-century polyphony the ideal diatonic
scale implies distinctions of intonation beyond the capacity of
any mechanical instrument with a limited number of notes. In
the Ionian mode or major scale of C the interval C–D is not
the same kind of whole tone as the interval D–E, but differs as
8:9 from 9:10.

The normal position for the supertonic is a 'major tone' (8:9)
above the tonic; but even so common a discord as the dominant
seventh will set up a conflict, the dominant requiring its fifth to
be as 9:8 above the tonic, while the seventh will want to make a
true minor third from a supertonic in the position of 10:9. Such
conflicts are about very minute distinctions, but every discord
produces them if it is dwelt upon. Nevertheless, the twelve notes
that human hands can negotiate within a span-stretched octave
suffice to express the most chromatic harmony with less average
inaccuracy than is cheerfully permitted in human singing and
violin-playing. Singers and violinists can and do constantly
achieve a purer intonation than that of keyed instruments; but
the only aesthetic issue between free voices and tempered instruments is the difference between a human intonation liable to
human error and an instrumental intonation with an inherent
systematic error. The human error is often not only accidentally
but deliberately in excess of the systematic error, for the slightest
vibrato is larger than the quantities involved.

The subject of just intonation is fatally fascinating to people
whose mathematical insight has not attained to the notion of
approximation. In art, as in mathematics, accuracy lies in estimating the relevant degree of approximation rather than in
unrolling interminable decimals. Music is no more to be heard
through Helmholtz resonators than pictures are to be enjoyed
through microscopes. The true musical ear will recognize the
real meaning of harmonies though the practical intonation con-
founds them with homonyms. Bach introduced no new musical
thought when he arranged *Das Wohltemperirte Klavier* to stimulate the adoption of equal temperament by providing music in
every major and minor key for which the keyboard had notes.

Systems of unequal temperament tuned the commoner keys as well as possible, in the hope that remoter keys would never be visited. Bach decided that it was better to have all keys equally out of tune than to have some keys intolerable. The miraculous modulations of his Chromatic Fantasia deliberately emphasize all the chords that were 'wolves' in unequal temperament, and thus Bach devoted his highest efforts of imagination to a humble practical purpose. But Marenzio had modulated as far in madrigals written in the purest golden-age polyphony. No true harmonic ideas are based on equal temperament, any more than a true geometry is based on exclusively rational quantities.

VIII. METHODS OF MODULATION

The commonest way of establishing a change of key is, as we have seen, to emphasize the dominant chord of the new key until only the new tonic can be expected. This we will call dominant modulation; leaving out of consideration how the new dominant is reached. (It was probably surrounded by its own dominant-of-dominant, which could be reached from various other directions.)

A more interesting type of modulation begins with Beethoven, arising out of hints given by Haydn and Mozart. It may be called functional modulation, and consists in placing indirectly related keys into positions which make their exact relation appear vividly. If the first chord of the second key is a dominant, the relation will still appear in high relief; but any further decoration of that dominant will reduce the result to an ordinary modulation. (Compare bars 22–3 of the first movement of Beethoven's 'Waldstein' Sonata with the drastic process of bars 37–8 in the first movement of op. 106.)

Functional modulation might well be called 'natural' if that term had not been commonly assigned to modulation within the five directly related keys, irrespective of method.

Mere juxtaposition of tonics will suffice for the purposes of a functional modulation. If Beethoven had wished to explain the presence of F sharp minor (vi♭) in the scheme of op. 106, the natural (or functional) process would consist of the following four chords:

Ex. 17

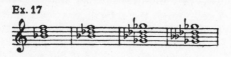

Closely akin to this method is Beethoven's dramatic way of

reducing a chord to a single note, and then building up therefrom a quite remote chord. (*See* opp. 90 and 81a.)

All such devices show the listener what is really happening.
The object of 'enharmonic' modulation is frankly to mystify. It
is popularly supposed to belong specially to tempered scales; but
it really presupposes just intonation. All discords, as we have
seen, set up a conflict in their intonation; and an enharmonic
modulation is merely a conflict so coarse-grained that it appears
in the notation by some such mark as a change from G♯ to A♭.
An ill-motived enharmonic modulation is like a bad pun; a great
enharmonic modulation is a sublime mystery. Here is the commonest pivot of enharmonic changes, the diminished seventh,
with its four vastly different resolutions:

Of course, these are really four different chords. If the true
theory of just intonation demanded that the minor scale should
be rigid, a chord of the diminished seventh would be much
harsher than the tempered scale makes it. But what really happens in just intonation is that two notes of the minor scale become
so unstable in the stress of discord that it becomes a small matter
to shift the strains to whichever notes you please. Even with a
limited keyboard the ear imagines a change of intonation when
the unexpected resolution appears. This is why chromatic intervals are difficult to sing; the singer loses confidence when he has
to aim at a note which will not stand still.

Not every change of notation represents a genuine enharmonic
modulation. Modulate diatonically from A to F: and transpose
your modulation down a semitone. You will start in A flat, but
if you have much to say in the second key you will probably prefer to write it as E, instead of F flat. Sad nonsense has been
written by many commentators on the most ordinary harmonies
disguised by convenience of notation.

Nevertheless, a merely notational change may eventually have
an enharmonic result, for it may be part of an enharmonic circle.
If the harmonic world is round, why should just intonation be
plane? Adjustments infinitely smaller than those of temperament will suffice to make the ends of an enharmonic circle meet
in the course of a long composition. The first movement of
Brahms's F major Symphony, played with its repeat, goes four
times round an enharmonic circle of major thirds (F, D♭, B♭♭
= A, F). Every time the key written as F returns it identifies
itself by the opening theme. If the pitch rose to G♭♭ we would

scarcely notice the fact after the intervening passages, and when the pitch had risen noticeably we should complain. Temperament keeps the pitch; but just intonation could do so by an even distribution of infinitely smaller adjustments.

It now becomes clear why keys a tritone fourth apart cannot become related. That interval (which modal musicians identified with the devil) constitutes the kink in musical space. It sets up an enharmonic short circuit; a modulation from C to F sharp is exactly the same as one from G flat back to C; and whichever key you start from, the other will sound like the dominant of a Neapolitan key instead of asserting its own rights. No sensible person forbids the modulation; its effect may be excellent, but it is not the effect of a key-relation.

IX. WAGNERIAN HARMONY

Wagner's sense of key is exactly the same as Beethoven's; but it has hours in which to exercise itself, whereas Beethoven's designs seldom stretch without break over fifteen minutes, and always show their purport within five. But take, for example, the conflict between two major keys a tone apart. The jealous Fricka *did* hope (in F major) that the domestic comforts of Walhalla would induce Wotan to settle down. Wotan, gently taking up her theme in E flat, dashes her hopes by this modulation more effectively than by any use of his artillery of tubas and trombones.

But the most distinctive feature of Wagner's harmony is his use of long auxiliary notes in such a way as to suggest immensely remote keys, which vanish with the resolution. (Chopin anticipates Wagner in what Sir Henry Hadow finely describes as 'chromatic iridescence'.)

On p. 68 is the evolution of the wonderful opening of *Tristan und Isolde*.

X. POST-WAGNERIAN HARMONY

The line of evolution traced thus far has, evidently, no *a priori* limits, though it has principles. Any new system is destined either to starve for lack of nourishment from the main sources of music or become absorbed in them. Systems derived from equal temperament are crude fallacies. The whole-tone scale which readily arises on the pianoforte, e.g., C,D,E,F♯. (=G♭, A♭, B♭, C), amused Debussy during a few dozen songs and short pieces, and played a much less predominant part in his *Pelléas et Mélisande* than is generally supposed. It is really no more a whole-tone scale than the diminished seventh is a major sixth bounding a series of minor thirds. Sir Walford Davies has pointed out that this scale is a six-note chord projected into a

Evolution of the opening of Wagner's Prelude to *Tristan und Isolde*

Ex. 19 — Three concords (tonic, first inversion of subdominant, and dominant of A minor, a possible 16th-century cadence in the Phrygian mode)

Ex. 20 — The same chords varied by a suspension (*)

Ex. 21 — Ditto, with the further addition of a double suspension (*) and two passing notes (††)

Ex. 22 — Ditto, with a chromatic alteration of the second chord (*) and an 'essential' discord (dominant 7th) at (†)

Ex. 23 — Ditto, with chromatic passing notes (**) and appoggiaturas (††)

Ex. 24 — The last two chords of Ex. 23 attacked unexpectedly, the first appoggiatura (*) prolonged till it seems to make a strange foreign chord before it resolves on the short note at *, while the second appoggiatura (†) is chromatic.

Ex. 25 — The same enharmonically transformed so as to become a variation of the 'dominant ninth' of C minor. The G♯ at * is really A♭, and * is no longer a note of resolution, but a chromatic passing note.

single octave and capable, like the diminished seventh, of an
enharmonic turn to each of its notes. Here is one of several
possible ways of showing the six resolutions of this scale:

Ex. 26

Enthusiasts for new systems are naturally infuriated when the
systems thus fade into the light of common or Wagnerian day.
Nevertheless, the pleasure given by every effort at revolutionary
harmony results from the fact that the new chords enter our
consciousness with the meaning they would bear in a classical
scheme. Not only Wagner but Bach and Palestrina lurk behind
every new harmonic sensation, and cannot long be prevented
from making sense of it. After sense has been made, the fundamental theorists will return and prove to us that many quite
commonplace chromatic progressions contain the triskaideka-
hyperhendekaenneaheptachord of . Ex. 26 with the omission of
not more than four of its notes.

Other new theories are not less quickly worn out, even when
invented by gifted composers. Scriabin, each of whose last five
sonatas is built round its own new chord, complained shortly
before his untimely death that he had, after all, not succeeded in
getting away from a sophisticated dominant seventh. This complaint recalls Philipp Emanuel Bach's criticism of Rameau's
theory, and its cause lies deep in the very nature of articulate
thought. If you wish to compose freely, do not fix your mind
on new harmonic propositions. Language is not extended by
declining to use what is known of it.

Arnold Schönberg's harmonic theory is often masterly in its
analysis of classical music, but it is extremely disappointing in
its constructive aspect. Not only does Schönberg think the
absurd old theory of 'added thirds' worth refuting, but he in-
vents a new theory of added fourths which has even less foundation. The theory of added thirds was no more scientific than a

classification of birds by the colour of their feathers. But birds
do have feathers of various colours, and classical music does build
up chords by sequences of thirds. Schönberg's theory rests on no
observation at all, for the piling up of fourths has no origin in
classical harmony and only a quickly exhausted melodic value.
However, it can be carried right round the tempered scale in
twelve steps and *ad infinitum* in just intonation. To find the composer of the *Gurrelieder* fathering such theories is as disconcerting as to discover Einstein telling fortunes in Bond Street.

XI. THEORETIC POSSIBILITIES OF THE FUTURE

Harmony has not yet found a place for so simple a natural
phenomenon as the seventh note of the harmonic series. Here
are the first sixteen notes from bass C as the fundamental. Many
a 'clang' contains them all in appreciable strength, yet no fewer
than three (besides the octave of No. 7) are outside our system,
Nos. 7 and 13 being much flatter than the notes here written,
and No. 11 much sharper.

Ex. 27

1 2 3 4 5 6 7 8 9 10 11 12 13 14 15 16

Again, though resultant tones are audible enough to save organ-
builders from the expense of 32-ft. pipes by means of devices
which reinforce the resultant tone and obliterate its generators,
they have played no acknowledged part in musical aesthetics.
A theory which builds upon them must abandon the hypothesis
that all harmony grows upwards from the bass. Abandon it by
all means if your musical intuitions inspire you with ideas based
on resultant tones—by which, however, you must mean something different from harmony whose ideal bass lies in its resultant
tones, for that will merely be another notion of fundamental
bass, differing from Rameau's, but again forcing you to regard
harmony as rising from the bass. And, after all, the hypothesis is
not a theory, but an experience. The language of music has, in
fact, taken shape without guidance from resultant tones; just as
the art of painting has, until recent epochs, made no conscious
use of complementary colours, except by instinctively avoiding
ugly or unintelligible effects.

Schönberg rightly says that *der Einfall*, the inspiration that
comes without theorizing, is the sole criterion of musical truth;
and perhaps some composers may have *Einfälle* so convincing in
their use of Nos. 7, 11, and 13 as to compel us to build new
instruments for them. And so with the use of a resultant-tone or

inverted harmonic system. The string quartets of Haba have
not as yet made quarter-tones sound convincingly unlike faulty
intonation. We must not blame our ears, which often appreciate
much smaller measurements. The just intonation of a Wagner
opera would comprise some thousand notes to the octave. The
question is not how many notes we use in the long run, but how
small a direct measurement is of interest to us. The carpenter
deals faithfully with the incommensurable when he so much as
fits a cross-bar to a square gate.

Many other modern harmonic tendencies are essentially matters of instrumentation. If, abandoning the polyphonic hypothesis, we use chords, simple or complex, as mere unanalysed
tone-colours, we can start a new polyphony with moving chords
instead of moving single parts.

Triplanar harmony and doubling of melodies in whole chords
R. VAUGHAN WILLIAMS, *Pastoral Symphony*

Ex. 28

Our problem, then, will be to keep the planes of tone distinct.
Organ mixtures, if not properly drowned by the fundamental
tones, would shock the boldest multiplanar harmonist by the
mess they would make of classical harmony.

Extremes meet, and we are recovering a sense of the values of
unharmonized melody; not melody which wants to be harmon-
ized, nor melody which achieves harmonic sense by draughtsmanship, but the austere achievement, far more difficult than any
atonality, of a melody that neither needs nor implies harmony.
And so we return to nature.

INSTRUMENTATION

INSTRUMENTATION is the aspect of music which deals with timbre, and with the technical possibilities and characters of instruments and voices. The treatment of the orchestra has for the last hundred years been the most popular branch of the art. Hence the vogue of the narrow term 'orchestration'. The colloquial word 'scoring' is the only adequate name for an art that ought to include all other aspects of timbre and performance, such as chamber music (q.v.), pianoforte writing, and organ registration.

Method of Study.—The first requisite for good scoring is an imagination exercised by training. Rules are not enough; and neither is mere practical experience. Schumann's scoring grew worse as experience discouraged him; and a student who masters good rules without training his imagination merely protects himself from learning by experience. Many musicians who ought to know better are doing serious mischief by denying the possibility of arm-chair score-reading. Exaggerated claims are harmless, for they are nearer to the truth of what an accumulation of study can achieve. The common sense of the matter is obviously this: the arm-chair reader can vividly imagine effects that he has heard; he can recognize similar effects when he sees them in a score that is new to him; and so with effort and practice he can realize the effect of known sounds in new combinations. The complexity of the combinations has, in reason, little to do with the difficulties of imagination; and familiarity with the type of music is always a paramount factor.

William Wallace, in *The Threshold of Music*, seemed to believe that modern progress in orchestration has produced new cerebral powers. This is a fallacy: listeners or conductors who have become familiar with Richard Strauss's orchestration will vividly imagine the sounds of a page of the master's latest and fullest scoring long before scrutiny has shown more than the main entries and the general type of colouring. But such readers may get nothing but abstract grammatical propositions from a page of Palestrina if they have never heard pure polyphony sung without accompaniment in a vaulted building. The music of each great period has its own proper scoring which sounds well under its proper conditions. The student should take opportunities of hearing each kind of music well produced; and he should multiply his experience by reading the scores of all periods, besides those of his own day. An imagination thus trained is obviously useful to conductors. It is not less useful to composers, for it is no mere antiquarian lore but a widely generalized capacity to

72

imagine correctly all kinds of significant musical sounds. Its possessor will never produce the woolly scoring of the unimaginative composer who goes by rule, and if he makes errors of calculation these will be remediable as errors of imagination are not.

Rules are useful in preventing errors of calculation. The only extant treatise on instrumentation that gives correct rules is the posthumous work of Rimsky-Korsakov. Starting with the proposition that good scoring is good part-writing, this brilliant and fantastic Russian composer lays down surprisingly severe rules for combining good part-writing with well-balanced orchestral values. At first it seems incredible that any free art could live on such terms; yet the marvellous purity of Mozart's orchestration supports Rimsky-Korsakov's system in an art a century earlier and far more complex. For there is less wonder that Rimsky-Korsakov's colouring should be pure since his ideas never overlap, and his hundreds of illustrations from his own works consist (except for a few scraps of recitative) exclusively of 2-bar or 4-bar phrases that repeat themselves. We shall not learn Mozart's art from this, and rules will not endow us with Rimsky-Korsakov's imagination. Nor was that imagination equal to distinguishing blunders from subtleties in the score of his friend Mussorgsky's *Boris Godunov*. Much less, then, is it to be trusted when he dismisses Beethoven's orchestration with the remark that the execution of Beethoven's ideas is far inferior to their conception. This really means that the narrow cross-section of Beethoven's ideas that comes within the aesthetic range of Russian ballet-music could have been scored more easily and brilliantly by a Russian composer in 1890. Apart from this, Beethoven is doubtless not infallible. But perkiness starves the imagination.

Pure Sixteenth-century Polyphony.—In the article HARMONY (q.v.) the grammar of pure polyphony is shown to be equivalent to the art of vocal scoring. A modern choir soon learns the truth of the sixteenth-century rules when it faces the task of unaccompanied rehearsal. The old rules secure singability as well as euphony. But they also leave the composer's imagination free for many subtleties. Our stereotyped full chorus of soprano, alto, tenor, and bass is roughly that of the sixteenth century, though we have forgotten the ways of the genuine boy-alto who delights in manly growls down to D and becomes shy above A in the next octave. The sixteenth century knew no other alto, and Palestrina has seventeen ways of grouping four parts and twelve different ways for three parts, besides equally various five-part and six-part grouping. In eight-part works for double choir the two choirs are often contrasted, as in Palestrina's motet and mass *Hodie Christus natus est*, where the second choir, led by the altos, makes a terrestrial antiphony to a choir of angels.

The infinite subtleties of sixteenth-century part-writing are beyond the scope of this article and very remote from the experiences of any instrumental music. But every conductor and every composer may learn much from Palestrina's and Lasso's devices of producing by part-crossing beautiful progressions that would be crude if the planes of tone were not kept distinct. In all later periods the distinction of planes of tone is a fundamental principle. In the sixteenth century it enters into these delicate intricacies, and appears more obviously in the rule formulated by the first composers for double and triple choirs, viz., that the harmony of each choir must be complete even when all are singing together. Lasso disregards this rule, but its common sense becomes evident when the choirs are on opposite sides of the building.

Archaic Instrumentation.—At the end of the sixteenth century monody arose. It was the art of non-polyphonal vocal declamation with an instrumental accompaniment. With characteristic acumen the Italian monodists promptly recognized that voices and instruments will not meet on the same plane of tone. Not all composers understood the new problems. The habit, in private performance, of using viols to replace missing voices in madrigals had gone far to make composers incautious in dealing with more penetrating instruments. The flat-backed viols with their husky and reedy tone (nowadays still noticeable in the double-bass) were already giving place to the royal family of the violin in all its sizes; this family was no longer on singing terms with voices; yet many composers at first saw no difficulty in using any instrument as equivalent to any other instrument or voice at the same pitch. Schütz (1585–1672) writes for triple and quadruple choirs of voices mixed with instruments. He writes the words under the instruments as well as under the voices; he often merely designates a part *Vox instrumentalis*; but he also takes the trouble to suggest *Tromba o flauto*, as if these instruments, in low register, had the same weight! Beauty often emerges from the chaos—associated with some practical suggestion that leaves us in doubt whether the composer knew what he achieved; as when Schütz proposes that his wonderful *Lamentatio Davidi*, a perfectly scored masterpiece for bass voice, four trombones, and organ, should be played with two violins an octave higher as a substitute for the first two trombones!

Continuo Instrumentation.—By the time of Bach and Handel instrumentation had become a mature art but an art depending on conditions no longer familiar to us. When these conditions are restored the resulting aesthetic system completely justifies itself. It recognizes that no group of instruments can make homogeneous harmony like a vocal chorus, but that all instrumental scoring consists normally of a top, a bottom, and a *tertium quid* which completes the harmony but remains in the background. Bass instruments support the bass; all other instruments, whatever their pitch, are aesthetically top parts, and their most elaborate counterpoint does not profess to make their tones blend. They are woven into patterns of coloured threads, not blended like the colours of a landscape. The *tertium quid* is provided by an organ or a harpsichord; and it obeys the normal grammar of choral harmony. Only a keyboard instrument can provide such harmony ready-made on one plane of tone. At the present day one of the commonest faults of unimaginative scoring is the habit of treating the orchestra like a four-part chorus. Continuo orchestration shows the true principle with drastic clearness, but it shelves the problem of how to keep subordinate parts in their places. The continuo player represents an army of slaves upholding an aristocratic civilization.

Besides gaining a capacity to attack discords boldly, the vocal chorus has undergone a radical change in the treatment of the bass voice when supported by instruments. When the tenor is low but still interior to the harmony, the bass is no longer obliged to go lower, but is free to sing in its upper register, crossing freely above the tenor but relying on instruments which double it an octave lower as the true bass. Bach and Handel never once cross the bass over the tenor in any other way; the tenor in such places never gives the true bass. And Bach's so-called unaccompanied motets thus show in every line that they were conceived as supported by at least an instrumental bass. In fact, unaccompanied choral writing practically disappears from classical music between Palestrina and Schubert. It appears modestly in part-songs, and is first taken fully seriously by Brahms, though some older conductors of choral societies had honourably kept up its tradition.

The basis of the continuo orchestra was, as now, the string band, an instrumental chorus of first and second violins, violas, and violoncellos, supported an octave lower by double basses which are never independent. Wind instruments did not form a complete mass of harmony but stood out against the strings in double or triple threads of each timbre, except when (as often in Handel) they doubled the strings. Flutes were used much more in their lower registers than we think fit in modern orchestration. In the organ loft of a vaulted building low flutes are more effective than in ordinary concert-rooms. The ordinary flute is called traverso. The term 'flauto', with the use of the treble clef on the bottom line, indicates the flute-à-bec, a kind of flageolet, with rather a higher range. Bach uses pairs of each kind in the *Matthew Passion* but not in the same movements.

Oboes are also used in threes or pairs, and the ordinary oboe alternates with a variety a third lower, the oboe d'amore, with the bell (and therefore the tone) of a cor anglais. Strauss has revived it. The real cor anglais figures in Bach's orchestra as the oboe da caccia or the taille. Some authorities tell us that one or other of these was not an alto oboe but a tenor bassoon. It is easier to relabel a museum specimen than to rewrite the whole of Bach's oboe da caccia music.

Bassoons hardly ever emerge from doubling the bass. The 'Quoniam' of Bach's B minor Mass is a bass solo accompanied by a horn, two bassoons, and continuo. It would be delicious if we could find proper acoustic conditions for it and could handle the continuo discreetly enough. A great moment is the rising of the spirit of Samuel in Handel's *Saul*, where the bassoons are as ghostly and awesome as the prophet's message. In large enough numbers they would also astonish us in Handel's scoring of the 'thick darkness' in *Israel in Egypt*. Handel, whose oratorio performances were on a large scale, must have had more reed-tone than string-tone in his orchestra; for he often had twenty oboes and twenty bassoons. Multiplication greatly mellows the tone of an instrument; and we, who seldom hear more than four oboes in unison, even in Mahler's Eighth Symphony, must not hastily judge our ancestors on this point.

Trumpets and horns, not being provided with modern valves, could produce only the natural harmonic series of the key to which their length of tube was set. That series does not close up into anything like a scale until the eighth harmonic. Accordingly trumpeters devoted themselves to acquiring extraordinary command of the delicate distinctions of high lip-pressures (*embouchures*) between the eighth and twentieth harmonics. A long mouthpiece, with a little play in its adjustments, enabled the trumpeter to correct the out-of-tune eleventh, thirteenth, and fourteenth harmonics. (This secret was already forgotten by 1785, so that Burney, describing the Handel Centenary Festival, tells us that whenever the G and G♯, alternately represented by the eleventh harmonic, were heard in 'The trumpet shall sound', displeasure was seen on every countenance.) Humbler players called themselves *Principal-bläser* and produced the lower notes to which the tight-lipped clarino-player could not descend. Horn-players developed a similar hazardous technique of high notes. In modern performances special training and special instruments are required for early eighteenth-century trumpet and horn music. A modern tendency to strain all instruments up to high notes has facilitated this revival. Trombones, when they occasionally appear in continuo orchestration, are treated exactly like choral voices, and are, indeed, mainly used in unison with the chorus. A soprano trombone at first completed the group, but Bach already had to replace it by some kind of slide-trumpet (*corno da tirarsi*).

Bach's full orchestra consists, then, of the string band (preferably larger than he ever had), oboes (ordinary or d'amore) in pairs or threes, flutes or flutes-à-bec in pairs or threes, bassoons (taken for granted) in unison with the basses, three trumpets (two clarini and one principal), three horns (not often used together with the trumpets), and a pair of kettle-drums. If the string band is large the wind parts, other than the trumpets, should be doubled, trebled, or (in festival performances) multiplied. The organ supplies the continuo in choruses, and the harpsichord supplies it in solo movements. The pianoforte is really (as Philipp Emanuel Bach already urged) better than the harpsichord, if only the player will avoid a self-assertive touch.

The orchestral combinations of solo movements range from Handel's perfunctory *tutti unisoni* to Bach's and Handel's richest schemes. Instruments obsolescent from incompatibility or feebleness live awhile in the arias and recitatives, protected from competition with the orchestra; and so we learn from Bach's *Passions* and *Trauer Ode* the use of the lute and viola da gamba, and from Handel's *Alexander Balus* the use of the theorbo, a large double-necked lute. Each movement has its own scheme of instrumentation as a set pattern which cannot change while the movement lasts.

The scheme of a chorus with independent full orchestra is in three planes of tone. These planes do not interfere with each other, and each plane has variants of the same harmonic scheme which would produce appalling collisions if all were projected on to a single plane (say, in an arrangement for two pianofortes). The principal plane is that of the voices. Above it, mostly higher in pitch, all the instruments that are not doubling the bass flourish with more rapid detail than the voices. Behind, and supporting the whole, is the continuo which moves more slowly than the chorus. The bass is common to all the planes, though it is enlivened by instrumental details. The results of this scheme, realized by competent execution under scholarly guidance, are as true in our age as they were when Bach and Handel wrote. Scholarship must show us the right conditions for performance, but it need not recover too precisely the actual original conditions. An old man who had been a chorister under Bach at Leipzig once told Wagner's teacher, Weinlig, how Bach's cantatas were performed. His account was, 'It went atrociously and we always got a flogging afterwards'.

Symphonic Orchestration.—Gluck laid down one of the cardinal principles of symphonic as well as dramatic orchestration when he said that instruments ought to be used according to dramatic vicissitudes. This means that for Gluck it is neither sufficient nor often possible to use them according to a set pattern. Another cardinal principle results from the disappearance of the continuo. This first happened merely by neglect, as the severe training needed for it repelled a generation of musicians excited by non-polyphonic styles. But mere neglect soon passed into a disposition to make the orchestra provide its own continuo. If old music sounded hollow without a continuo, why should not new music contrive better? This at once put many instruments into categories unrealized by Bach and only sporadically realized by the eclectic Handel. An instrument could now have two values: one, the old cantabile function; the other a capacity to provide unobtrusive notes for the background. Holding-notes for the horns revealed a wonderful beauty and usefulness in this way, with all a singer's power to swell and diminish the sound.

The bassoons became the hardest-worked wind instruments in the early symphonic orchestra, for they could do everything required of continuo-work, from doubling the bass to supplying the many notes the natural horns could not reach. Their tone, so beautifully if unwittingly described in *The Hunting of the Snark* as 'meagre and hollow but crisp, like a coat that is rather too tight in the waist, with a flavour of will-o'-the-wisp', had a most useful capacity for vanishing; and 'too tight in the waist' is a very apt description of instruments which, like the bassoon and the viola, show in their half-veiled tones the results of a compromise between the dimensions proper to their pitch and the practicable stretch of human hands.

The viola had at first a curious position in the early symphonic style. That style was so unpolyphonic that the viola could for a long time find nothing to do but to double the violoncello in the upper octaves as the basses double them in the lower. The result is so good that in early symphonies it is carried out mechanically, even where it takes the violas above the second violins. But Mozart uses this primitive device with full imaginative insight in mature works where he hardly less often divides the violas into two independent parts.

The trumpets of the symphonic orchestra have become degraded to the fanfares and signallings of the *Principal-bläser*. The clarino player was finally ousted by players of a cheap substitute called the clarinet, which could play high trumpet parts with ease, if with rather a vinegar tone. But the clarinet had a wide compass; these trumpet-sounds were its worst. Below them it had a rich cantabile octave, and below that a few rather dull notes; and below these a coldly mysterious and reedy lowest octave, the chalumeau register. The dull middle notes proved astonishingly useful for continuo purposes; they are higher than the bassoon can attain without self-assertion, and they are not limited like the horn notes. Gluck uses the clarinet only in this neutral region; and even Mozart gives the instrument nothing better when the orchestra is in the key of D. This primitive treatment survives as late as Beethoven's Second Symphony, and was revived by him in quite a late work, the fugal overture *Zur Weihe des Hauses* (op. 124).

But when Mozart uses clarinets in the keys of A major, E major E flat, and B flat he reveals the clarinet as richer and more resourceful than any other wind instrument. The chalumeau octave is deliciously nutty in arpeggios, and dramatically hollow in sustained notes. The cantabile octave is magnificent (see the trio of the minuet of the great E flat Symphony, for its contrast with echoes on the flute and with low arpeggios on the second clarinet). The military high notes (or 'fife sounds') Mozart does not care for. Beethoven's view of the clarinet is less sympathetic than Mozart's, his idea of its cantabile register being just a tone too high. Schubert understands it perfectly.

The oboe can never efface itself. Run through the individual wind-parts of some such encyclopaedic score as Wagner's *Meistersinger*, and you will be astonished at the unfailing beauty of the oboe parts and at the large tracts of drudgery in the excellent, uncomplaining clarinets.

The flute has no power in its lower octave and blends with other instruments in none, except, paradoxically, with extremely high Bach-like trumpet notes (if the experiment were ever tried). But in its top octave (from A to A) it is a very adequate and euphonious treble to the wind-band, and gains greatly by doubling. Haydn hardly ever writes his orchestral flutes high enough and often seems to expect low notes to be heard under conditions that would not have satisfied Bach. It is possible that his long period of experiment at Esterhazy did him less good than he or historians have thought. His Esterhazy symphonies show that he had a primitive orchestra diversified by astonishing solo players. He was able at Esterhazy to produce horn-passages that would astonish Bach. But in the world outside he found that orchestras, though better in the rank and file, were seldom troubled by virtuoso members. In his last symphony the theme of the finale is a typical and easy horn tune, but he dare not give it to the first horn of Salomon's London orchestra except under cover of a tutti! All his mature scoring is full of strokes of genius but deeply marked with signs of disillusion.

Beethoven's Instrumentation.—Beethoven enlarged the range of orchestral thought more than any composer between Gluck and Wagner. The circumstance of his deafness made him the victim of some miscalculations; and pedantic views of orchestration lead many critics to exaggerate these into grounds for a worse perkiness than Rimsky-Korsakov's damaging patronage of Beethoven's scoring. Two things must be learnt by everybody who wishes to understand Beethoven; first, that errors of calculation are not the same thing as errors of imagination; secondly, that a symphony is not an opera. Beethoven's errors of calculation are no greater than those of any composer who has not been able to hear a rehearsal of his own orchestral work. Their correction, as shown by Weingartner (*Ratschläge*), is equivalent to any pianoforte player's control of his own touch, and would amount to little more than a conductor's ordinary exercise of his skill were they twice as extensive.

Errors of imagination do not exist in Beethoven's art; and only a school of criticism by rule of thumb would suppose that they did. Compared with Mozart's, Beethoven's scoring is rough, redundant, and capricious. But Beethoven's ideas are not Mozart's and can be expressed neither in Mozart's nor in Wagner's scoring. When critics tell us that bars 5–8 of the first movement of Beethoven's Eighth Symphony are badly scored, all they mean is that to let two oboes and a flute crowd in upon a quiet phrase in the clarinet is not a proper way to score the first fateful appearance of a Wagnerian leitmotive, which may not be heard again for an hour. But it is an admirably dramatic and symphonic way to score a formal phrase which is going to be shouted at the top of the full orchestra immediately afterwards. The conductor need only say four words to the oboes, 'Let the clarinet through', and the passage becomes perfectly clear. But it is already intelligible without any such precaution, and only bad playing can spoil it.

The symphonic orchestra which suffices for Beethoven, and for Brahms two generations later, consists of strings, pairs of flutes, oboes, clarinets, and bassoons, one or two pairs of horns, a pair of trumpets, and kettledrums. Trombones, reserved for climaxes, are used in spacious three-part harmony, and Beethoven requires them in three sizes, alto, tenor, and bass. For lack of the alto trombone many of Beethoven's top notes must nowadays be lowered; and then our smart young orchestrators blame Beethoven for his ill-balanced chords. The full wind-tone is extended upwards by the dangerously shrill piccolo, and downwards by the contrafagotto, which gives the bass a richness without asserting itself. The big drum, cymbals, and triangle are called 'Turkish music' and, when used at all by Beethoven, are used according to Viennese ideas of Turkishness. Beethoven's intentions, whatever we may think of their execution, cover the whole field of symphonic art; and it is to dramatic orchestration that we must look for any addition to his range of thought.

Dramatic Orchestration.—The change from continuo-orches-
tration to the symphonic style was, as we have seen, essentially a
change towards drama. Hence the dramatic and symphonic styles
do not become separated at once; and with Mozart, who was
equally happy in both, they are not easy to distinguish. The
distinction is, even in Mozart, a paradox to people who think that
opera is the most dramatic form of music. Sonatas and symphonies, even by Mozart, turn out to be far too dramatic for the
stage. The fight at the beginning of *Don Giovanni* is perfectly
adequately represented in musical sequences which would be too
cold for any but his earliest symphonies. Theatre music will no
more stand a symphonic environment than stage scenery will
stand daylight.

And yet there is no limit to the refinement of dramatic orchestration whether in Mozart or Wagner. The gradations that a
symphonic composer uses in twenty bars must be spread over a
hundred in any continuous part of an opera, even on Mozart's
scale. Here we already have a reason why opera should encourage
very delicate gradations. Wagner's scale is given by the three
minutes of the chord of E flat at the beginning of *Das Rheingold*;
but still more significant is his management of a tensely emotional
quarter of an hour with no more orchestra than strings and two
horns, without double-basses, in the first act of *Die Walküre*. His
enlargements of the orchestra all have an ultimate effect of puri-
fying the timbre and so removing complications from the method
of scoring. There was nothing new in large orchestras: both
Mozart and Beethoven had rejoiced in performances with double
wind; and in Wagner's early Dresden days Spontini requisitioned
douze belles contrebasses for the performance of his operas. The
experienced Wagner of Bayreuth is contented with eight.

A great stimulus was given to all orchestration by the invention of ventil trumpets and ventil horns. When these instruments
thereby acquired a complete scale, the aesthetics of all brass instruments needed reconsideration. Unimaginative composers of
course saw no difficulty. A trumpet penetrates everything else
like a red-hot poker, so why not give it the melody in every tutti?
Wagner thought otherwise; he felt that brass tone was coarse
unless it was used in large harmonic masses, and he accordingly
invented new brass instruments to make the masses complete
and coherent. Meanwhile he took his wind instruments in threes
instead of twos. Already in the comparatively simple scores of
Der Fliegende Holländer and *Lohengrin* this greatly clarified the
colour-scheme. Half the art of scoring for wind instruments in
the classical symphonies consists in making the best of the fact
that instruments of contrasted tones will not make homogeneous
triads when taken in couples. In *Tristan und Isolde* the threefold

arrangement (two oboes and cor anglais: two clarinets and bass clarinet) adds its advantages to the maturest Wagnerian harmony, with a polyphony as profound as that of Beethoven's last quartets. In the tetralogy of *Der Ring des Nibelungen* Wagner takes his wind groups in fours, and introduces his new brass instruments. They originated in the bass-tuba, which had come to replace the grotesque ophicleide and the still more primitive serpent as a bass to the trombones. These makeshifts had served Mendelssohn's purpose and failed to serve Berlioz's. The tuba could put an imposing bass below the trombones. Its tone is fat and puffy whereas that of the trombone is red-hot. A sensitive ear may notice, and a wise ear may refuse to notice, that the tuba is putting a black line below the red. But Wagner saw the possibility of a new aesthetic value here; and so in his tetralogy five tubas ranging from contrabass to high tenor show as clear a contrast from trombones as oboes from clarinets (Rimsky-Korsakov utterly fails to grasp this point).

The composers, having learnt new powers from such enlargements, can henceforth use these powers without extra apparatus. The orchestration of *Die Meistersinger* is the most complex in all Wagner, just because it is written for Beethoven's orchestra plus one tuba and a harp, and, of course, the now ubiquitous ventil horns, the most perfect of all continuo-players. In *Parsifal* the extra tubas are abandoned but the remaining bass-tuba has permanently won its independence of the trombones.

It seems paradoxical to leave Berlioz out of account in a history of instrumentation. Yet, short of a detailed appreciation of his individual strokes of genius, all that can be said of him is that he drew attention to the subject in an epoch-making but capricious treatise, and that he achieved all that was possible to a highly imaginative musician who happened to hate polyphony. And that is more than some critics might expect. But it cannot have much direct influence on more ordinary musicians.

Post-Wagnerian Instrumentation.—A great many loudly proclaimed 'new' tendencies in orchestration are nothing but the discovery of some single elementary principle. It would be quite easy to write a history of post-Wagnerian scoring in which single characteristics from each of the historic schools here described were assigned haphazard, one to each living composer; and quite impossible to argue against its results. The silliest *a priori* theories seem incontrovertible if we forget how music is actually made. If, for example, we believe that music is made for instruments instead of instruments being built to make the best music they can, we may come to believe in the theory ascribed to Stravinsky, that each instrument should produce no passages that are not peculiar to its own timbre and inappropriate to any other.

This is as if no gentleman should ever say anything that could be said by a lady; and vice versa.

When we have dismissed all such precious nonsense, several real phenomena remain. New harmonic ideas, like multiplanar harmony, depend inextricably on instrumentation as surely as did the classical grammar of counterpoint. Less important is what Richard Strauss has called al fresco orchestration. This means a perception that there is not only safety in numbers, but a high aesthetic value in the average result of sixteen wild-cat attacks at a passage that no individual can play properly. It is doubtful whether that is the real reason of the splendour of such passages. For one thing, the splendour is enhanced by rehearsal, and in the best orchestras the players eventually learn such passages fairly accurately.

Mahler made a systematic study of the possibilities of very large orchestras; almost a quarter of the size of that of our Crystal Palace Handel Festivals, but with music specially written for them. His Eighth Symphony is a choral symphony requiring at least 750 performers, and going much more satisfactorily with 1,000. Berlioz never really contemplated anything larger. Such propositions are not decadent; they are severely disciplinary and require an imagination of the highest efficiency. On a large scale most orchestral colours fade—especially horns, which must be greatly multiplied if they are to tell.

More fascinating to most artists, and more practical in the present lean years,[1] are the aesthetics of small groups and chamber-orchestras. But this is a subject which cannot be pursued here. It is as much as a young composer's prospects are worth to come before modern critics without a new aesthetic system of his own invention. But a general article cannot deal with such private affairs.

[1] 1927-30.

MADRIGAL

AS a definite musical art-form, the madrigal was known by the middle of the fifteenth century. It developed on the same lines as the Motet (q.v.), some early examples even combining an ecclesiastical canto fermo in the tenor with secular counterpoint in the other parts. Thus Josquin's *Déploration de Jehan Okenheim* (*see* MUSIC) might be called a madrigal if the term were used for compositions to French texts at all. But by the middle of the sixteenth century the Italian madrigal had become the highest form of secular music, and the name was appropriated to Italian compositions regardless of the form of the words. Only Yonge's *Musica Transalpina* saved the title for English composers, and this by providing singable English texts for Italian compositions. When Lasso sets Marot's madrigals he calls his compositions *chansons*. On the other hand, when Palestrina composes Petrarch's sonnets to the Virgin in memory of Laura, the result appears as a volume of *Madrigali spirituali*. The fame of these made elegiac madrigals, spiritual or secular, as common as livelier kinds.

The term means a polyphony not inferior to that of the motet, and thus distinguishes madrigals from *ballets*, *villanellas*, *frottolas*, and other fantastic trifles. Masses were often founded on the themes of madrigals, with little more scandal than when they used the themes of motets (*see* MASS; MOTET). Some of Palestrina's masses remained in high favour even though they were avowedly founded on madrigals with almost *risqué* texts.

In the seventeenth century the new dramatic style of Monteverdi and the eclectic experiments of Schütz put the breaking-strain upon the madrigal. It had already been overworked in the attempt to make music-drama by a choir behind the stage with pantomime in front. Vecchi, a great polyphonist, laughed this to death in his *Amfiparnasso* (*see* OPERA).

Later uses of the term seldom have a definite meaning, though there was a remarkable vitality in the mid-nineteenth century efforts of De Pearsall, in pure madrigal style; while the *Madrigale spirituale* in Stanford's oratorio *Eden* has the beauty of pure scholarship.

MASS

1. *Polyphonic Masses.*—As an art-form the musical Mass is governed by the structure of its text. The supremely important parts of the Mass are those which have the smallest number of words, namely the opening *Kyrie*; the *Sanctus* and *Benedictus*, embodying the central acts and ideas of the service; and the concluding *Agnus Dei*. A sixteenth-century composer could best write highly developed music when words were few and such as would gain rather than lose by repetition. Now the texts of the *Gloria* and *Credo* were more voluminous than any others which sixteenth-century composers attempted to handle in a continuous scheme. The practical limits of the Church service made it impossible to break them up by setting each clause to a separate movement, a method by which Josquin and Lasso contrived to fill a whole hour with a penitential psalm. Accordingly the great masters evolved for the *Gloria* and *Credo* a style midway between that of the elaborate motet (adopted in the *Sanctus*) and the homophonic reciting style of the Litany.

This gave the Mass a range of style which made it to the sixteenth-century composer what the symphony is to the great instrumental classics. Moreover, as being inseparably associated with the highest act of worship, it severely tested the composer's depth and truthfulness of expression. The story of archaic and decadent corruptions in polyphonic Masses is touched upon in the article MUSIC (section iii). In the twentieth century a decree of Pius X again inculcated the restoration of the Palestrina style to its proper position in liturgical music. But the trouble with modern settings of the Mass is not the decadence of an old art but a fundamental incompatibility between the modern orchestra and a good liturgical style.

The sixteenth-century Mass was often written for a definite day, and when the composer bases its themes on those of his setting of an appropriate motet (q.v.) for that day, the whole musical service becomes a single tissue of significant themes. Thus, Victoria wrote for All Saints' Day a motet, *O quam gloriosum est regnum*, and a Mass with the same title and on the same themes. The motet is given as an illustration to the article on that subject; and the accompanying examples (pp. 86–87) show the relation between the themes of the Mass and those of the motet.

2. *Instrumental Masses in the Neapolitan Style.*—The Neapolitan composers who created classical tonality and instrumental art-forms (*see* MUSIC, sec. v) created a style of Church music best known (but not always best represented) in the Masses of Mozart

Ex. 1 Themes of Victoria's *Missa: O quam gloriosum est regnum.* The words quoted above each theme are these of the motet of the same name. See illustration to MOTET

Kyrie ('In quo cum Christo')

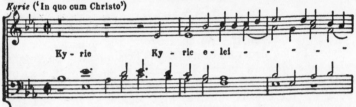

Ky - rie   Ky - rie e - lei - - - -

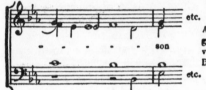

son

Also recognizable in the Gloria at 'in gloria Dei Patris'; in the Credo at 'et vitam venturi saeculi,' and in the Agnus Dei at 'Qui tollis peccata mundi'

Ex. 2 Christe ('quo cumque ierit')

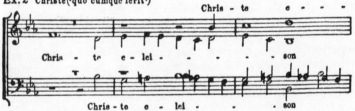

Chris - te e - - -

Chris - te e - lei - - - son

Chris - te e - lei - - son

- lei - - - - son

etc.   Also in the Gloria at 'Filius Patris'

Ex. 3 Kyrie ('sequuntur Agnum')

Ky - ri - e

etc. Also in the Gloria at 'tu solus sanctus ' and in Agnus Dei at etc. 'miserere nobis'.

Ex. 4 *Gloria*

qui se - des ad dex - te - rum Pa - - - tris

Ex. 5 *Hosanna* (variation of 'quocumque ierit' in bass and tenor)

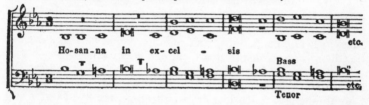

Ho- san - na in ex- cel - sis

and Haydn. By this time the resources of music were such that
a reasonably expressive setting of the *Gloria* and *Credo* would
overbalance the scheme. Only a very small proportion of
Mozart's and Haydn's Mass music may be said to represent
ideas of religious music at all, though Haydn defended himself
by saying that the thought of God always made him feel irre-
pressibly cheerful, and he hoped God would not be angry with
him for worshipping Him accordingly. The best (and least
operatic) features of such unabashed music are those which
develop the polyphonic aspect of the Neapolitan style. Thus
Mozart's most perfect example is his extremely terse Mass in F,
written at the age of 17, and scored for four-part chorus and
solo voices accompanied by the organ and two violins mostly in
independent real parts. This scheme, with the addition of a pair
of trumpets and drums, and occasionally oboes, forms the normal
orchestra of eighteenth-century Masses. Trombones often played
with the three lower voices.

3. *Symphonic Masses.*—The enormous dramatic development
in the symphonic music of Beethoven made the problem of the
Mass with orchestral accompaniment liturgically insoluble. Yet
Beethoven's second Mass (in D, op. 123) is not only the most
dramatic ever penned, but is, perhaps, the last classical Mass
that is thoughtfully based upon the liturgy. It was intended for
the installation of the archduke Rudolph as Archbishop of Ol-
mütz; and though not ready until two years after that occasion,
it shows much thought for the meaning of a church service,
unique in its occasion and therefore exceptionally long. Immense
as was Beethoven's dramatic force, it was equalled by his power
of sublime repose; and he was accordingly able once more to put
the supreme moment of the music where the service requires it
to be, viz., in the *Sanctus* and *Benedictus*. In the *Agnus Dei* he

writes as one who has lived in a beleaguered city. Beethoven read the final prayer of the Mass as a 'prayer for inward and outward peace', and, giving it that title, organized it on the basis of a contrast between terrible martial sounds and the triumph of peaceful themes.

Schubert's Masses show rather the influence of Beethoven's not very impressive first Mass, which they easily surpass in interest, though Schubert did not take pains, like Beethoven, to get his Latin text correct. The last two are later than Beethoven's Mass in D and contain many splendid passages, besides a dramatic (though not realistic) treatment of the *Agnus Dei*.

Weber's two Masses (G and E flat) are excellent works; the larger one (in E flat) achieving an ecclesiastical style as good as Cherubini's and much less dry. Otherwise, the five Masses and the two Requiems of Cherubini are the most important works of their period. Those that were written within Beethoven's life-time made him regard Cherubini as the greatest master of the day. Since Schubert's time the Viennese tradition of Mass music has been worthily represented by Bruckner. Dame Ethel Smyth's Mass (1890) owes nothing to tradition, but is undoubtedly a work inspired by its text.

4. *Lutheran Masses.*—Music with Latin words is not excluded from the Lutheran Church, and the *Kyrie* and *Gloria* are frequently sung in succession and entitled a Mass. Thus the four Short Masses of Bach are called short, not because they are on a small scale (which they are not), but because they consist only of the *Kyrie* and *Gloria*. Bach treats each clause of his text as a separate movement, alternating choruses with groups of arias; a method independently adopted by Mozart in a few early works and in the great unfinished Mass in C minor. This method, carried throughout an entire Mass, will fit into no liturgy; and Bach's B minor Mass must be regarded as an oratorio.

The most interesting case is the setting of the words: 'Et exspecto resurrectionem mortuorum et vitam venturi saeculi. Amen.' The greatest difficulty in any elaborate instrumental setting of the *Credo* is the inevitable anti-climax after the *Resurrexit*. Bach contrives to give this anticlimax a definite artistic value; all the more from the fact that his *Crucifixus* and *Resurrexit*, and the contrast between them, show him at the height of his power. To the end of his *Resurrexit* chorus he appends an orchestral ritornello, formally summing up the material of the chorus and thereby destroying all sense of finality as a member of a large group. After this the aria 'Et in spiritum sanctum', in which five dogmatic clauses are enshrined like relics in a casket, furnishes a beautiful decorative design, as a point of repose.

Then comes a voluminous ecclesiastical fugue, 'Confiteor unum baptisma', leading, as through the door and world-wide spaces of the Catholic Church, to that veil which is not all darkness to the eye of faith. At the words 'Et exspecto resurrectionem mortuorum' the music plunges suddenly into sublime and mysterious modulations in a slow tempo, until it breaks out as suddenly into a vivace e allegro of broad but terse design, which comes to its climax rapidly and ends as abruptly as possible, the last chord being carefully written as a short note without a pause. This gives finality to the whole *Credo* and contrasts admirably with the coldly formal instrumental end of the *Resurrexit* three movements farther back. Now, such subtleties might be thought beyond the power of conscious planning. But Bach's vivace e allegro is an arrangement of the second chorus of a Church cantata, *Gott, man lobet dich in der Stille*; and in the cantata the chorus has introductory and final symphonies, and a middle section with a da capo!

Until fairly late in the nineteenth century the Sing-Akademie of Berlin (and perhaps other choral societies in Germany) maintained a laudable tradition according to which its director glorified his office in a Lutheran Mass (*Kyrie* and *Gloria*) for sixteen-part unaccompanied chorus. Some of these works (notably that of C. F. C. Fasch) are very fine.

5. *The Requiem.*—The *Missa pro defunctis* or Requiem Mass has tended to produce special musical forms for each individual case. The text of the *Dies Irae* imperatively demands either a dramatic elaboration or none at all. Even in the sixteenth century it could not possibly be set to continuous music on the lines of the *Gloria* and *Credo*. Fortunately, its Gregorian canto fermo is very beautiful and formal; and the sixteenth-century masters either, like Palestrina, left it to be sung as plainchant, or set it in versicles (like their settings of the *Magnificat* and other canticles) for two groups of voices alternatively, or for the choir in alternation with the plainchant of the priests.

A *Dies Irae* with orchestral accompaniment cannot avoid illustrating its tremendous text regardless of ecclesiastical style. But it is a sour view that denies the title of great Church music to the sublime unfinished *Requiem* of Mozart (the Italian antecedents of which would be an interesting subject) and the two important works by Cherubini. These latter, however, tend to be funereal rather than uplifting.

Of later settings, Schumann's belongs to the days of his failing power; Henschel's is a work of great sincerity and reticent beauty; while the three other outstanding masterpieces renounce all ecclesiastical style. Berlioz seizes his opportunity like a musical E. A. Poe; Dvořák is eclectic; and Verdi towers above both in flaming sincerity, no more able to repress his theatrical idioms than Haydn could repress his cheerfulness.

Brahms's *Deutsches Requiem* has nothing to do with the Mass for the dead, being simply a large choral work on a text compiled from the Bible by the composer.

MELODY

MELODY is the organization of successive musical sounds in respect of pitch (Gr. μελωδία, a choral song, from μέλος, tune, and ῷδή, song). In its most primitive state it already requires rhythm (q.v.); but it can develop freely without the aid of harmony, which removes it into a wider category. Thus a 'melodic scale' is a scale that is not based on an harmonic system; and thus we call ancient Greek music 'melodic'. The popular conception of melody as 'tunefulness' is modern and depends on symmetries of harmony and rhythm that seldom occur in recorded music before the seventeenth century, and are accidental, if frequent, potentialities in older folk-music. For us a melody is the surface of a series of harmonies, and an unaccompanied melody that fails to imply clear harmonies is felt to be strange and vague (*see* Ex. 1 and 2). Harmonic rationality and sym-

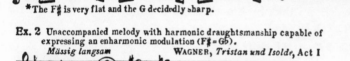

Ex. 1 Non-harmonic melody; a bagpipe tune refractory to any harmonization beyond drones A and E.

Slow   *'MacRimmon's Lament'*

*The F♯ is very flat and the G decidedly sharp.

Ex. 2 Unaccompanied melody with harmonic draughtsmanship capable of expressing an enharmonic modulation (F♯ = G♭).

Mässig langsam   WAGNER, *Tristan und Isolde*, Act I

etc.

Westwärts schweift der Blick; ostwärts streicht das Schiff.

metrical rhythm thus combine to make a tuneful melody an epitome of musical form. The historical process is from the smaller to the greater. See SONATA FORMS for the gradations between such melodic forms as that of *Barbara Allen* (Ex. 3) and the larger dance forms of the suite, and for the gradation between these and the true dramatic forms of the sonata.

Ex. 3 *'Barbara Allen'* (showing the germ of binary form in the balance between A¹ on the dominant and A² on the tonic).

Lastly, the most narrowly melodic element, the rise and fall of pitch, is a capacity of the human voice, and in later forms is enlarged not less by the characteristics of instruments than by rhythm, harmony, and form. Thus modern melody is the musical surface of rhythm, harmony, form, and instrumentation; and, if we take Wagnerian leitmotives into account, we may as well add drama to the list. In short, melody, whether it be in an inner part or on the top, is the surface of music.

An immense number of musical resources are manifested on the melodic surface; and the following definitions and illustrations will be found to cover a very wide ground. In fact, one of the principal dangers that beset the teaching of composition has been the notion that the logic of music can be placed in melodic relations without regard to rhythm (especially in its larger aspects of phrasing) as well as harmony.

1. A *theme* is a melody, not necessarily complete in itself, except when designed for a set of variations (q.v.), but recognizable as a pregnant phrase or clause. Thus a fugue-subject is a theme, and the expositions and episodes of the sonata forms are more or less complex groups of themes.

2. A *figure* is the smallest fragment of a theme that can be recognized when transformed or detached from its surroundings. The grouping of figures into new melodies is the main resource of 'development' or 'working-out' in the sonata forms (*see* Ex. 5–10) besides being the means by which fugues are carried on when the subjects and countersubjects are not present as wholes. In sixteenth-century polyphony, melody consists largely of figures which are thus broken off from a canto fermo. (*See* CONTRAPUNTAL FORMS.)

Ex 4 Melody in keyboard polyphony, requiring two parts to complete the sense.

BACH. *Das Wohltemperirte Klavier,II, Fugue* 15

Ex. 5 Main theme of the first movement of Beethoven's Trio in B♭, Op. 97.

Ex. 6 Figure A of above developed in a new polyphonic 4-bar phrase.

Ex. 7 Further sequential developments of A.

Ex. 8 Development of C with B.

Ex. 9 Further development of B by diminution, in combination with the trills derived
from C.

Ex. 10 Further development of B by diminution and contrary motion (inversion).

3. A *sequence* is the repetition of a figure or group of chords
at different levels of pitch. A *real sequence* repeats the initial
group exactly, and therefore changes its key. Thus in the first
movement of Beethoven's 'Waldstein' Sonata bars 5-8 are a
step in real sequence below bars 1-4. A *tonal sequence* repeats
the figure within the key, and modifies details accordingly,
tolerating things that would be inadmissible in the initial group.
In the first movement of the 'Waldstein' Sonata the theme, with
a brilliant counterpoint above, is treated in tonal sequence forty
bars from the end. Repetition at the same pitch is not sequence.
Thus, in illustration, there are no sequences in Ex. 1, but Ex. 4,
7, 9, and 10 contain tonal sequences.

4. *Polyphony* is harmony made of melodic threads. Some classical melodies are polyphonically composite, requiring an inner melody, appearing through transparent places in the outer melody, to complete the sense. This well suits the pianoforte with its evanescent tone, but is even more frequent in music for earlier keyboard instruments, as in the keyboard works of Bach (*see* Ex. 4). Beethoven often divides a melody between voices in dialogue, as in bars 35-42 of the first movement of the 'Waldstein' Sonata.

5. (*a*) *Conjunct movement* is movement along adjacent degrees of the scale (Ex. 5, Fig. B).

(*b*) *Disjunct movement* often tends to produce arpeggio types of melody, i.e., melodies which trace out a chord, as in Ex. 11, 12.

The rigid devices of inversion, augmentation, and diminution are illustrated in CONTRAPUNTAL FORMS and FUGUE.

The musical examples 5-10 show how Beethoven can develop a theme to results unrecognizable but for the intermediate steps.

Ex. 11   BRAHMS, Quintet, Op, 34

Ex. 12 A and B² diminished

Ex. 13

Ex. 14 *The Rhinedaughters' Toy*   WAGNER, *Das Rheingold*

Ex. 15 *The Nibelung's Talisman.*

Ex. 11–16 show a later kind of metamorphosis requiring no intermediate steps, though the process in Wagner's *Ring* motive is
gradual.

Ex. 16 *Walhalla*

MOTET

A MUSICAL art-form of paramount importance in the sixteenth century. The word is of doubtful etymology, and probably has more than one origin. Thus *motulus* suggests *modulus* or melody, and probably connects with *motetus* or *motellus*, which designates one of the middle parts in early vocal compositions. On the other hand, the Italian word *mottetto* (diminutive of motto) suggests the French *mot* (in the sense of *bon mot*) and is associated with a profane art-form contemporary with the *conductus* and *rondel* of the thirteenth and fourteenth centuries.

The only mature art-form denoted by the word motet is that of sixteenth-century pieces of liturgical polyphonic music in one or two (rarely more) continuous movements. The word is, however, used for any single Latin-text composition in continuous form, not set sectionally verse by verse, and not forming a permanent part of the Mass. Thus Palestrina's *Stabat Mater* is included among his motets; though the text is metrical and rhymed, and the style is that of the homophonic litanies. The title of motet is also loosely used for non-ecclesiastical works, such as the dedicatory motet at the beginning of Palestrina's fifth book.

The most important kind of motet is that which is written for a particular holy day. Such motets are sung between the *Credo* and the *Sanctus* of the Mass. They are often founded on the Gregorian tones of their texts, and the Mass is founded on the same themes, thus giving the whole service a musical unity which has never since been approached in any Church music even under Bach. When a motet was not founded on Gregorian tones it was still possible for the composer to design a Mass on the same themes, and the titles of sixteenth-century Masses, when they do not indicate a secular or diplomatic origin, indicate either the motet or the Gregorian tones on which they are founded. The accompanying illustration is one of the most perfect examples existing, and the illustration in the article MASS shows how Victoria uses the themes of this motet in his Mass with the same title. In the present illustration, the bar-strokes (unknown in sixteenth-century part-books) are drawn irregularly so as to show the free rhythms. Typical points are the runs and slow triple rhythm at 'gaudent'; the note-against-note swinging rhythm at 'amicti stolis albis' and the naïve illustration of 'sequuntur Agnum'. When such a motet is associated with a Mass it is a crime to perform the Mass without it. Sometimes one composer founded a Mass on another composer's motet; thus Soriano's fine Mass *Nos autem gloriari* is based upon a motet by Palestrina, and Palestrina's Mass *Quem dicunt homines* is on a motet by Willaert. When a motet was in two movements the second movement always ended with the last clauses of the first, both in text and in music, producing a distinct impression of da capo form. In later times the term motet indicates any piece of Church music of clearly single design, regardless of language or of place in a liturgy.

Original notation a 3rd lower, but this is about the pitch intended. The note is Hypo-
mixolydian (VIII). The first note in the treble is a Long ⎕ , = 2 breves = 4 semibreves.

T.L. DA VICTORIA. First Book of Motets

O ____   quam glo-ri-o ― ― ― ― ― sum

O ____   quam glo-ri-o ― ― ― ― ― sum

in quo cum

est reg ― ― ― ― ― ― ― num   in

in quo

est reg ― ― ― ― ― num   in quo cum Chri ― ― ―

Chri ― ― ― ― ― ― ― sto, in quo,

quo   cum Chri ― ― ― ― sto, in quo cum

in   quo cum Chri ― ― sto,

― ― ― sto,   in quo   cum

in quo   cum Chri ― ― ― sto

Chri ― ― ― sto, in quo cum Chri ― sto, gau ― ― ―
gau ―

Chri ― ― ― sto, in quo   cum Chri ― sto, gau ― ― ―

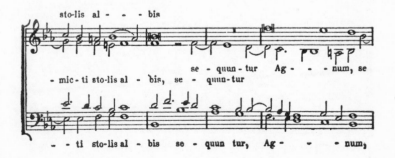

MUSIC

THE Greek μουσική (*sc.* τέχνη) from which this word is derived was used comprehensively for all the arts of the Nine Muses. Contrasted with γυμναστική (gymnastic) it included the culture of the mind as distinguished from that of the body. Thus the singing and setting of lyric poetry formed but a small, if a central, part of a 'musical' education which ranged from reading and writing to the sciences of mathematics and astronomy, besides all the arts of literature. The philosophers valued music, both in the ancient general sense and in our restricted sense, chiefly as an educational element in the formation of character; so that we obtain little light from them on the pure aesthetics of the Greek art of musical sounds.

I. INTRODUCTION

The present article deals mainly with the musical art-forms matured by European civilization since the fourteenth century. More ancient music is discussed frankly as beyond our power of appreciation except in the light of prehistoric origins. Our Western art of music stands in the unique position that its language has been wholly created by art.

Music owes but little to nature in the form of acoustic science, and still less to the sounds that occur outside works of art. It is already a mature musical art that selects the acoustic facts, just as in painting it is art that determines the selection of optical facts. Wise critics have, since Ruskin's day, abandoned the attempt to settle *a priori* how much of nature an aesthetic system ought to digest; and music differs only in degree from literature and the plastic arts in independence of nature.

Yet the difference is often important. Perspective existed as a science before it was taken up by painters, and as a human experience before it became a science. The naïve Western spectator has seen enough of it in pictures to make him resent its neglect, whether in modern art or in the masterpieces of China and Japan. In music the nearest analogy to perspective is the system of tonality developed by the great composers from Alessandro Scarlatti to Wagner. (*See* HARMONY.) Every step in its evolution has been fiercely contested; and even twenty years after the end of Wagner's long career not every responsible musician was ready to admit Wagnerian tonality as a legitimate enlargement of the classical system.

If we set aside language and the organized art of music, the power of distinguishing sensations of sound is no more complex than the power of distinguishing colours. On the other hand sound is the principal medium by which most of the higher animals both express and excite emotion; and hence, though until codified into human speech it does not give any raw material for elaborate human art, it suffices for bird-songs that are as long prior to language as the brilliant colours of skins, feathers, and flowers are prior to painting. Again, sound as a warning or a menace is an important means of self-preservation; and it is produced instantly and instinctively.

All this makes musical expression a pre-human phenomenon in the history of life, but is unfavourable to the early development of musical art. Primitive music could mysteriously reawaken instincts more elemental than any that could ever have been appealed to by the deliberate process of drawing on a flat surface a series of lines calculated to remind the eye of the appearance of solid objects in space. But the powers of music remained magical and unintelligible even in the hands of the supreme artists of classical Greece. We may be perfectly sure that if the Greeks had produced a music equivalent to the art of Palestrina, Bach, or Beethoven, no difficulty of deciphering would have effectively prevented us from recovering as much of it as we have recovered of Greek literature. Some enthusiasts for Oriental lore assure us that long ago the Chinese knew all about our harmonic system but abandoned it after they had exhausted it. This need not worry us. The Oriental aristocrat conceals in his politeness a profound contempt for our efforts to patronize his culture; and that contempt is justified when we show such ignorance of our own music as to suppose that a music of similar calibre could have utterly disappeared from a living nation whose most ancient plastic art and literature command our respect and reward our study. When we trace the slow and difficult evolution of our harmonic system, we cease to wonder that it was not evolved sooner and elsewhere, and we learn to revere the miracle that it was evolved at all.

II. NON-HARMONIC AND GREEK MUSIC

Music before the rise of a harmonic system is of two kinds, the unwritten or extemporaneous, and the recorded or scientific. At the present day the music of races that have not acquired Western harmony often pleases us best when it seems most extemporaneous. Tradition can go far to fix the forms and even the details of a performance that may, without the aid of words or dance, last for hours. With words or dance, music becomes more capable of being fixed by writing; but the first musical problems are as far beyond conscious reasoning as the origins of language. Birds solved them before human beings; and folk-music can show real beauty when the systematic music of its day is arbitrary and uncouth. Moreover, folk-music, together with the present music of barbarous races and Oriental civilization, can give us materials such as anthropology uses in reconstructing the past from its vestiges in the present.

For us the music of ancient Greece is by far the most important branch of musical archaeology. Unfortunately the approach to this most difficult subject has been blocked by lack of co-ordination between scholarship and musicianship; and the ascertained truth is less instructive to the general reader than the history of opinions about it. These opinions begin to be interesting when they are expressed by musicians whose music we can understand. The natural tendency of such musicians was to suppose that Greek music was like their own; and each advance in knowledge is marked by disillusion. The first difficulty presented by ancient Greek writers was sufficiently disconcerting. The Greek terms for 'high' and 'low' were found to be reversed. Our own meaning seems founded in nature; and science confirms it. Our 'high' or 'acute' notes demand tense vocal cords and correspond to vibrations of 'high' frequency. A great sixteenth-century composer, Costanzo Porta, inferred a mystery here, and argued that the Greeks had mastered the art of a totally invertible polyphony, such as Bach afterwards displayed in two fugues in *Die Kunst der Fuge*. Porta accordingly wrote a four-part motet (*Vobis datum est cognoscere mysterium*) which could be sung upside down: and his contemporary Vincentino composed four-part motets in each of the three Greek *genera*, diatonic, chromatic, and enharmonic. (*See* Hawkins's *History of Music*, i. 112, seq.) They are as good as any other music written on *a priori* principles, and the enharmonic motet may be commended to some of our modern experimenters in quarter-tones. But they represent as much knowledge of Greek music as we possess of the inhabitants of Mars.

The truth must be sought by other methods, and by far the most promising is the study and comparison of the present scales of nations, whether barbarous or cultured, who have not come into contact with the classical harmony of the West.

A readable account of musical origins may be found in Parry's *Evolution of the Art of Music*. Following the researches of A. J. Hipkins and A. J. Ellis, Parry illustrates the fact that most of the primitive scales, notably the pentatonic scales prominent in Scottish and Chinese music, are built around the interval of a downward fourth (as from C to G), which was probably the first melodic interval to become fixed in the human mind as being simple enough but not too wide. A scale would begin to form by the accretion of other notes near the bottom of this interval. Now take another fourth with similar accretions below the former, either conjunctly (as G to D below the C–G) or disjunctly (as F–C). The resulting scale will either fill or include an octave, it does not matter which; for the filled octave of the conjunct tetrachord contains in another position the notes of the included octave of the disjunct tetrachords, as can be seen in the combined series C, A, G, E, D, C, A, G. And the octave was recognized from the outset as a limit after which a musical series repeats itself.

The Greeks' three *gener*: of scales were the diatonic, the chromatic, and the enharmonic. Of these the diatonic divides the tetrachord most evenly, as E, D, C, B:A, G, F, E. This gives us our diatonic scale in what Palestrina would call the Phrygian mode. The Greeks found that all its notes could be traversed (as a knight's move can traverse our chessboard) in a series of intervals which they call concords. (They thought of them only as successions, not combinations of sound.) These were the fourth (in the ratio of 4:3); the fifth (3:2); and the octave (2:1). (Our own 'perfect concords' are in these ratios.) Scales with chromatic tetrachords (E, C♯, C♮, B:A, F♯, F♮, E) could also be traversed by the concordant intervals, but not so easily. The enharmonic tetrachords, which only the most accomplished singers could sing, were beyond the reach of perfect concords; and for us they would need a special notation, as E, C, B′, B; A, F, E′, E♮; where B′ and E′ signify something like quarter-tones above the B♮ and E♮. Yet this difficult scale was said to be the oldest of all; which seems not unlikely when we observe that it gathers three notes closely to the bottom of the tetrachord, leaving a gap of a major third from the top. Eliminate the quarter-tones, and there remains a pentatonic scale E, C, B: A, F, E, which is more likely to be the earliest filling out of the downward fourth than the scales in which the auxiliary note is a whole tone away. And if this nucleus had the prestige of a mystic antiquity musicians would feel a pious pride in mastering the difficulty of filling it up like the other genera.

If authorities on Greek music would abandon their habit of writing scales and reckoning intervals upwards, their results, whether correct or not, would become much more lucid. For, as Parry points out, it is only our harmonic system which makes us think of scales as normally rising; and when a musician applies the term 'cadence' to chords that rise from dominant to tonic he contradicts the literal meaning of the word.

Until the most recent times classical scholars have ruthlessly closed the door upon all hope of further light from the comparison of Greek data with the phenomena of extant non-harmonic

folk-song and Oriental scales. If such a comparison is to have
any meaning we must assume that the now universal phenomena
of modes existed in ancient Greece. Modes, as far as non-
harmonic melody is concerned, are various cross-sections of a
standard scale. Thus, Scottish music shows very clearly five
pentatonic modes. Adding the octave to complete the scale,
these are, (1) C, A, G, F, D, C; (2) D, C, A, G, F, D; (3) F, D,
C, A, G, F; (4) G, F, D, C, A, G; (5) A, G, F, D, C, A. In
the article HARMONY the ecclesiastical modes of pure polyphony
are given with their fondly-imagined Greek names. Pre-
harmonic music without modes is contrary not only to our
Western prejudices but to the whole trend of anthropological
research. In these circumstances classical scholars, under the
guidance of D. B. Monro, crushed all hopes by deciding that the
Greeks had no modes at all, but that either their ἁρμονίαι or their
τονοί (the terms, whatever they mean, are not synonymous) were
mere transpositions of the three genera into various pitches, just
as our 'keys' are transpositions of our pair of major and minor
modes.

When Monro published his *Modes of Ancient Greek Music* in
1894, musicians had learnt too well the lesson that Greek music
must not be expected to make sense. They would never dispute
a point of classical scholarship; and it did not occur to them that
Monro might be just so innocently familiar with modern music
as not to realize that he might as well impute high-church tendencies to Alcibiades because of 'the splendour of his liturgies'
as impute to the ancient Greeks a system of keys related by mere
transposition. But musicians could only suppose that even the
most unprejudiced anthropological comparison of extant scales
was no more able to prevail than Macfarren's Victorian assump-
tions could do in a dispute with Monro. Fortunately in 1916
Mr. G. H. Mountford, in a degree thesis, satisfied classical
scholars that Monro was in error and that the Greek modes
were modes in the universal and proper sense of the term.

Miss Kathleen Schlesinger found, by experiments with a
monochord, a means of producing modes on mathematical principles. Certainly the Greeks did measure musical intervals
mathematically on a string; certainly Miss Schlesinger's system
is among the very first things that could have happened in that
way; and its results produce many phenomena that ought to have
occurred in ancient Greek music. There is, for instance, a remarkable passage in Plato's *Republic* (VII. 531) where Socrates
gibes at the pedantries of the merely practical musicians who
spend hours in arguing whether this and that note are too near
to allow another note between them. And Miss Schlesinger's
various scales comprise between them notes quite close enough

to explain how the practical musician could get into difficulties about what was obvious to the philosopher. Miss Schlesinger, moreover, tuned a pianoforte on the basis of her theory, and the result is acoustically very interesting. So much then, for *a priori* theory and practical experience. If Miss Schlesinger's results are not Greek they ought to have been.

The other line of approach is through the experience of setting the choruses of Greek tragedy to a modern music which confines itself to a strict representation of the metre and sets strophe and antistrophe to the same melody. The composer should not attempt Greek modes, on whatever theory, or he will achieve nothing better than an effect of singing 'We won't go home till morning' on the supertonic of a minor key and with a beat missing. Instead of thus warping his imagination the composer should translate all that modern culture enjoys in Greek poetry into a music that he can enjoy; restricting himself mainly to one note to a syllable and, while making his instrumental accompaniment as beautiful as he likes, straying into no by-paths of musical tone-painting other than the most natural symbolisms. The Greek rhythmic forms prove musically fascinating, and there is full scope for fine melody within them. The strict correspondence of strophe and antistrophe causes difficulties which reveal much. Even a unisonous accompaniment, such as the Greeks had, can glide over a difference of punctuation or indeed a running on of the sense between strophe and antistrophe, as at the end of the enormous first chorus of *Agamemnon*; and the technique of such compromises closely resembles that of Schubert and Brahms in strophic songs, and has the subtlety of Greek simplicity. Aristophanes, in *The Frogs*, laughs at the interlinear θραττο θραττο θρατт (or 'plunketyplunk') of the Aeschylean lyre. The passage seems to indicate something more extensive than a merely connective tissue; but exaggeration is not unknown in comedy.

More difficult and therefore still more instructive are the occasional contrasts of sentiment between strophe and antistrophe. In another chorus in *Agamemnon* the pretty ways of a lion-cub are to be sung to the same music as the tale of disaster that befell the man who adopted it when, on growing up, it behaved as might be expected. The highest point of pathos in the first chorus, one of the supreme things in poetry, is the moment where the description of the sacrifice of Iphigeneia turns into a reminiscence of her singing in her father's halls and then runs on into the antistrophe, with the words 'The rest I saw not, nor will I tell'. After which the same music has to express the pious hope that the queen who now approaches shares the wishes of the chorus for the welfare of the land she holds in trust.

From Plato we learn that musicians degraded themselves by imitating the roaring of lions and the whistling of winds. But what was the Greek criterion for the singing voice? Certainly very different from ours; for Aristotle says that certain high-pitched modes (but what is 'high' in this context?) are suited to the voices of old men. An age-limit is the only criterion the heartless modern critic has for the voices of old men. Be this as it may, the safest inference from it is that every educated Greek was expected to sing well as an integral part of the art of speaking well. Perhaps our modern contrast between the singing and the speaking voice did not exist. Nowadays it is not uncommon to find a high soprano speaking normally around the A or G below the treble staff.

III. HARMONIC ORIGINS

The latent harmonic sense of the Greeks is shown in the fact that their diatonic scale was amenable to the Pythagorean science of harmonic ratios. And we cannot suppose that no notice was taken of the combined sounds resulting from reverberation in halls and caverns, or from striking several strings of the lyre at once. Yet the fact remains that outside the orbit of our own Western music of the last six centuries we know of no harmonic system that has advanced beyond drones below the melody and cymbals (our Authorized Version is right in reading 'tinkling cymbal') or bells above it.

Music, as we now understand it, consists in the interaction of three elements as inseparable (but not as interchangeable) as the three dimensions of Newtonian space. The Greeks knew two, rhythm and melody, which are as ancient as human consciousness and evidently have their meaning for some other animals. But non-harmonic melody is a very different thing from melody that implies harmony. (*See* MELODY exs. 1 and 2 with their discussion.) When we hear an unaccompanied folk-song we involuntarily think of it as the top line of a series of harmonies. If it is really pre-harmonic it will prove unamenable to that interpretation, and then we shall think it quaint. Neither the quaintness nor the harmonic interpretation ever entered into its intention. Life is too short for Western musicians to devote much of it to the violent mental gymnastics of thinking away the harmonic ideas that have made Western music enjoyable throughout five centuries. We may perhaps widen our experience by going back another two centuries; for it was agreed by all the musicians in Vienna that a concert of 'Gothic' music was their most interesting musical experience of the year 1928.

In the article HARMONY the main steps are indicated by which medieval musicians advanced from doubling melodies in fourths and fifths (as the unoccidentalized Japanese are said to be doing now) to an aesthetic system of polyphony that demands complete independence in its melodic threads and forbids consecutive fifths and octaves as barbarous. The details of this evolution are abstruse; but two main issues may be mentioned here. Polyphony could not have been established without fixed scales and a repository of known melody for composers to work upon.

The scale was set in order in Graeco-Roman times by Ptolemy the astronomer, who flourished A.D. 130 and from whose time the history of the 'ecclesiastical modes' becomes continuously traceable until the records of music are secured by the art of printing.

The necessary repository of melody was supplied by the ancient plainsongs of the Church, many of which claimed to have come uncorrupted from the music of Solomon's temple and certainly had a continuous history reaching back to early Christian services in the catacombs of Rome. In A.D. 384 a large body of these 'tones' was set in order by St. Ambrose. According to a tradition accepted, after some 'historic doubts', by good authorities, St. Gregory revised and enlarged the Ambrosian collection; and the whole corpus of Gregorian music undoubtedly familiarizes Roman Catholics of to-day with a music enormously more ancient in its origin than any harmony. This music forms the principal melodic foundation of Palestrina's polyphony; but by his time it had become corrupted, and we must look to the Solesmes edition of 1904 for the text and method of singing plainsong in the perfection it is held to have attained shortly after the death of St. Gregory. The essential difference between the Ratisbon tradition (which we may loosely call Palestrinian) and that of Solesmes is that the Palestrinians impatiently curtailed the flourishes of the plainsong much as Palestrina did with the Gregorian themes he used in polyphony; whereas the Solesmes method restores the free speech-rhythm which makes the flourishes (or melismata) possible in a rapid delivery. Some of these melismata are very extensive, and the Palestrinians (who gradually developed the modern organist's habit of providing each note of a Gregorian melody with a separate chord) had some excuse for mistaking them for corruptions of style.

The Gregorian tradition did not stand alone. There was an ancient Visigoth (or 'Spanish') tradition; and there are the traditions of the Eastern Church. Professor J. J. W. Tillyard has shed much light on Byzantine music, including a promising opening in the deciphering of the earliest *Neumae*, diacritical signs above the words, supposed to indicate musical notes. He uses the method of interpreting the past from vestiges of primitive usage in the present. Controversies as to the number of modes, whether eight or twelve, raged till late in the sixteenth century. The *Dodecachordon* of Glareanus settled the question in favour of twelve, as its name implies. Meanwhile composers developed polyphony by ear and got no help whatever from the theorist. Quite independent of modes and entirely practical was the hexachord scheme developed in the eleventh century by Guido d'Arrezzo.

The general reader may learn something of the hexachord system very pleasantly from the music-lesson in *The Taming of the Shrew*. Hortensio's gamut says '"Gamut" I am, the ground of all accord ... "D sol re", one clef [i.e. sign, or key], two notes have I "E la mi", show pity, or I die'. 'Gamut' is a survival of Greek tradition; for the bottom note of the Greek scale was identified with the bass G, and this 'ground of all accord' is an octave below the Ut of the hard hexachord. Hence it is Gamma-ut.

D is Sol in the hard hexachord $\left\{\begin{array}{llllll} G, & A, & B, & C, & D, & E \\ Ut & Re & Mi & Fa & Sol & La \end{array}\right\}$ and

Re in the natural hexachord $\left\{\begin{array}{llllll} C, & D, & E, & F, & G, & A \\ Ut & Re & Mi & Fa & Sol & La \end{array}\right\}$. It has

two names but only one position or 'clef', unlike B which has to be flattened in the soft hexachord (F to D). (Morley, writing in 1597, calls A flat the B clef.) E is La in the hard hexachord and Mi in the natural hexachord.

Between Fa of the natural hexachord and Mi of the hard hexachord a dissonant tritone fourth exists. It gave great trouble to medieval musicians, who assigned it to the devil. *Mi contra Fa est diabolus in musica.*

To the early harmonic and contrapuntal processes alluded to in the article HARMONY some details must be added. The famous unwritten songs of the aristocratic troubadours or *trouvères* of the twelfth and thirteenth centuries undoubtedly set the fashion in melody, and probably set it in the direction of *Sumer is icumen in*; that is to say, in the Ionian mode (that *modus lascivus* which is identical with our major scale) and in a lilting trochaic rhythm.

♩ ♩|♩ ♩

Sumer is icumen in contains no technical feature that has not been found in other compositions of its period, but nothing within two centuries of it achieves either its euphony or its easy handling of canon in four parts on a canonic bass in two. Its consecutive fifths which sound licentious to us were in its own day the sole justification of the scheme.

   It confirms other evidence that the imperfect concords (thirds
and sixths) must have obtained squatter's rights in music in spite
of theorists; for a very early practice known as ghimel or gymel
consisted in singing in thirds. This is not merely doubling, for
the third must oscillate between major and minor according to
its position in the scale; and this adjustment requires an advanced
harmonic system. When scholars tell us that singing in thirds
was traditional in Britain before the Roman Conquest, we must
demur, especially when they tell us (in Grove's *Dictionary of
Music and Musicians*, third edition) that we must not expect to
find written records of 'so simple a process'. Similarly we must
not expect to find ancient Greek written records of so simple a
process as steam locomotion. Still, let us not be unduly sceptical
as to the extent to which popular licence and unrecorded extem-
porization could advance beyond all the theoretic lore that scribes
will record.
   The troubadours disdained both the practice of accompaniment (which they left to their servants) and the art of scientific or
written music. Not until the time and work of Adam de la Hale,
surnamed the Hunchback of Arras (*c.* 1230–88), can we trace
the development of the troubadour into the learned musician.
Nearly a century later, when literature is unbending from its
universal Latin and becoming truly universal by becoming ver-
nacular, we find the poet Machault, who stands with Petrarch
among Chaucer's masters in the technique of verse, producing
music that marks a technical advance discoverable by grim toil of
expert analysis. But so far we may pardonably dismiss all such
archaic work (except *Sumer is icumen in*) with Burney's sly comment on the earliest piece of recorded music known to him: 'It
is not of such excellence as to make us greatly regret the loss of
such music; though the disposition of those who were pleased by
it may have been a great blessing to them.' When music is too
archaic or inaccessible to give us aesthetic data more may be
learned from the disposition of those who were pleased by it than
from its recorded technical data.
   Before the middle of the fifteenth century music had passed
for ever out of the stage at which we need know other things of
the composer than his music. As early as 1437 an Englishman,
John Dunstable, had acquired a European reputation. The
Golden Age of the sixteenth century had no use for archaic music,
and Morley in his *Plaine and Easie Introduction to Practickall
Musicke* quotes Dunstable much as we might now quote Bach if
all Bach's works were lost except for traces of contemporary hostile criticisms and awe-inspired laudations. To call Dunstable
the 'inventor of counterpoint' is no better than to call Cadmus
the inventor of the alphabet. But he is the earliest composer

whose polyphony is in direct line with that of the Golden Age; for
Dufay, the first important master of the Netherlands, where the
true polyphonic tradition was for long thought to have originated,
is now known to have died in 1474, twenty-one years after Dunstable. And when Dr. Walker, in his *History of Music in England*,
praises a motet by Dunstable for its extraordinary distinction of
style, he is indulging in no pious fancies but is describing permanently intelligible aesthetic values. By the end of the fifteenth
century counterpoint was substantially fixed, practice was still
imperfect, and aims were uncertain, but skill was increasing, and
in the sixteenth century we leave archaic music behind.

IV. THE GOLDEN AGE

From this point onwards the history of music is best studied in
the masterpieces of the art. Each period has its own art-forms.
Articles relevant to the Golden Age are HARMONY, Section iii;
INSTRUMENTATION, Section ii; CONTRAPUNTAL FORMS; COUNTER-
POINT; MADRIGAL; MASS; and MOTET.

The external history of music is not so easily brought into true
relation with the art as popular legends would have it. Everybody is familiar with the story of the drying-up of polyphony in
the foolish ingenuities of Flemish contrapuntists until, at the
behest of the Council of Trent, Palestrina wrote the *Missa Papae
Marcelli* in a pure and simple style which convinced the authorities that polyphonic music could be devout. The facts are not
quite so simple. Undoubtedly there was a great deal of barren
ingenuity in the work of the lesser Flemish masters; and the
great Obrecht himself had written Masses in which the liturgical
text is drowned beneath five other texts which each voice sings to
other plainchants and themes of old songs. The secular tunes
thus freely introduced were not always sung as canti fermi too
slow to be recognized. Recognition sometimes even led to the
singing of the original words. One old song, 'L'homme armé',
became the string round which every possible ingenuity crystal-
lized in the composition of the Mass. There is no reason to doubt
that the state of Church music both deserved and received the
serious attention of the Council of Trent.

On the other hand, not all Flemish music was silly, and many
of the quaintest canonic devices were really nothing but harmless cryptography applied to music that was composed on purely
artistic lines. Burney discovered this when, with his usual flair
for good illustrations, he quoted some dry ingenuities from
Okeghem (or Okenheim) and followed them by the wonderful
Déploration de Jehan Okenheim, by that master's great pupil
Josquin des Prés, who is the first unmistakably great composer

and who has been well named 'the Chaucer of music'. No
listener can fail to recognize, from anything like a competent
performance, the spontaneous beauty and poetic depth of this
music, throughout which, while the other voices sing an elegy in
French, the tenor intones in Latin the plainchant of the Requiem
beginning on a note *a semitone lower* than the liturgical pitch, and
continuing in the wailing melodic mode thus produced. Burney
had the wit to see that the 'canon' *un demiton plus bas* did not
mean that some other part was to answer the tenor in canon, but
was merely the 'rule' for reading the cryptogram, the tenor
being written at the normal pitch.

Many Flemish devices are well calculated to give coherence
or climax to a large composition. One voice may wander up and
down the scale with a single figure and a single motto-text while
the other voices tell their whole story in polyphony. For instance,
declaim the words *Miserere mei Deus* in monotone rising one
step just for the first syllable of *Deus*. Start on the fundamental
note of the scale, and at intervals repeat the phrase a step higher
each time. After reaching the fifth degree go down again. Josquin's *Miserere* is a setting of the whole of Psalm li., woven round
a tenor part entitled *Vagans* and constructed on this plan. It is
one of the first mature masterpieces in the history of music.
Palestrina's art is too subtle for rigid Flemish devices; but once,
in one of his finest motets, *Tribularer si nescirem*, he uses Josquin's *Miserere* burden in exactly Josquin's way. Lasso is
thoroughly Flemish in both sacred and secular music; and in a
motet on the resurrection of Lazarus he makes a soprano *Vagans*
cry *Lazare, veni foras* from the beginning of the narrative until
the chorus reaches these words, and joins with them in trium-
phant polyphony.

We must not, then, be misled by the ecclesiastical tradition
that condemns Flemish music wholesale. In any case the concern of the Church authorities was liturgical rather than artistic.
The bishops would have been for the most part glad enough to
see Church music restricted to the note-against-note style of
Palestrina's litanies, *Stabat Mater*, *Improperia*, and last book of
Lamentations. A very sublime style it is, and Tallis's Responses,
in their authentic form, are a noble illustration of it. But, as Dr.
Jeppesen (*The Style of Palestrina and the Dissonance*) has clearly
shown, Palestrina's *Missa Papae Marcelli* shows special signs of
being a deliberate demonstration that a high degree of polyphony
can be reconciled with clear choral delivery of the words. Certainly the ecclesiastical authorities did not long succeed in preventing the use of secular themes in Church music.

Many great musicians of to-day have a musical culture which
ignores the Golden Age; and a knowledge of Palestrina is still

Ex.1. *La Déploration de Jehan Okenheim*, for soprano, male alto, two tenors, and bass
(Barred according to the main rhythms)
Phrygian mode transposed

JOSQUIN DES PRÉS

*Or 'de trépas'

‡ The distribution of the words is uncertain. Perhaps these repeated notes are a realistic sob.

considered, as it was in the days of Bach and of Beethoven, rather
an out-of-the-way speciality. This is like a culture based on
Latin and sceptical of Greek; good as far as it goes, but limited
and cocksure, like an eighteenth-century gentleman's artistic
impressions of the Grand Tour. An illustration of the most perfect style of the Golden Age is appended to the article MOTET.

V. THE MONODIC REVOLUTION AND ITS RESULTS

Until Palestrina's art attained its height, the path of progress
in music for the best part of two centuries was that of purity. It
was not the free and bold spirits but the idlers and dullards who
broke rules and disliked contrapuntal forms. The Hispano-
Roman style of Victoria and Palestrina was not everything. It
was not secular (though Palestrina's madrigals make him as
supreme in that form as in Church music), and it was not, like
our glorious English polyphony, experimental or racy of the soil.
But it was metropolitan, and the boldest of our Tudor composers
would have been no such fools as not to hold it supreme. But
already before the death of Palestrina a new music was groping
towards the light; and for this music the path of progress was no
more that of purity than the path of omelette-making is that of
the conservation of egg-shells.

Eve's apple was not more fatal to man's earthly paradise than
the rise of instrumental music and dramatic solo declamation was
to the hope of continuing the Golden Age of music into the seventeenth century. The revolution did not consist in this detail or
that. To say that Monteverdi 'invented' the dominant seventh,
or that any one else invented it, or that any such invention could
revolutionize music, is like saying that Shakespeare revolution-
ized drama by inventing strange oaths. The important point is
not the technical names of the details but their meaning. When
Lasso was young some experiments in chromatic music had been
made by Cipriano de Rore, and were eagerly imitated by Lasso.
But what is Lasso's object in being the first person to write such
an out-of-the-way note as A♯? Simply to express the words
novum melos. Very different from such intellectual playthings is
the purpose of the powerful discords of Monteverdi's madrigal
Cruda Amarilli and of the monodic lament of Ariadne which
drew tears from the spectators of his opera *Arianna.*

In the *Encyclopaedia Britannica* article, MONTEVERDI, will be
found further remarks on his importance and on his coincidence
in place and time with the creators of the violin. (*See also* OPERA
in this book.) The Palestrina style henceforth became the right-
ful privilege only of those composers who, either having mastered
it before monody arose, or, like our own Orlando Gibbons, living

in regions too remote for it to penetrate, could still compose polyphonically from impulse and not from asceticism. Orlando
Gibbons did, in fact, try some monodic experiments, which are
poor enough.

An impulsively eclectic composer is another matter; and in
uncouth, illogical Germany a giant such as Schütz could almost
fill the century before the birth of Bach and Handel, with a life's
work ranging from the pure polyphony of his Venetian master
Gabrieli to the exploitation of all his 'astute friend' (*scharfsin-
niger Freund*) Monteverdi's new principles in most gigantic efforts
in mixed vocal and instrumental polyphony. From Schütz we
can extract no such system as that which makes Monteverdi a
favourite subject in musical history; but in Schütz's chaos the
elements may at any moment come together in some strange work
of art that fits into no historical or technical scheme but speaks
clearly to us through its own coherence. Schütz's 'astute friend'
always knows what he is doing and whither his work is leading;
but, except in a madrigal here and there, which was not his
proper business, he does not produce a convincing work of art
so often as Schütz who seems to have no proper business at all.
It is to the astute, logical Italians that we must look for the progress and consolidation of musical art in general during the
seventeenth century; but we must not let the enthusiasm of historians make us think that such a century of progress was a period
of great music. The historians themselves are apt to neglect the
intrinsic values of the seventeenth-century compositions and to
estimate them merely for their tendency towards something that
was to take convincing shape later. The early seventeenth century was, in fact, musically not unlike what we have so far experienced of the twentieth; the eyes of musicians and music-
lovers were at the ends of the earth prophesying Wagner, when
all that the whole century could finally achieve was the da capo
form of aria.

Monteverdi and his fellow monodists had, in no mood of
caprice, moved in the one direction that was universally important for music; yet their formless declamation soon palled, and
its method survived only by becoming codified into the formulas
of recitative, which are happy idealizations of Italian speech-
cadence, and which survive as dramatic idioms in all music even
at the present day. The 'invention' of recitative has been
ascribed to this or that monodist, with as little room for dispute
as when we ascribe the invention of clothes to Adam and Eve.
Any vocal music which, whether from inability or from disin-
clination, avoids organizing symmetrical melody, will be called
recitative. When Wagner was still a subject of controversy, critics
on both sides used to say that *Das Rheingold* was all recitative.

Two tendencies converged to make music become formal after the 'first fine careless rapture' of monody was spent. First, the dramatic stage, with baroque scenery in magnificent development as early as 1667, in Cesti's *Pomo d'Oro*, greatly encouraged the ballet; so that when serious musicians cultivated the stage they also cultivated dance-music. This, however, was less important than the rise of the violin. Monteverdi had already understood its importance; and one symptom of the decadence of polyphony had been the growing habit of solo-singers to sing the top parts of madrigals with all manner of ridiculous flourishes. Persons less legendary than King Cole felt the fascination of the 'tweedle-dee' of the fiddle; the great Dutch polyphonist Sweelinck used to adorn his organ works with passages of 'imitatio violinistica'; and the last quarter of the seventeenth century saw the brilliant work of Biber with his queer abnormal violin-tunings, and the sober classical 'sonate da chiesa' and 'sonate da camera' of Corelli. Artistically as well as morally this development of the violin was healthier than that of the voice, wherein coloratura singing tended to become an acrobatic monstrosity though it had first been regarded as a means of emotional expression. A talent for the violin was no danger to a boy; but a beautiful voice put a boy in deadly peril in an age when all the great opera-singers were *castrati*. Even Haydn had a narrow escape in his youth.

And yet there is, on the whole, more beauty than decadence in the vast mass of solo vocal music produced between 1630 and 1760. That period takes us from the advent of mature instruments and instrumentalized music to a time beyond the death of Handel. Except for the device of the ground-bass (*see* VARIATIONS) the first form that emerged from chaos organized itself on a method of balance between a solo voice and a group of instruments, together with a development of melodic form by means of a firmly established classical key-system. The result was the classical aria, one of the most effective art-forms ever reduced to the capacity of normal musicians. It entirely destroyed the dramatic character of opera for a whole century; but this has been lamented with unnecessary vehemence. With the exception of the early monodic works and of Purcell's *Dido and Aeneas*, opera before Gluck is not an art-form at all; it is merely a name for the spectacular conditions under which the eighteenth-century public could be induced to listen to a string of thirty arias by one composer who could either handle no other forms or find no listeners for them. The article ARIA shows the intimate connexion of this form with that of the concerto. Other art-forms developed in the seventeenth century for use in the eighteenth are discussed under CANTATA, OPERA, ORATORIO, SONATA, SONATA FORMS, and SUITE. Matters of style and texture are discussed in

CHAMBER MUSIC, HARMONY, and INSTRUMENTATION. Among the monodic composers are Caccini, Cavalieri, Cesti, Peri, and Monteverdi, besides Artusi and Banchieri, who wrote against Monteverdi's earlier works with well-grounded demonstrations of their subversive effect on pure polyphony. The survival of polyphony in grimy and pompous decadence is represented by Pitoni, and later and more as a renascence by Lotti. Early violin music is represented by Biber and Corelli.

The short career of Purcell ends twenty years after the death of Schütz and ten years after the birth of Bach and Handel. Almost any random quotation from Purcell might be by a composer of the calibre of Bach or Handel. Purcell is one of the greatest contrapuntists that ever lived; one of the greatest inventors of themes; one of the greatest masters of declamation; and a completely mature master of early orchestration. And his fellows in the English music of the Restoration, Pelham Humfrey, Child, and Blow, were no mean spirits. Burney devotes an entire plate in his *History of Music* to examples of 'Dr. Blow's crudities'; and later historians need look no farther afield for examples of intelligent prophecy. But our Restoration music lacks one thing; and that is power of composition. Purcell, in small dance-forms and short lyrics, is unsurpassable. But his only chance of getting through a sustained movement is when he writes on a ground-bass. In this fascinating forlorn hope of English music we see the fruit of nearly a century of bold endeavour ripening a generation too soon. Parry ascribes the patchiness of Purcell to the subtle humour of Charles II in sending his best chorister to learn from Lully, the master of the French ballet-opera, how to write English Church music. But Lully is not patchy, and Purcell's music is a crazy-quilt, purple with foreshadowings of the music of the future.

VI. BACH, HANDEL, AND THE NEAPOLITAN SCHOOL

If all music between 1685 and 1759 were annihilated except the work of Bach and Handel, the ordinary music-lover would miss nothing but a large collection of decorative and decorous violin music and a still larger collection of arias; and to most of these favourite *gemme d'antichita* the mid-nineteenth-century editor has contributed much of their lusciousness. For us the age of Bach and Handel is the age of nobody else in music. But the contemporaries of Bach and Handel thought of Handel as a fashionable opera-writer who with advancing years developed choral music as a pious fad; while nobody thought of Bach except people within coaching-range of Saxony, where Bach was known as a wonderful organist and an impracticably deep scholar. The polyphony of Bach and Handel stands almost alone in an age when polyphony was utterly unfashionable. It was inculcated as a staple subject in musical education; but to carry it into mature art was to discuss Latin grammar in the drawing-room. The opportunities and the difficulties of early symphonic orchestration alike arose from the neglect of polyphony after 1750. Apart from Bach and Handel, that neglect can be traced much further back, and it characterized musical connoisseurship much later; so that Burney could say of Philipp Emanuel Bach that wherever he got his beautiful and natural style from it was not from his father, for that eminent organist, though profoundly versed in all devices of canon and fugue, was so fond of crowding all the harmony he could into both hands that he must inevitably have lost melodic grace.

The vast and accurately-perfected aesthetic system of Bach and the improvisatorial opportunist eclecticism of Handel are discussed under various headings in this book. But, while this information covers the aesthetic values of the period, it tells us little of its historic trend. We must not look for light from the 'spirit of the age' as shown in its politics or even in its religious history. Palestrina writes, from habit and preference, a devout music which neither Luther nor the Council of Trent could blame as representing the spirit of the age; and Bach achieves the ideal Lutheran music while Voltaire is at the court of Frederick the Great.

The music that pleased the contemporaries of Bach and Handel was that which continued, not too elaborately, the Neapolitan tradition founded by Alessandro Scarlatti. Lully (an Italian by birth) took this tradition to France, and transformed Italian opera by encouraging the French taste for the ballet. Rameau, greatest of classical French composers and epoch-making theorist, carried on the Lully tradition in opera, and joined forces with the exquisite school of *clavecinistes*, whose leader, Couperin, was admired and imitated by Bach in his suite-forms. Italian violin music and concertos in the Neapolitan style were produced by composers who were also great players. The enormous industry of Bach and Handel was nothing unusual. Arias could be written as easily as letters, and distributed by thirties in operas. Oratorios and Church music, though less fashionable, were more highly organized; mainly because they kept choral music in being. And thus the Neapolitan tradition of choral music passes straight into the polyphony of Mozart, quite independently of Handel and wholly ignoring Sebastian Bach, of whom Mozart knew not a note until he was grown up. Meanwhile cultured Europe was unvexed by doubts as to who were the immortals. The Handel-Bononcini rivalry had been little more than a nine-

days' wonder. Six years after Handel's death, the seven-year-old
Mozart in London dedicated his violin sonatas to Queen Char-
lotte in the hope that under Her Majesty's protection *je devien-
drai immortel comme Haendel et Hasse*. Graun would probably
have been the third name of European repute; and Telemann,
the most voluminous composer of his voluminous day, was a
great figure in his own country. As for Bach—everybody in
London knew Mr. J. C. Bach, of the Bach and Abel concerts,
and report said that his father had been a great musical
scholar.

Behind the dignified musical history, but not (like Sebastian
Bach) aloof from it, vital forces were at work in comic music-
drama. This was admitted by way of intermezzi between the
acts of serious operas. One of these intermezzi, *La Serva Padrona*
by Pergolesi (known in the nineteenth century by his conventional
Stabat Mater for two-part female chorus), not only broke from
its moorings, like many other intermezzi, but found its way to
Paris where it created a furore of popular success and precious
disputation dividing musical Paris into Buffonistes and Antibuffonistes. Except for the untimely blossom of English opera
in the hands of Purcell in the previous century, this is the only
moment at which opera after Monteverdi and before Gluck (with
all respect to Rameau) becomes a genuine art-form instead of a
concert on the stage. Rameau is equally important in three
capacities as a master of French opera, a livelier master of instrumental music, and a great theorist. German beginnings of
serious and comic music-drama were sumptuously inaugurated
at Hamburg by Keiser, whose influence is traceable in Handel's
first opera *Almira*.

VII. THE RISE OF DRAMATIC MUSIC AND THE SONATA STYLE

The fashionable distaste for polyphony was a mere negative
force in the early eighteenth century. The positive force was, as
in the monodic revolution a hundred and fifty years earlier, an
impulse towards drama. Unlike the monodists who, when they
rejected polyphony, had no power of composition beyond the
single musical sentence, the eighteenth-century musicians could
easily cover ten minutes with a well-balanced form; and the
problem of making such forms dramatic was no longer confined
to the monodist's problem of making them rhetorical. On the
contrary, the rhetoric had to be demolished; for the action of
drama is not the action of rhetoric.

The distaste for polyphony was no unfavourable condition for
the rise of dramatic music; it was the inverse aspect of a growing
sense of contrast in various textures cheap and valueless in them-

selves. The rest of the story is told in the articles, INSTRUMENTA-
TION, HARMONY, OPERA, and SONATA FORMS.

It is inadequate to call Gluck a 'reformer' of opera. Music
itself was not dramatic before Gluck made it so. Hence it is a
mistake to separate Gluck's 'reform' from the whole process of
the development of the sonata style. Lastly, we miss the whole
meaning of that style unless we realize that as soon as it arose
the purely instrumental music became more dramatic than any
drama. At the same time it also became more powerfully architectural than any earlier music. The art comprised in the works
of Haydn, Mozart, and Beethoven constitutes one unbroken
aesthetic system, more universal in emotional range than any art
since Shakespeare, and as perfectly balanced as the arts of ancient
Greece. Until the end of the nineteenth century it would have
seemed a paradox to maintain that Beethoven's work belonged to
the same aesthetic system as Haydn's and Mozart's; for critics
were slow to escape from the habit of estimating works of art by
the face value of their subjects and the dignity of their language.
And the language of Haydn and Mozart corresponds with that
of the comedy of manners, while Beethoven is the most tragic
composer that ever lived. Nevertheless the huge expansion which
music underwent at Beethoven's hands was no revolution, and
the popular idea of Beethoven as a revolutionary artist is based
on two errors: first, the commonplace habit of seeking parallels
between the works of genius and the personal eccentricities of
their authors, and, secondly, the inadequacy of orthodox doctrine
on musical forms. This inadequacy results from the fact that
the doctrines are contemporaneous with the compositions and are
accordingly hostile to all but the easiest conventions. A proper
grammar of a classical art requires something of the attitude of
the unjustly despised Byzantine scholars who sacrificed aesthetic
pleasures in humble devotion to the task of securing the texts. It
is when the languages are dead that they live for ever and suffer
no corruption.

We need not expect scholarship in the orthodoxies that were
current as to musical forms used in the lifetime of the classics
themselves. (See FUGUE for a demonstration of the irrelevance of
traditional doctrine on that art-form.) Still more impertinent is
our orthodoxy on sonata forms. It ignores the differences between Haydn and Mozart which are as radical as any innovation
Beethoven introduced; and, having thus cut away all ground
for appreciating Beethoven, treats him as the central symphonic
classic, and also as a stupendous revolutionary. This result is
correct as far as it goes: central classics can be stupendous revolutionaries. But correct pious opinions are the healthier for facts
that can give us a right to them, and the beginning of the nine-

teenth century was unfortunately the beginning of an age of
humbug in musical education. One consequence is that many a
musical revolt purports to revolt against the classics when its
nearest contact with classical forms has been the perky generaliza-
tions of text-books by writers who regarded the great masters as
dangerous, and who deduced their rules from the uniform procedures of lesser composers. Now these procedures were often
derived from one or two popular works by the greatest men: thus
Beethoven himself produced one model sonata (op. 22)—if its
'first subject' had only been long enough. And if Mozart's great
C major Quartet had not such a subversive introduction it might
(and did) serve as a jelly-mould for all the quartets of Spohr.
Take another jelly-mould from Spohr, and you have classical
tradition.

But now comes the fundamental difficulty in all attempts to
distinguish the classical from the pseudo-classical. Every individual work must be judged on its own merits. No generaliza-
tions are trustworthy. Many movements by Mozart are as alike
as peas. But, being alive, they are not as alike as buttons. With
Mozart and Haydn the individuality of each work is all-important
for the critic, and if he neglects this all that he says about the
common form is superficial. On the other hand, the materials of
Beethoven's work developed so rapidly that he seems to be driven
to invent a new technique for almost each composition. Hence
the external differences become obvious; and unless the critic
penetrates to the common form he is lost.

With the symphonic classics we enter the period when these
considerations become important; for there is no gulf between
that period and our own. No musical art known to Haydn has
suffered, as did the art of Bach, a period of total eclipse; nor, on
the other hand, has it preserved a character that Haydn could
have understood. Not much light is shed on Haydn and Mozart
by calling them court composers, and little more on Beethoven
by calling him a child of the French Revolution. In an age of
court patronage Bach the theologian had been inspired to write
warlike music not more by ancestral memories than by scriptural
texts of war in Heaven. Mozart and Haydn were restive in the
service of courts, and their musical language was that of the
comedy of manners when it was not racy of the soil. In Paris,
where musicians might be expected to know most about the
French Revolution, the modest, lovable Etienne Méhul (famous
for the biblical opera *Joseph*) produced his prettiest comic operetta
Le Jeune Sage et le Vieux Fou in the year of the Terror; and on
French music the immediate effect of these tremendous days was
the rise of a new type of sentimental opera concerning the hair-
breadth escapes and sufferings of the political prisoner rescued

by the heroic wife. Hence Cherubini's *Les Deux Journées* (*The Water-Carrier*) and Beethoven's *Fidelio*. Genius is the wind that bloweth where it listeth. In Bach's day Beethoven would have been the musical interpreter of the Apocalypse; and in this twentieth century Bach would be something like Dr. Schweitzer.

When we contemplate the impassable gulf that separates Bach's art not only from Haydn's and Mozart's but from the apparently more kindred spirit of Beethoven, we find it hard to realize that contemporaries were unaware of any catastrophic development. In the case of choral music a little study shows us that its forms and language remained Neapolitan. Haydn's and Mozart's masses are flamboyant Neapolitan music; and Michael Haydn, who was merely decorative as an instrumental composer, was rightly thought by his brother to be the better man at Church music. Again we regard Philipp Emanuel Bach as bridging the gulf between his father's and the new art; but Philipp Emanuel was writing quite mature sonatas in the year of his father's B minor Mass and his last set of sonatas was produced in the year of Mozart's *Don Giovanni*. Clementi, born in the year after Bach's death, was an infant prodigy of eight when Handel died; he had developed an extraordinary massive and genuine pianoforte technique (more powerful than beautiful) when he encountered Mozart in a musical tournament, and he survived Weber, Beethoven, and Schubert. Nothing can be gained by a further attempt to summarize this 'Viennese' period. We may call it the period of the sonata and of Mozartean comic and French romantic opera. More particular information is given in the technical articles in this book.

VIII. THE ROMANTIC PERIOD

With the romantic period comes the development of lyric music in the forms of songs and short pianoforte pieces. Schubert, Weber, Spohr, Mendelssohn, and Schumann would be the romantic composers in this sense, and many contemporaries would have added Cherubini to the list, for they thought of him not as the martinet who directed the Paris Conservatoire but as the composer of *Les Deux Journées*. Romanticism was thrilling and classicism was cold.

But this list traverses another sense of the term which opposes the romantic to the classical. The classical is in this connexion identified with both formalism and mastery. Mendelssohn and Spohr chose romantic subjects to no purpose; their mastery was unromantically slick (there is no other word for it) and Spohr's forms were more thoroughly ascertained than anybody else's except those of Mozart's brilliant pupil, J. N. Hummel. Mendelssohn's forms were free; but he never got into difficulties, so how could anybody recognize his freedom? Philipp Emanuel Bach's vein of sentimental rhetoric was not only typically romantic but enabled him to write some genuinely lyrical songs. J. Schobert is another romantic writer who influenced Mozart at an impressionable time of his boyhood. Every thrilling modulation in Beethoven's music was romantic, and so were the double-bass passages at the beginning of Cherubini's Overture to *Les Deux Journées*.

But the facts are more interesting than this generalization. Mastery is not the line of cleavage that ranges Spohr and Mendelssohn on the one side and Schubert, Schumann, and Chopin on the other. Beethoven's later tonality and polyphony had made music ready for lyric forms which he himself adumbrated in a few of his *Bagatelles* for pianoforte and in some sporadic good things among his songs. Mendelssohn and Spohr took up songwriting and produced in that line masterpieces for the drawing-room. We ought not to despise the drawing-room. Schubert became the supreme master of song, and Schumann achieved greatness there as in his pianoforte lyrics; but you might as well think of Keats and Shelley as writers for the drawing-room.

Another line of cleavage separates Schubert from Schumann and Chopin as fundamentally as it separates him from Mendelssohn and Spohr. When Schumann and Chopin handle the large classical forms they show obvious weaknesses. Schumann makes an effective new artificial sonata form out of his stiff, antithetic, epigrammatic style, as a man might construct a landscape in mosaic. Chopin merely shows that he has taken the sonata forms uncritically from Hummel, though the first two movements of the B flat minor Sonata are almost as happy in their classical form as the Ballades are in Chopin's unique way. But Schubert's large forms have only the weaknesses of youth, and their positive qualities and tendencies set him above all schools and indicate that if he had lived we should not so readily have closed an historic chapter with Beethoven. The mastery that Schubert lacks is not anything that Spohr could have supplied. Younger composers with new worlds to conquer could with some truth accuse Spohr of playing with classical forms as one might play chess; but they could never have so accused the Schubert that died young or the Schubert that might have reached old age.

We do not know what Mendelssohn might have achieved if he had lived longer. His influence on the musicians he knew personally was wholly stimulating and good. But he too seemed able to play chess with symphonies, oratorios, and songs with and without words, while other composers were grappling in their music with real life, perhaps confined to one narrow art-medium

like Chopin, or, like Schumann, deserting lyrics for larger forms
or some artificial hypothesis, or, like young Berlioz, kicking right
and left against all teaching and all criticism while dreaming new
wonders of orchestral sound, and correctly dreaming the practical
means to them also.

Meanwhile a greater than Berlioz was arising, a dreamer of
new sense as well as sound. Mendelssohn and Schumann saw
only the beginning of Wagner's development, and could not feel
very sure that this voluble and stormy reformer of music-drama
was really likely to achieve anything better than the tinsel of the
astute Meyerbeer who dominated the world of cosmopolitan
opera. The early style of Wagner is indeed an alloy of many
metals besides iron and potter's clay; but even in the 'forties his
work marks the eclipse of the first romantic period and the dawn
of another and greater epoch.

The art-forms peculiar to the Romantic period have no definite
names, though composers began to use many literary titles, such
as Ballade, Romance (already used by Mozart for slow movements in sonata form), Nocturne, and the like. Dance-rhythms,
especially those of Poland, were brought into prominence in the
pianoforte music of Chopin. Mendelssohn's invention of the
Song without Words was very successful, but the notion is too
facile to lead far, or always, even in Mendelssohn's hands, to
justify its existence. Fantastic titles, used in the eighteenth century by the French *clavecinistes*, assumed great prominence in the
pianoforte works of Schumann, who created a new type of long
connected cycles of epigrammatic little pieces. The article PRO-
GRAMME MUSIC concerns this period vitally. The crowd of pianoforte composers whose brilliance on that instrument obstructed
all wider musical prospects include the respectable Hummel, the
less respectable Steibelt, the flimsy Woelfl, and the Irish writer
of beautiful pre-Chopin nocturnes, John Field.

IX. THE WAGNERIAN DEVELOPMENT AND THE RENASCENCE OF CLASSICAL FORM

Wagner formulated his principles of music-drama long before
he matured his musical style. It is impossible to understand the
musical history of the second half of the nineteenth century until
we frankly admit that the composers of instrumental music saw
in Wagner, not only the subversive operatic theorist and erotic
dramatist, but the composer who was popular because of the
Salvation Army religiosity of the end of the *Tannhäuser* Overture,
and the downright vulgarity of the entr'acte before Act III in
Lohengrin. His theories and methods might be controversial, but
these lapses never were.

Strange to say, Wagner received something like recognition from the doyen of classical champions, Spohr, whose attitude to Beethoven had been merely condescending, but who saw in *Der Fliegende Holländer* and *Tannhäuser* interesting, if faulty, works which well deserved painstaking production at his theatre at Cassel. Schumann too, after joining in the general hostility towards *Tannhäuser*, frankly recanted and praised its many noble features. Personally he and Wagner did not get on well; he found Wagner too talkative and Wagner found that Schumann had nothing to say. Later on, when Wagner was in exile, *Lohengrin* found a powerful champion in Liszt at Weimar.

Liszt presented another problem to sober musicians. Wagner himself at first saw nothing in Liszt but the virtuoso who, when asked for music, would give you a fantasia on *Robert le Diable*. On the other hand, persons who became bitterly hostile to all the musical tendencies that Liszt fostered went out of their way to declare that no such wonderful interpretations and technique as Liszt's pianoforte playing had ever before been heard on any instrument or orchestra. All Liszt's gestures were superb, from his monumental immobility at the pianoforte to his princely and often really self-sacrificing generosity to other musicians. And at the age of 37 he made the most superb of all his gestures in giving up playing in public. And so the one incontrovertible power of his art became a legend and his actual activity became the championship of unorthodox artists. He took to composing on a more ambitious scale than that of the marvellous pianoforte virtuoso; and became himself the leader of a new development of romantic music. Although he took little pleasure in counterpoint he had none of Berlioz's clumsiness in harmonic texture; and his orchestration, in which his first efforts had the secret assistance of Raff, was always brilliant and novel, though it never caught the Berliozian fire or plumbed the Wagnerian deeps. Liszt realized no more than did Berlioz the true musical purport of the new ideas which his symphonic poems and Berlioz's symphonic-dramatic phantasmagorias were putting forward under all kinds of literary and pictorial names. While the new romantic composers purported to be devoting instrumental music to the illustration of literature (*see* PROGRAMME MUSIC), they were really struggling with a new musical time-scale.

As we have already seen in the present article and in the discussion of HARMONY, musical history may be traced in terms of the time-limit over which the listener's memory is brought into play. In the sixteenth century that limit is from accent to accent; by the end of the seventeenth century it ran from phrase to phrase. The great architectural forms of Bach could stretch it easily to six minutes, and in extreme cases to ten. The rise of

the dramatic sonata style did not greatly enlarge the time-scale;
for there are few well-constructed sonata movements that exceed
a quarter of an hour, though on no smaller scale could Beethoven
have prepared the famous harmonic collision that gave such
offence in the first movement of the 'Eroica' Symphony. Now
this ten-minute time-scale obviously compelled musicians to
handle the action of an opera by means of conventions.⌐ (*See*
OPERA.) It is less obvious that it also produced a similarly conventional artifice in the relation of sonata forms to their emotional
content. A design may complete itself in ten minutes while
raising emotional issues that cannot be dealt with in less than
forty. And so the sonata forms are grouped in from two to four
(rarely more) movements as artificially as the musical sections of
classical operas. Wagner's enormous achievement in music-
drama consisted essentially in giving music the same time-scale
as that of the drama. As with all first solutions of an art-problem,
he achieved an extreme case, for his drama became cosmically
slow. But from *Das Rheingold* onwards every Wagnerian opening
instantly, and without any introductory gestures, lays down the
lines of its vast time-scale, to the utter bewilderment of his contemporaries, who continued to expect *Das Rheingold* to show its
pattern on Beethoven's time-scale, just as Beethoven's contemporaries had heard seven pianissimo bars on the chord of E flat,
not as that vaulted vacancy appears in the middle of the Andante
of the C minor Symphony, but as it would have sounded if it
were intruded into an andante by Mozart.

Nobody else before Richard Strauss achieved Wagner's mastery of his new time-scale; and few, if any, of his contemporaries,
whether hostile or friendly to him, realized its existence. Liszt
was trying, in his symphonic poems, to make a music that filled
its half-hour or forty minutes continuously; but his first effort of
the kind, *Ce qu'on entend sur la montagne*, spends the first twenty
of its forty minutes in a series of introductions, and the remaining
twenty in retracing the series backwards. And his more successful efforts, such as *Orpheus* and *Les Préludes*, are either essentially
lyric or not on the new time-scale at all. He never achieved so
effective a symphonic poem as Schubert had already long ago
unwittingly produced in the 'Wanderer' Fantasia. Musicians
who might not have been repelled by new doctrines of musical
form found Liszt's style even more demi-mondaine than that of
the early works of Wagner; nor did Liszt show any tendency to
purify it. Moreover, he rivalled Meyerbeer in the efficiency of
his press bureau, by which he made propaganda, often in his own
fluent French, more generously for others than for himself.

Meanwhile another musical development was arising, conscious
of its continuity with the past and, like Judaism as defined by

Matthew Arnold, tinged with emotion in the morality of its aesthetic principles. Joachim, as great an interpreter on the violin as Liszt on the pianoforte, at first found in Liszt a congenial friend, until he saw his compositions. These horrified him, and the horror completed an estrangement already begun by his dislike of the atmosphere of Liszt's press bureau. He and his younger friend Brahms were united not only in general musical taste but in personal devotion to the heroic widow of Schumann, who, after her husband's tragic and lingering death, was bringing up a large family on the proceeds of her concerts. These three artists soon came to regard the musical atmosphere of Weimar, where the *Lisztianer* gathered around their master, as unhealthy. In the correspondence and mutual criticism of Brahms and Joachim the word *Lisztisch* became synonymous with 'devilish'; and indeed it is true that any characteristic Lisztian and many Wagnerian idioms would have a disgusting effect if intruded into Brahms's music. To-day we can be wise after the event and find matter for regret in the drastic outspokenness of Joachim and Brahms, which elevated matters of taste into questions of artistic honour. If Liszt could have been contented with *sachlich* criticism on definable issues of technique without requiring attestations of sympathy and enjoyment, and if Joachim could have resolved matters of taste into questions of artistic proportion, the neo-classical and neo-romantic musicians would have joined forces instead of condemning each other. Similar economies might be effected in nature if lions could be converted to vegetarianism.

The controversy was unequal, in two compensating ways. Wagner had a tremendous, if acrid, fluency in prose and did not care where his vitriol might alight. Moreover, Wagnerian and Lisztian music was much easier to write about, whether in attack or defence, than music which had no literary aspect. Brahms, like Wagner, needed and found friends who adored his music, but he hated the idea of a press bureau and snubbed anybody whose compliments aroused the least suspicion of flattery. These drawbacks had their own compensation. It might be difficult to write as interestingly about Brahms as about Wagner; but Wagner, whether in exile or enthroned at Bayreuth, had Wagnerian music-drama as his whole province, while Brahms reigned over the whole of the rest of music, instrumental, choral, and lyric. If criticism came to persecution, on the whole the neo-classics had the worst of it; for Brahms had no equals since Joachim gave up composition, and the position of a champion of classical forms was easily confused with that of a persecutor of the prophets of progress. As a matter of fact, Brahms was no anti-Wagnerian and was annoyed when his friends bracketed Wagner with Liszt.

But, apart from the clash of flying inkpots, the recognition of
Brahms was assured by two facts: first, the propaganda of his
work not by words but by consummate and authoritative performance, and second, the very fact that his music required an
experienced love of music for its understanding. A man might
become an enthusiastic Wagnerian or even a well-equipped conductor of Wagner's music and be as the brutes that perish about
symphonic orchestration, choral music, chamber music, songs,
and all pianoforte music except Chopin. But it was long before
any musician could venture to tackle Brahms's music on any
basis except that of the most comprehensive musical culture and
technique. Brahms lived long enough to become worshipped
unintelligently; and after his death (in 1897) the reaction was
more evident than the fashionable worship had been. There are
signs that the reaction is over by now.

The Wagnerians felt deeply that their propaganda was incomplete for lack of a master of purely symphonic music. This they
found in Bruckner. Brahms was appalled by the clumsiness of
Bruckner's forms, and the most official Wagnerians admitted the
frequent lapses of their symphonic master. On the other hand
Bruckner's Nibelungen-tetralogy openings to his symphonies
obviously dwarfed the terse themes of Brahms. By the time
Brahms and Bruckner had come into their own, the public had
long lost all sense of form in its appetite for bleeding gobbets of
musical butcher's-meat hacked from the living body of Wagnerian
music-drama, and served up in concert rooms as *Waldweben*,
Karfreitagszauber, and *Walkürenritt*. After this it was pedantry
to quarrel with any symphonic composer's form so long as his
openings were vast enough. Brahms was no pedant; obvious
weakness of form and style did not deter him from being the first
to recognize Dvořák; and he was drastic in his rebuff of anybody
who thought to flatter him by talking against Wagner.

The song-writer Hugo Wolf (1860–1903) became recognized
too late to be made use of as a lyric-pawn in the Wagner-Bruckner
party politics of music. As far as his theory of song can be
summarized, it consists in the application of Wagnerian declamation to lyric poetry. If his practice were not better than this
essentially prose theory of verse-rhythm (*see* RHYTHM) and the
perky censorship of classical musical declamation that goes with
it, Hugo Wolf's art would not have survived his short and ailing
life. But it is deeper than the theories on which it is supposed
to rest and its apparent revolt from lyric melody only partly
conceals a powerfully organized lyric form, and does not at all
conceal a great gift of characterization.

While these great issues were being debated in Germany, the music of other countries was awakening from long sleep or outgrowing infancy and provinciality. France had, since Rameau, been remarkably content to have its music dominated by foreigners. Before Rameau, French opera was established by the Italian Lully. After Rameau it was reformed by the Austrian Gluck. Early nineteenth-century French classicism was dominated by the Italian Cherubini. Another Italian, Rossini, was in the prime of his life absorbed by Paris; and the result was *Guillaume Tell*, with its rich orchestration and grandiose forms. But the crown of French opera was imposed on it by the German Jew Meyerbeer. The pretensions of the native French composers were more modest, except for the volcanic eruptions of that typical *méridional* Berlioz. The popularity of Gounod (1818–93) rested on the same misunderstanding of the meaning of art as the vogue of Doré in the capacity of an illustrator of the Bible. *Faust* was a success. Another development, more improvisatorial, uncertain of its style, but fundamentally sincere, was initiated by the Belgian, César Franck (1822–92). From him, and not from the more prolific and facile Saint-Saëns, originates the main stream of modern French music. His style has too much affinity with Liszt to please the musicians who continue to regard Liszt as the author of all modern musical evil; but he achieved mastery in a wide range of forms all his own and he never wrote for effect.

In Italy music since Rossini was long contented to imitate the things in which Rossini was imitable. These were the mechanical cultivation of *bel canto* and the use of a full orchestra to support the voice in a thick unison of the melodic instruments, with a brassy dance-rhythm in the rest, and the big drum and cymbals to mark the rhythm. The genuine melodic inventiveness of Bellini and Donizetti did little to improve the other categories of the art; but in Verdi (1813–1901) a new genius was arising together with the Risorgimento. In *Rigoletto*, *Il Trovatore*, and *La Traviata* Verdi's dramatic sincerity triumphs over the defects of a musical texture which still clings to traditional squalor, though strokes of genius occur unpredictably in the orchestration of many passages. In *Aïda* the style silences all cavil; and in *Otello* (written at the age of 74) and *Falstaff* (written at the age of 80) Verdi creates a new kind of opera, Wagnerian in its perfect continuity and dramatic movement, but utterly independent of Wagner's style and method.

Bold prophets in Beethoven's time had been heard to say that a great musical future was in store for Russia. The fulfilment of this prophecy was long delayed, for when Rubinstein averred that

Michael Glinka (1803–57) was the equal or the superior of
Haydn and Mozart, he expressed an opinion which could have
occurred only to a Russian, and then only as a patriotic paradox.
Rubinstein himself achieved only a weak cosmopolitanism in his
voluminous compositions, though his pianoforte playing remained, for all its waywardness, till near the end of the century,
as the most monumental power of interpretation on that instrument since Liszt. The first composer to make a genuinely Russian music recognized over the whole civilized world was Tchaikovsky (1840–93), whose symphonies were held by some critics
to have eclipsed those of Brahms. This was the eclipse of drama
by melodrama. The true merits of Tchaikovsky are now eclipsed
by the rising reputation of his less immediately successful contemporaries. Mussorgsky (1835–81) had the posthumous fortune to have his two great operas, *Boris Godunov* and *Khovan-
tchina*, revised by Rimsky-Korsakov (1844–1908), the most
brilliant contemporary master of pure orchestral colour and
texture. This was unquestionably good fortune in so far as it
speeded these unconventional works on their way into the wide
world; but something like indignation has accompanied the more
recent study of Mussorgsky's original scores, with the discovery
that besides altering clumsinesses Rimsky-Korsakov constantly
meddled with features in his friend's style that were far beyond
his comprehension.

The nineteenth century was over before any musician on the
Continent could be persuaded that there were composers in
England. Schumann had repeated St. Gregory's pun about
Angles and angels when he hailed Sterndale Bennett as 'ein
englischer Componist'; but the trials of English musical life dried
Bennett up. All who knew and loved him denied hotly that his
music reflected Mendelssohn's; and perhaps, to-day, a leisurely
study of it might vindicate his independence. Macfarren (1813–
87), who succeeded Bennett in his educational offices, was a
widely cultured musician whose influence for good was frus-
trated by his violent conservatism, which co-existed with a fatal
readiness to be led by faddists. (*See* HARMONY.) The renascence
of English music began in the work of Parry (1848–1918) and
Stanford (1852–1924). They put an end to the provincial absurdities of our British oratorio tradition, and consistently set great
literature in a way that revealed to contemporary poets that the
antithesis between musical and general culture was false. They
also had wide and deep influence as teachers of composition.

Still, recognition of English music on the Continent was rare
and capricious. Englishmen wrote Church music for the stage,
stage music for the Church, organ music for the orchestra, and,
as far as we had any orchestral ideas at all, orchestral music for

the organ. The one famous English composer who could be understood on the Continent, as saying intelligible things in fit terms, was Sullivan, with his Savoy operas. And his serious colleagues and critics urged him with owlish solemnity to produce no more light masterpieces but to go on with his serious and luscious Golden Legends and Martyrs of Antioch and generally to consummate the final merging of English music into 'The Lost Chord'. We may thankfully hope that that chord is now lost for ever; but the Savoy operas live, and might, without delay to their popularity, have risen to the position of great music if Sullivan had had enough steadfast love of music to finish those parts of his work to which the public did not listen; if for example, he had provided his operas with better orchestral introductions than the perfunctory pot-pourris of their favourite tunes which he calls overtures and which are quite as long as artistically decent overtures would have been.

It is customary to explain the failure of all but the most recent British music by saying that the native art was crushed by the ponderous genius of Handel. It is a great pity that the united ponderosity of Handel and the middle-weight Mendelssohn could not avail to dam the output of oratorios by composers who might have become good song-writers or even acquired some knowledge of orchestration beyond that of choral accompaniment. The complaint of foreign domination is nonsense. No country has had its music so long and so completely dominated by foreigners as France; and French music has always remained exclusively French and has made thoroughly French artists of the foreigners who dominated it. The traces of foreign influence on English music have always been the echoes of individual phrases or mannerisms. While we have echoed, as the fashions change, Mendelssohn, Brahms, and Debussy, we have learnt no technical lessons from them. Such mechanical echoes show no foreign domination, but are the best proof of an inveterate provincialism and the kind of ignorant and irritable independence that goes with it. Since music ceased to be an integral part of an Englishman's culture (about the time of William and Mary), our musicians, as a rule, began its serious study far too late. The language of music cannot be begun at the age of nineteen like courses in law or medicine. Our universities have played a considerable part in shaping British musical destinies; but a mighty Oxford treads on the tongue of the encyclopaedist who would pursue this topic.

XI. MUSIC OF THE TWENTIETH CENTURY

The twentieth century inherited the last development of the nineteenth in the symphonic poems and operas of Richard Strauss.

Much acrid controversy at first raged around the details of his style, which dashed through all the traffic regulations of classical part-writing. And nothing was easier than to identify all carping critics with Beckmesser and to accept humbly Strauss's own self-portrait as the hero of *Ein Heldenleben*. The elements that were sensational in Strauss's symphonic poems have become so familiar that we are in some danger of underestimating the importance of these works as real achievements of the problem in which Liszt failed; not the trivial problem of programme music, but the vital problem of writing purely instrumental music on the Wagnerian time-scale. The power of composition in these works is unquestionable and remains eminent in their facile aftermath, the *Alpen-Sinfonie*, which, designed before the War of 1914, appeared in 1915. But Strauss had eclipsed the fame of his symphonic works by his operas, which began to be important with *Salome* (1905), a setting of Oscar Wilde's play. Then came the long and fruitful partnership with Hugo von Hofmannsthal which enabled poet and musician to prove the possibility of many different kinds of modern opera, Wagnerian and non-Wagnerian. The purity of the Straussian metal has been strongly alloyed with worldly wisdom in every phase of Strauss's career: in the period of the good boy of the conservatoire; in the romantic symphonic poet of *Tod und Verklärung*; in the timely musical adaptation of Wilde while he was still a new discovery on the German stage; in the seizing of the opportunity presented by Hofmannsthal's *Elektra* after its triumph as a play; and not least in the later phase of naïve melodiousness. Nevertheless *Die Frau ohne Schatten* is perhaps the most noble gesture in music since 1918. From the twilight of *fin-de-siècle* and recent erotic art and from its always selfish and sometimes abnormal sexual preoccupations, *Die Frau ohne Schatten* breaks away with a heroic plea for normal love and life. Unassailable by any cavil that does not write itself down as ignoble, musically, this is Strauss's grandest and most grandly realized opportunity for beauty. As a theatrical spectacle it is a gorgeous pantomine, no more disturbed by its allegorical meaning than *Die Zauberflöte*, which it in some ways intentionally resembles. *Die Aegyptische Helene* (1928) descends from this high level into all manner of cleverness in its stage-technique and of facility in its music.

Whatever has been gained in the twentieth-century music, Strauss presents an almost solitary example of mastery of movement. Elsewhere, neither in academic teaching nor in new musical developments does any sense of movement seem to be cultivated. The vast cosmic movement of Wagner is attempted, in Bruckner's fashion, by composers who seem to think that huge dimensions can impress us as huge without any reference to human measurements. The best work of Sibelius shows a true sense of cosmic movement and a real freedom and economy in the forms by which this is expressed. With other modern composers the most curious musical inhibition is that which makes them continue to write sonata works in the four classical movements with a rigidity unknown to Mozart, Haydn, and Beethoven, though the modern matter has no more connexion with sonata form than Wagnerian music-drama has with the da capo aria.

This lack of necessity in form is nowhere more conspicuous than in the whole work of Max Reger, who is usually regarded as the Brahms of the twentieth century. His untimely death happened when he was evidently about to change his style. He was a pupil of the most mechanically systematized musical scholar of recent times, Hugo Riemann; and any one who has groaned in spirit at the sight of one of Riemann's instructive editions of a piece of classical music may easily recognize in Reger the traces of Riemann's teaching. Every external feature of the classical art-forms is present without any trace of the classical reasons for it. Everything has been worked out from one detail to the next as if it had been plotted on squared paper ready marked by some one else with points of reference.

Whatever is to be learnt from Reger, it is not the meaning of classical art-forms. And much is to be learnt from Reger. His texture is inevitably thick, for its systematic completeness vetoes the suggestiveness of the highest art. But it is astonishingly sonorous, and its numerous notes are the fewest and most effective for its ponderous purpose. Every instrument is treated according to its natural technique; and while the player who claims that he can read Reger at sight is probably mendacious, he will enjoy his instrument the better for playing Reger well. The fundamental reality of Reger is that he is not only a sincere artist but a consummate rhetorician. But this age must be very ill-informed about the foundations of music if it elects Reger as its Brahms.

There is at present no Brahms; the twentieth century must enlarge its musical experience before another renascence of classical form can either be expected or recognized when it comes. It might be as likely to come from Russia as anywhere; the gigantic geniality of Glazunov has remained with us, active in the composition of brilliant classical and symphonic polyphony, and generously stimulating to younger composers; and the efforts of young artists to find out things for themselves may lead to something more fundamental than revolt against academicism or than the still narrower academicisms that young revolutionaries are apt to set up among themselves.

Scriabin's later harmonic system has been touched upon in the

article HARMONY, section x. At this point we may sum up the
lessons of three harmonic revolutions distributed over five centuries of musical history in the generalization that whenever a
composer becomes permanently preoccupied with harmonic
ideas, his power of composition is in great danger of paralysis.
The reason for this lies deeper than the nature of music itself.
Similar tendencies in literature reduce the power of sentence-
building to that of the first Ollendorfian exercises. Scriabin's
Chopinesque but stiff style of composition was fortunately well
mastered by him before he doomed himself to discover that the
harping on any chord, however strange and novel, in the long run
only produces the effect of a sophisticated dominant seventh.
Before his style receded into its theosophical fastnesses Scriabin
had achieved, in his Fifth Sonata and in his orchestral *Poème
d'Extase* (both inspired by a literary poem from his own pen), works
of powerful impulse that could not have been written on earlier
harmonic and rhythmic resources.

The chances of producing permanently living work are heavily
weighted against the composer who confines his art to things
which he alone can understand. The Russian Ballet gives abun-
dant vital occasion for music as long as it deals intelligently with
drama, fairy-tale, fable, and life; and the young Stravinsky found
in it inspiration for music that remains intelligible apart from the
spectacle. In *Pétrouchka* he produces rhythms and tones that
enhance the moods of a fascinating pantomime; but the concert-
goers who profess to enjoy it without ever seeing the ballet show
themselves to be of the tribe who will gaze 'as ducks that die in
tempests' at anything they are told to admire.

Self-deception and dry-rot set in when the designers as well
as the composers of the ballet retire into the arbitrary kingdom
of abstractions which they call symbolic and which common
sense calls nonsense. Opinions will never unite about where the
line should be drawn; but the twentieth century will differ from
all other periods of human history if a large percentage of its
most precious nonsense does not vanish into the limbo of mere
nonsense before its generation becomes middle-aged.

The art of Debussy made its mark without any such artifices.
Some aspects of it are discussed in HARMONY, section x; but
Debussy would have indignantly repudiated the resolving of his
whole-tone scale as a six-part polyphonic chord, though he himself cannot resist the impulse to resolve it on to a pentatonic
scale, which is itself constructible as a chord. Debussy's propagandists believed him to be more closely confined to his special
system than was the case. Eclecticism was always breaking in
without any damage to the aesthetic coherence of the style. It is
probable that Debussy's art, discreetly anthologized, will remain

vital when the work of the more voluminous and hard-headed Ravel will have become no more distinguishable from an echo than Sterndale Bennett is from the echo of Mendelssohn. Independent origin does not settle such questions. Cyril Scott has been called the English Debussy, but he began to form his style before Debussy was known.

One of the eternal questions in aesthetics is the proportion of means to ends. The War of 1914 tragically dictated to all artists a preference of the study of reduced rather than of increased resources; yet performances on the scale of the Handel Festivals in the Crystal Palace continue at London, though the music for organizations of even half that size has never yet been composed. Here, then, is material for a real and strenuous aesthetic discipline; and the zeal of Mengelberg has created in Holland a great vogue for the vast works in which Mahler, while writing for existing conditions, set himself the task of pioneer-work in the aesthetic and technical principles of music designed for one thousand performers and upwards. Taste is of secondary importance in such an enterprise, and Mahler is likely to be underrated in countries where naïve sentimentality and boyish grandiosity encounter the inhibitions of a musical culture that thinks itself wiser. Mahler was one of the greatest orchestral and opera conductors that ever lived. On the total value of his compositions tastes may agree to differ, but this century has seen no more strenuous idealist. The main stream of music still flows within the Wagner–Strauss limits and seldom requires one hundred and fifty instrumental players. Arnold Schönberg's *Gurrelieder* (a large song-cycle for chorus and soli, the great success of which is held to be a hindrance to the spread of his later and more revolutionary gospel) requires an extraordinary orchestra; but the polyphony that requires fifty staves for its notation implies detail rather than mass.

The performance of Elgar's *Dream of Gerontius* at Düsseldorf in 1902, its enthusiastic reception there, and finally the generous speech of Richard Strauss then delivered in its honour, inaugurated the recognition of modern English music on the Continent, and gave English critics and audiences a not unneeded lesson after their lukewarm reception of it at its inadequate first performance at Birmingham. Elgar's rich and subtle orchestration is not more remarkable than the wealth of his invention of themes. His contemporary, Bantock, is a prolific composer in a style far easier but not less personal and sincere, in which the influence of Strauss and the schematic purity of Rimsky-Korsakov's orchestration may be traced by their technical results but not by mannerisms.

In Italy the masterful personality of Boïto (1842–1918) de-

veloped in the nineteenth century, but his musical ideas anticipate the twentieth. He wrote brilliant libretti to Verdi's last
works and those of younger composers, and achieved extraordinary musical fame by two operas, *Mefistofele* and the posthumous
Nerone. These have taken their place among the historic documents of musical Italy on the strength of less actual musical
content than any other operas in existence. Their aristocratic
refinement and flair for atmosphere is unquestionable. Very
different is the full-blooded efficiency of Puccini (1858–1924), in
whose hands Italian opera advanced in the estimation of a public
that was in all countries becoming too experienced in music to
be satisfied with perfunctory orchestration and histrionic convention. The razor-edge intellect of the great pianoforte artist
Busoni (1866–1924) achieved important results in compositions
for the pianoforte, the orchestra, and the stage, in spite of the
energy he spent in demonstrating how much more cleverly the
classics would have been written if they had possessed his
advantages. If Casals could have his way, the musical awakening
of Spain would be a leading feature in the history of the modern
art.

In England there are encouraging signs that musicians are
beginning to think for themselves without confusion between
independence of academic tradition and independence of truth.
Gustav Holst's interest in oriental subjects was (like Bantock's)
no whim for *chinoiseries* but a true expression of the nostalgia of
the West for the East. His *Hymn of Jesus* is worthy of its awe-
inspiring Byzantine eucharistic text. Vaughan Williams, with less
of Holst's wide and clear-sighted exploration of pre-harmonic
regions, composes with consistent nobility on a large scale and
in a style that it would be an impertinence to try to trace to its
various historic origins.

Thus the work of doctrinaires is not all that is happening in
modern music; and, in any case, music is in the happy position of
existing, like architecture, on practical terms which forbid mere
lunacy to flourish unchecked. A large proportion of modern
musical developments have been tested by enthusiastic and
capable public performers almost before the ink of the manu-
script was dry. Immediately before the last war, Rutland
Boughton's small-scale Glastonbury festivals of music-drama
were a stimulus of incalculable importance in the history of
modern British opera; and on the Continent the younger composers of chamber music have had the help of knight-errants in
the masterly Amar Quartet which, with Paul Hindemith as viola
and his brother as violoncello, spared no pains to secure for the
most difficult experiments (such as the quarter-tone works of
Haba) a perfect performance. Hindemith himself is one of the

boldest and most masterly experimenters, if indeed, he is not the master of them all. It is very significant that his vocal writing, which seems to contradict all previous orthodoxies, stays uncommonly firmly in the vocal memory once it is mastered; whereas many otiose modulations in the Lisztian music of the 'seventies, such as the part-songs of Cornelius, sink in pitch however much choirs may practice them. The young masters who sternly renounce romance make a romantic gesture in the very act.

Much has been said as to the fructifying or deleterious influence of jazz. The highest class of jazz-band is undoubtedly composed of sensitive artists; but the conductor of a symphony orchestra in a musically not metropolitan town will, if he engages for a symphony concert the gentleman who handles the percussion apparatus of the best local jazz-band, discover that that artist's methods are entirely extemporaneous, and that, except with a drumstick, he has never clashed the cymbals otherwise than flat on to the top of the big drum, and never counted rests in his life. Ordinary jazz-music distributes its rhythmic surprises over the most imperturbable eight-bar ambling trot that ever lulled the rhythmic sense to sleep. Most drugs that begin with a stimulating action end as narcotics.

XII. PROBLEMS OF THE FUTURE

The explorers of new musical intervals are hampered by having to deal with classical keyboards and other practical limitations. Perhaps they would do well to investigate Miss Schlesinger's pianoforte-tuning, already mentioned in connexion with Greek music; for, whether it be Greek or not, it is scientific and therefore more natural than most of the experiments that composers have yet tried in the way of quarter-tones. But new instruments cannot be so readily produced as in the eighteenth century. Harpsichords and early pianofortes were *made*; but pianofortes are now *manufactured*. Emmanuel Moor's duplex-coupler pianoforte has enormously extended the resources of the instrument without compelling the player to unlearn the classical technique. But its progress is impeded by the commercial difficulty of promoting an improvement that cannot be added as an extra apparatus to existing and standardized pianofortes, and its reputation is damaged by the tendency to expound it as a device that makes existing feats of technique nugatory, a policy that infuriates the pianoforte virtuoso and ignores the great new possibilities of the invention.

Resonators have been invented for many instruments. The claim that by such devices one violin can sound like sixteen ignores the real effect of the multiplication of instruments, which consists far more essentially of a change in quality of tone than of a mere increase of volume. No resonators, phonograph disks, or loud-speakers for wireless transmitters will ever replace the quality of sounds that combine in the ear from the various directions of their dispersed orchestral sources. The listener need only put his hands around his ears while listening to an orchestra in a concert-room, and he will realize that a 'gramophone effect' is little more than the result of cutting off the waves that reach the ear from other than the frontal direction.

The main importance of 'wireless' lies in the fact that it appeals viva voce to millions without producing the phenomena of crowd-psychology. Here and there it leads to a revived interest in intimate early pianoforte music that would never satisfy modern ears in the concert-room, and a new fact in musical aesthetics is the beauty of microphonically-magnified tones of very faint instruments such as the clavichord. Wireless has undoubtedly increased the number of fireside music-lovers; but it needs careful administration to prevent it from a tendency to cut off orchestral music at the source, for many of the new music-lovers prefer tinned music at the fireside to live music in the concert-room. It is urgently necessary that the wealthy supporters of music should be made to see the folly of the notion that good music should be expected to pay its way commercially.

Wireless music may prove less subversive than another revolution by means of the microscopic study of phonographic records. There is nothing to prevent the eventual production of music directly in terms of the track of the phonograph-needle. That is to say, the composer, untrammelled by the technique of instruments, will prescribe all producible timbres in whatever pitches and rhythms he pleases, and will have no more direct cooperation with the craftsman who models the phonographic wave-lines than the violinist has with Stradivarius. The crudest beginnings of this new method of composition will be enormously important; but its highest development will still leave the handling of human voices and instruments supreme as the infinite source of inspired music.

OPERA

OPERA, a drama set to music, as distinguished from plays in which music is merely incidental.

Italian Beginnings.—The historian, Doni, tells us that in the last years of the sixteenth century a group of amateurs held meetings at the house of the Bardi in Florence with the object of trying experiments in musical declamation by solo voices supported by instruments. Hitherto the ónly high musical art was unaccompanied choral music; though its expression was perfect within its own limits, those limits were such that within them, dramatic music was as inconceivable as dramatic architecture. But the literary dilettanti who met at the house of the Bardi were not mature musical artists, and no technical scruples interfered with their glorious project of restoring the musical glories of the Greek tragedy. Vincenzo Galilei, the father of Galileo, warbled the story of Ugolino to the accompaniment of the lute, much to the amusement of expert musicians; but he gained the respectful sympathy of literary listeners.

The first public production in this 'monodic' style was Jacopo Peri's *Euridice* (1600), which was followed by a less successful effort of Caccini's on the same subject. Feeble as were these efforts, they impressed contemporary imagination as infinitely more suggestive of life and passion than the forlorn attempts then in vogue to provide good music for a music-drama by means of a polyphonic chorus behind the scene, with actors in dumb-show on the stage. As Parry happily points out in this connexion, the laying of a foundation stone suggests a future so inspiriting as to exclude all sense of the triviality of the present achievement. A great master of pure polyphony, Orazio Vecchi, had already, in 1594, the year of Palestrina's death, laughed the madrigal-opera to extinction in his *Amfiparnasso.* The woodcuts which adorn its first edition show how the actors sang or mimed in front, while the other singers completed the harmony behind the stage.

With the decadence of the madrigal, Monteverdi brought a real musical power to bear on the new style. At the beginning of the seventeenth century no impressionable young musician could fail to be profoundly stirred by Monteverdi's *Orfeo* (1602), *Arianna* (1608), and *Il Combattimento di Tancredi e Clorinda* (1624), works in which instruments were used with the same archaic boldness, the same rhetorical force, and the same lack of artistic organization as vocal style and harmonic resources. So explosive was the spark of Monteverdi's genius that the next step necessary for the progress of opera was a development of forms, not only non-dramatic but anti-dramatic.

The types of monody conceivable by the pioneers of opera were codified in the system of free musical declamation known as recitative. This is said to have been used by Emilio del Cavalieri as early as 1588. Formal melody, such as that of popular songs, was as much beneath the dignity of monody as it had been beneath that of the highest forms of polyphony; but in the absence of any harmonic system but that of the Church modes, which was ruined by the new unprepared discords, formal melody proved a godsend as the novelty of recitative faded. Tunes were soon legalized at moments of dramatic repose; it was in the tunes that the strong harmonic system of Neapolitan tonality took shape; and by the early days of Alessandro Scarlatti, before the end of the seventeenth century, the art of tune-making had blossomed into the musically safe and effective form of the aria (q.v.).

The poet Metastasio realized that there was nothing unnatural in a scheme of drama which allowed each stage of the action to culminate in a tableau marked by a burst of lyric poetry and lyric music. Some thirty such tableaux would give occasion for thirty arias (including a few duets, rarely a trio, and only once in Handel's forty-two operas a quartet) while the connecting action and dialogue were set in recitative. Metastasio devoted his whole life to opera-libretti on this plan, which he executed with consummate skill. He was far from satisfied with the way in which most composers set his texts. The scheme was fatally easy for small musicians and did not stimulate the higher faculties of great ones; while great and small were equally at the mercy of singers.

Before this stagnation of baroque opera there was a provincial outburst of life in the wonderful patchwork of Purcell's art (1658–95). In the early *Dido and Aeneas* he and the humble Nahum Tate (of Tate and Brady) produced, perhaps, the most perfect opera before Gluck. Dryden was less accommodating. He had been so disgusted by the stupid vanity of the fashionable Monsieur Grabu, that when he wrote *King Arthur* he insisted on arranging that the musical characters should be quite independent of the main action; and with the infliction of this condition upon Purcell, English opera was relegated to a permanent musical squalor which even endured long enough to ruin Weber's last work, *Oberon*, in 1826.

Gluck.—Another sign of life was present in the farcical operas and intermezzi or comic entr'actes of certain Neapolitan composers (for example, Leo, Pergolesi, and Logroscino), one of which (Pergolesi's *La Serva Padrona*) occasioned the war of Buffonistes and Antibuffonistes in Paris (*see* MUSIC, sec. vi).

The forms of music known before 1750 were architectural or decorative, but essentially non-dramatic. Baroque opera required something more than reform, and the opportunity for progress came with the rise of the sonata style. The music of Gluck's time was too firmly organized to be upset by new discoveries; in fact the chief need for opera was retrenchment in rhetorical forms. Gluck, as Handel had remarked of his early works, was no contrapuntist, and to the end of his life this hampered him in 'jining his flats'. But he had a genius for phrasing (*see* RHYTHM) which went far to promote dramatic movement, and another aspect of this was a sense of symphonic form as vigorous as could find scope in opera at all; while his melodic power was of the kind which Matthew Arnold calls 'touchstones of poetry'.

The lasting effect of his work on French music left the course of Italian *opera seria* unchecked. Mozart's *Idomeneo* is the grave of some of his greatest music, including many genuinely dramatic strokes, and his perfunctory *Clemenza di Tito* is the last *opera seria* that contains any music worth extracting. The unmistakable influence of Gluck could not save *Idomeneo*; and Mozart's triumphs belong to the comedy of manners, until he entered the transcendental world of *Die Zauberflöte*. His first impulse was inveterately musical, and his power of dramatic movement and characterization grew steadily without always preventing him from yielding to singers and indulging himself in dramatically vicious musical luxuries. But after his first exuberant German opera, *Die Entführung aus dem Serail*, it is not so easy as it seems to catch Mozart napping. He is a dangerously subtle parodist, and in *Cosi fan tutte* the heroic coloratura arias of the virtuous Fiordiligi and Dorabella are the arias of ladies who do protest too much; and in *Die Zauberflöte* the vocal fireworks of the Queen of Night are the rhetoric of a formidable person, who, we are told, 'hopes to cajole the people with illusions'.

Mozart.—Mozart's operas are organized so thoroughly on the basis of their libretti that it is a serious mistake, not made by scholars like Jahn, to underrate the wits of his literary collaborator, Da Ponte. Goethe did not even underrate the rapscallion Schikaneder, but took the symbolical aspects of *Die Zauberflöte* so seriously as to sketch a sequel to it. Since boyhood Mozart never wrote an opera without thoroughly controlling its dramatic movement. Where he relaxes the relaxation is complete. The movement in *Die Entführung* is intermittent and the static elements excessively favoured, but the movement exists and is powerful. In *Figaro*, the fourth act, with its tangle of assignations in the garden, has five arias in succession, which would make a mere concert on the stage if they were all performed; but there is an ironic dramatic tension behind the last of them (*Deh vieni non tardar*); and when the librettist provides action Wagner is not as quick as Mozart in his timing of the details and the whole. One of Wagner's English propagandists, Hueffer, cited the duet in which Cherubino and Susanna are trying to find a way out of the locked room before the Count returns, and accused Mozart of keeping the Count waiting at the door until this effective piece of music had run its formal course. But every stage manager finds that Mozart has barely given Cherubino time for a natural hesitation before jumping out of the window, in spite of Susanna's terrified protest.

The Qualities of Opera.—And here we may profitably consider what are the qualities necessary for success in opera. It is notorious that the absolute value of the music comes last, if it is a factor of success at all. Unquestionably it is a factor in immortality; and the music of *Idomeneo* is immortal, though that opera is revived only in Mozart festivals. But operas cannot wait for immortality, and can manage on quite flimsy music to achieve as much immortality as musical history has given time for. It might be thought that success depends on dramatic power; and this is nearer the truth. But dramatic power comes only third in the conditions, and coherence is not necessary at all.

Two qualities take precedence of dramatic power as conditions for success in opera; one is the theatrical sense, and the other the histrionic sense. They are inseparable but not identical. The theatrical sense can thrill the listener before the curtain rises, as in the modulation to F major at the end of the overture to *Don Giovanni*; the histrionic sense can save the stage manager the trouble of telling the actors what to do with their hands. The beginning of Rossini's *Barbiere* is an excellent example, especially when compared with that of Paisiello's setting, which dominated the stage until Rossini's ousted it. Paisiello's opening is good music for any moderately cheerful situation, Rossini's opening consists of a scale rising for nine notes and descending again, with long halts and water-beetle glides. Actors may be defied to walk on during this music with any steps but those of conspirators! And the scoring (which is so perfunctory that literally half of the bulk of the opera is expressed by abbreviations) gives in perfection the theatrical atmosphere of a night scene. The same ridiculous scale in another ridiculous rhythm hisses up and down in thirds *sul ponticello* (close to the violin bridge) while Basilio describes the destructive effects of a well-managed calumny. Poor Paisiello's famous duet between two stammerers was no asset wherewith to outbid Rossini's ubiquitous histrionic sense in the contest for popularity.

But when brilliant writers tell us that Rossini is superior to Mozart in the sense of pace, it is high time to study the elements of Mozart's art. Three senses of pace enter into music. There is that of the athlete, relying on his own limbs, the limbs of his horse, or the wheels which he directly controls. There is that of the passenger reclining in his car. And there is the cosmic motion of the stars among which our own humble earth moves hundreds of times faster than a cannon ball, yet takes several minutes to traverse its own diameter. Of these three senses of movement that of the passenger in his car is equivalent to repose, and to nothing else; while cosmic movements, discernible in Bach, Beethoven, and Wagner, must be related to human measurements before they mean anything at all. The one directly exhilarating sense of movement is that of the athlete; and we are asked to believe that Rossini exemplifies this when Figaro rattles his 'Largo al factotum' at some nine syllables a second, immovable for six minutes except for semaphore gestures once in twelve bars, to the right when the music halts on the dominant, to the left when it halts on the tonic. No, let us be accurate; there is another tradition which identifies the tonic with the right and the dominant with the left. Mozart's *Figaro* contains one piece of patter-singing even faster than 'Largo al factotum', but he pronounces judgement on this kind of movement by giving it to the decrepit Dr. Bartolo ('se tutto il codice dovesse leggere', &c.).

The decline of *opera seria* and *opera buffa* led to an approximation between tragic and comic styles till the distinction became too subtle to be distinguished by any but experts. Dance rhythms became the only Italian forms of accompaniment, and vocal scale exercises remained the last resource of the dying Desdemona. Yet Rossini retained so much histrionic force that an English spectator of his *Otello* is recorded to have started out of his seat at the catastrophe, exclaiming 'Good Heavens! the tenor is murdering the soprano!' And in times of political unrest more than one opera became as dangerous as censorship could make it. An historical case is brilliantly described in George Meredith's *Vittoria*. But what has this to do with the progress of music? The history of Italian opera from after its culmination in Mozart to its subsidence on the big drum and cymbals of the Rossinians is the history of 'star' singers.

Verdi's art, both in its burly youth and in its shrewd old age, changed all that. He reformed nothing except by slow experience; but he gradually found a meaning for everything. Even the vile Italian brass is used in his last works in just the same style as in his earliest, with the enormous difference that he appreciates its brutality and uses it only where brutality is wanted. Verdi's development belongs to a later stage of operatic history.

France.—After Mozart the next forward step in operatic art was again made in France. The French histrionic atmosphere had a stimulating effect upon every foreign composer who visited Paris. Rossini himself, in *Guillaume Tell*, was electrified into a higher dramatic and orchestral life than the rollicking rattle of his serious and comic Italian operas. The grave defects of its libretto were overcome by unprecedented efforts at the cost of an entire act. Anywhere but in Paris Rossini's music would have pulled a worse drama through or else failed outright; but in Paris the composer found it worth while to learn how to rescue his best music from failure.

The French contribution to musical history between Gluck and Rossini is of austere nobility worthy of a better crown than Meyerbeer's music. If Cherubini and Méhul had had Gluck's melodic power, the classics of French opera would have been the greatest achievements in semi-tragic music-drama before Wagner. As it is, their austerity is negative, failing to achieve beauty rather than rejecting what is irrelevant. The histrionic sense is good, but the sense of movement rejects patter-singing without achieving anything more real. Cherubini's *Medée*, *Les Deux Journées*, and *Faniska*, however, did achieve grand musical forms and had a great influence on Beethoven.

Beethoven's *Fidelio* gives occasion to consider the function of the librettist, who obviously has the composer at his mercy unless the composer is prompt to get the upper hand. Mozart learnt betimes to bully his librettist. Beethoven did not; and the expansion of Bouilly's pretty *opéra comique*, *Fidelio, ou l'amour conjugal* into the powerful *Leonore* (afterwards renamed *Fidelio*) was executed according to Beethoven's general intentions but with many blunders in the *mise-en-scène*. French *opéra comique* is not comic opera, but opera with spoken dialogue. It thus includes Cherubini's tragic *Medée* and Méhul's biblical *Joseph*. It has a tendency (which culminates in Bizet's *Carmen*) to arrange that much of the music should happen more or less as it might occur in an ordinary play. For instance, necessary antecedents may be told in 'that dear old song which I am never tired of hearing', whereupon the family history follows in a ballad. Other occasions for music are the plighting of troth in a little private ceremony, the entry of a company of soldiers, and, less realistically, ordinary entries and tableau-situations in general, until we recapture the Metastasio scheme. Opera, viewed from this point, lacks opportunity for great musical forms which can deal with more than one action; but the influence of Mozart's wonderful concerted finales was not to be resisted, and Cherubini's librettists arranged that the second act in *Les Deux Journées*, *Lodoïska*, and one or two other operas, should end with continuous music for something like twenty minutes, with various changes of action. The last act French taste did not allow to expand, and in all French operas the end is perfunctory; whereas Mozart and Beethoven love to expatiate on the final happiness.

It is not known where the concerted finale originated, since its reputed invention by Logroscino is not borne out by his extant works; but it is already fully developed in the second act of Mozart's *La finta Giardiniera* (written at the age of 18). In his first *Singspiel, Die Entführung*, Mozart ends the second act with a highly developed quartet, while the whole opera ends with a vaudeville, i.e., a series of verses delivered by each character in turn, with a burden in chorus; followed by a short movement for full chorus. But in his other *Singspiel, Die Zauberflöte*, the finales to both acts, like those in *Figaro, Don Giovanni*, and *Cosi fan tutte*, cover so much action within their half-hour's extent that it would evidently cost Mozart little effort to extend the finale backwards over the whole act and so to achieve, without transcending his own musical language, the perfect continuity of Verdi's *Falstaff*. This would have suited neither his singers nor his public; but we do not know how he might have crushed opposition if he had lived longer and had seen the possibilities of French opera, with its thrilling tales of heroic adventure.

Fidelio.—As fate befell, Beethoven took the problem in hand too late. The original libretto of Fidelio was by the author of *Les Deux Journées*, and was on the usual French lines with (as Brahms once put it) vaudeville turns for each person in succession. Two acts were occupied with the love of the jailer's daughter, Marcelline, for Fidelio, the mysterious new assistant, really the disguised wife of the hero, who has been secretly imprisoned by the villain, and whom she has been seeking for two years. She reluctantly uses Marcelline's delusion in order to further her design of penetrating to the lowest dungeons of this jail, where a mysterious prisoner is being starved to death. In the original libretto a trio begins on the occasion of the father's giving his blessing on their engagement. And on the operatic vaudeville scale this is well enough timed. But Fidelio-Leonora's heroic project and the martyrdom of her Florestan in Pizarro's dungeon are themes too sublime for this light style of opera, which was all very well for the adventures of the hero of *Les Deux Journées*, carted out of Paris in his humble friend's water-cart. It was the sublime themes that attracted Beethoven; and in *Leonore* (as his opera was first named) his librettist, Sonnleithner, tried to expand them without the necessary recasting of the whole action. So the trio of plighted troth was begun earlier, so as to take in half of the previous conversation, which dealt with the project of getting permission for Fidelio to assist in the work of the dungeons, and with Fidelio's imperfectly suppressed excitement thereat. We thus have the music bursting into the conversation in an inexplicable way; and two revisions barely saved the first two acts even when an experienced dramatist named Treitshcke compressed them into the first act of *Fidelio*.

The rest, from the rise of the curtain on Florestan in the dungeon, was not beyond mending; and spectators who are insensible to its power should confine their criticisms to the costumes of the box-holders. *Fidelio* is one of the most important works in the history of opera; and the *Messiah* has not a firmer hold of the British public than *Fidelio* has of every class of unspoilt music-lover in Germany. The story is one of the finest ever put on the stage, and everybody in Germany knows it; which is fortunate, since nobody could ever make it out from the action, until it begins to explain itself in the dungeon scene. But in the first act the mystery is a mere puzzle, and even if Fidelio's disguise is as transparent as most operatic male parts for female voices, the spectator has no evidence beyond the playbill that she is other than the strangely embarrassed lover of the adoring jailer's daughter.

The difficulties of *Fidelio* are thus very instructive. Turn back from it to the almost nonsensical *Zauberflöte* and observe how perfectly the comings and goings of Mozart's music explain themselves. Music begins naturally on the rise of the curtain, and stops naturally with the exits of all the characters except the youth who is lying unconscious. He revives, wonders where he is, hears a distant piping; and the approach of the bird-catcher, Papageno, explains the piping and is accompanied by the orchestral introduction to his song. Later on, three veiled ladies give the hero a miniature portrait of the princess he is to rescue. He gazes at the portrait and falls in love; the orchestra heaves two sighs and Tamino's love-song begins. The scene darkens, the Queen of Night appears, enthroned among stars, pours out her woes and promises her daughter to the hero. She vanishes. Daylight returns. Tamino, wondering whether it was all a dream, is encountered by poor Papageno who, punished for his lies with a padlock on his mouth, can only sing *hm, hm, hmm*; another perfect occasion for music, worked up in a quintet in which the three veiled ladies remove his padlock and instruct him and Tamino how to set forth on their quest. And so from point to point the happy nonsense proceeds, always right and effective in matters the mishandling of which may ruin the finest story.

Coordination.—These are the matters in which Sullivan, with his Gilbert, is as right as Wagner. It makes little difference whether the opera be with spoken dialogue, with dialogue in the secco-recitative of *opera buffa*, with the accompanied recitative of Gluck and of Weber's *Euryanthe*, or in absolute Wagnerian continuity. The composer will always have to demand from his librettist an effective timing of the chief musical opportunities, and from himself a royal punctuality in the relation of his music to the drama. Wagner's advice to young opera-writers was to begin with *Singspiele*. The *a priori* critic complains that spoken dialogue and music are on irreconcilably different planes; and so they are when the transitions are mishandled. But Mahler, one of the greatest opera conductors of all time, did not think the planes incompatible. He insisted on being his own stage manager (which laudable example has been followed by Sir Thomas Beecham), and he rehearsed every word and every pose in the dialogue of *Fidelio*.

Secco-recitative, i.e. recitative accompanied on the pianoforte (or harpsichord), is no bad medium when it is properly done, namely, at the pace of spoken dialogue and, on the part of the conductor (who takes the pianoforte), with a light touch and some discreetly humorous 'gagging'. Modern composers, of course, might as well attempt prehistoric Chinese as try to revive this convention. With accompanied recitative and other more highly organized music the composer begins to lose the clear outlines of the problem of timing his chief musical events; and the wisdom of Wagner's advice appears. For only in the *Singspiel*, with *Freischütz* and *Zauberflöte* as examples, and with *Fidelio* as both an inspiration and a warning, do we see the bones of opera laid bare.

These principles are more important than any details of chronological operatic history. The reader who has grasped them can afford to ignore most of the patriotic and political aspects that have made this or that opera famous. *Der Freischütz* was the first German opera that had a truly German subject; and Wagner, speaking at a reburial of Weber's remains, said that there never was a more German composer. Very true, but that did not prevent Weber from following *Freischütz* by *Euryanthe*, his greatest effort, on a subject of chivalry ruined by an incompetent librettist; nor from contributing his swan song, *Oberon*, to the English stage and the English operatic tradition which, ever since the time of Dryden and Purcell, inculcated an utter incoherence in the musical scheme. Weber's distress at being made to compose separate numbers as Planché sent them to him, with no information as to their order or context, was surpassed only by his disgust at finding that Planché was quite right in thinking that such information did not matter.

Euryanthe, with its elaborate accompanied recitative and its thirteen distinct leitmotives (to anticipate the Wagnerian term), is an opera on lines hardly less advanced than those of Wagner's *Lohengrin*. Weber retains the outward appearance of the division into separate numbers, as arias, duets, finales, and so on; but the division is becoming artificial, and some vestiges of its real purport are useless. For example, the condemnation of *Euryanthe* at the end of the second act is expanded by Weber into a longish movement merely because he does not realize that a short outburst would suffice to round off the whole act far more grandly than a self-contained finale.

Wagner.—With Wagner's *Der Fliegende Holländer* extremes meet. It purports to be divided into nine 'numbers', but the musical traces of such divisions are only a nuisance, and the formal expansion of the Dutchman's duet with Senta is as out of place as a Punch and Judy show, besides being very poor music. On the other hand, the division into three acts is a grudging concession to the brutal necessities of the first performances, for Wagner conceived and executed *Der Fliegende Holländer* as a one-act opera, with continuous music during its changes of scene. It has been divided into three as if by a butcher's chopper, cutting off the curtain music at the first available tonic chord, and restarting it at the cut or a little earlier. The opera ought always to be performed in one act. Spohr's comment on it was that it had too few full closes and rounded-off forms. This shows how far it still seemed recognizable to him as a classical opera.

Wagner's mature work solves the problem of a music on the same time-scale as the drama. Every other feature of Wagner's art results naturally from this. Musical dialogue becomes completely realistic, to such an extent that Wagner could not at first (in *Die Walküre*) make up his mind to let his lovers sing together. He overcame this scruple in *Tristan*, and so recovered the classical art of making a composite emotional tableau. This he developed to unprecedented heights in *Die Meistersinger von Nürnberg*. The continuity of such highly organized music demanded a rational organization of recognizable themes. What more inevitable principle could organize them but that of association with personal and dramatic ideas? Thus Wagner's system of leitmotive grew up as naturally as the thematic organization of sonatas. The illustrations at the end of the article MELODY give a typical example of his handling of a theme in various contexts. Other aspects of his music are illustrated in HARMONY and INSTRUMENTATION.

Not only was Wagner his own librettist, but he succeeded in making clear and cogent upon the stage stories and ideas that no dramatist, musical or non-musical, had thought possible before. It is always a mistake to suppose that the libretto, however contemptible as literature, can be neglected in the enjoyment of an opera, however great as music. But Wagner's dramas, with all their affectations and amateurishnesses of style, are pieces of epoch-making stage-craft and overwhelming tragic powers, except *Meistersinger*, which achieves the yet higher mark of a comedy full of kindly wisdom and bathed in sunshine, with no shadows deeper than moonshine; for even its poor little villain, Beckmesser, is only a critic.

It was not Wagner's fault that so many of his *epigonoi* neglected his advice and, instead of writing *Singspiele*, refused to tackle anything smaller than continuations of the sorrows of Wotan. Lighter forms of opera prospered, nevertheless. Bizet first wrote *Carmen* as an *opéra comique*. It is doubtful whether it has been improved by the compression of its spoken dialogue into accompanied recitative, though this is well done and the recitatives have their points. It carries to an extreme the device of rationalizing the musical occasions; for if it were performed as a play an enormous amount of the music would still remain as songs or dances. *Meistersinger* is almost as full of songs and choruses on the same realistic basis.

The last works of Verdi have a complete Wagnerian continuity, but they reveal that unless the music is inveterately polyphonic the leitmotive system is Wagner's private affair, which need concern nobody else.

Modern Opera.—Space fails for anything like a complete review of modern opera; but it may be noted that the prevalence of Wagnerian continuity eventually enabled composers to take extant dramas and set them without any extensive remodelling at all. If the operas *Pelléas et Mélisande*, *Salome*, and *Electra* are compared with the original plays by Maeterlinck, Wilde, and Hofmannsthal, it will be found that the poets have suffered less from Debussy and Strauss than dramatic authors usually suffer from actor-managers. Debussy has omitted Maeterlinck's difficult and not musical first scene of the servants who, having heard of the prince's approaching return with a strange bride, must be speaking after the following scene, in which Golaud first meets Mélisande in the forest. By omitting the first scene Debussy secures an opening in the right atmosphere but loses the basis of the entry of the servants in the last scene of all. Here history repeats itself, for Weber offended the librettist of *Freischütz* by refusing to compose an opening scene with the hermit who appears as *deus ex machina* at the end. In both cases the composers are right, though the sacrifice is serious.

Debussy and Strauss have so treated these three plays that they are better acted when given as operas than when given without music. No actress except an opera singer ever has her declamation and movements so superbly timed, and timed permanently to the tenth of a second, as in these wonderful pieces of musical stage-craft. The methods of the two composers are

poles asunder, and Debussy's language is, as has been said elsewhere, the exact opposite of Maeterlinck's. Yet from his opposite direction Debussy reaches the Maeterlinckian world. He has
no leitmotives, hardly even a recurring figure. Strauss uses the
whole Wagnerian system, together with his own al fresco technique (the term is also his own, *see* INSTRUMENTATION, last section).

In later works Strauss and Hofmannsthal have shown that they
accept no limits to the number of different kinds of opera that
one composer may write. An annotated catalogue would be required to keep pace with the various types of modern opera from
the parodistic to the tragic and the symbolical.

A few final definitions may serve to fill up lacunae in an
account which has deliberately sacrificed historical order to the
laying down of a few broad aesthetic criteria. Besides the matters already defined the following particulars should be noted:

1. *Singspiel* originated in farces, such as Dittersdorf's *Doktor
und Apotheker*. But in France the *opéra comique*, which corresponds to *Singspiel*, had no comic origin at all, but arose from
the refusal of the *Académie de Musique* to allow rival companies
to infringe its monopoly of *Grand Opéra*, or opera in which every
word is sung and even the recitatives have orchestral accompaniments.

2. French *Grand Opéra* has had a continuous history from the
foundation of the *Académie de Musique* in 1669 to the present day.
It absorbed the works of Meyerbeer, which so infuriated Wagner
by producing 'effects' without assuming any responsibility for
causes. And this is all that can be said of Meyerbeer here.

3. *Opéra bouffe* has no historic connexion with *opera buffa* but
is the offshoot of vaudeville music in the early classical sense
described above. Its chief representative on the Continent is
Offenbach, and it is the ancestor of the Savoy operas of Gilbert
and Sullivan.

4. *Melodrama* is the use of an orchestral accompaniment to
spoken dialogue. It is promising in theory, but generally disappointing in effect, because the speaking voice becomes dragged
by the music into an out-of-tune sing-song. Benda never let the
voice speak during any notes except a long-sustained chord.
Mozart, after one example in an unfinished opera, *Zaide*, dropped
this form, though he admired Benda's essays so much that he
put them under his pillow during his travels. Other classical
examples are significantly short and cautious. There is one in
Fidelio which quotes from earlier movements in a thoroughly
Wagnerian way. But the device is more prominent in incidental
music to plays, as in Beethoven's music for Goethe's *Egmont*.
Mendelssohn's music for *A Midsummer Night's Dream* contains

the most brilliant and resourceful examples yet achieved; but they are beyond the musical capacity of the English non-operatic theatre, which, however, has practised the worst style of the method, till it has become a disease spreading an operatic continuity of bad music over large tracts of our drama.

In every period of musical fermentation the art of opera, while it has failed to sift good composers from bad, has instantly sifted the men of real ideas from the aesthetes and faddists; Monteverdi from the Prince of Venosa, Gluck from Gossec, Wagner from Bruckner on the one hand and Liszt on the other. As the ferment subsides laziness levels opera sooner than anything else; but every revolutionary principle that enters into music to destroy and expand must, first or finally, seek its ratification on the stage.

See also ARIA, OVERTURE, INSTRUMENTATION.

ORATORIO, the name given to a form of religious music with chorus, solo voices, and orchestra, independent of, or at least separable from, the liturgy, and on a larger scale than the cantata (q.v.). Its history is involved in that of opera (*see* ARIA and OPERA), but its antecedents are more definite. The term is almost certainly derived from the fact that St. Filippo Neri's Oratory was the place for which Animuccia's settings of the *Laudi Spirituali* were written; and the custom of interspersing these hymns among liturgical or other forms of the recitation of a Biblical story is one of several origins of modern oratorio. A more ancient source is the use of incidental music in miracle plays and in such dramatic processions as the twelfth-century *Prose de l'Âne*, which on 1 January celebrated at Beauvais the Flight into Egypt. But the most ancient origin of all is the Roman Catholic rite of reciting, during Holy Week, the story of the Passion according to the Four Gospels, assigning the words of the Evangelist to a tenor, distributing all *ipsissima verba* among appropriate voices, and giving the *responsa turbae*, or utterances of the whole body of disciples (e.g. 'Lord, is it I?') and of crowds, to a chorus. The only portion of this scheme that concerned composers was the *responsa turbae*, to which it was permitted to add polyphonic settings of the Seven Last Words or the eucharistic utterances of the Saviour. The narrative and the parts of single speakers were sung in the Gregorian tones appointed in the liturgy. Thus the settings of the Passion by Victoria and Soriano represent a perfect solution of the art-problem of oratorio. 'Very tame Jews' is Mendelssohn's comment on the sixteenth-century settings of 'Crucify Him'; and it has been argued that Soriano's and Victoria's aim was not to imitate the infuriated Jews, but to express the contrition of devout Christians telling the story. On the other hand, ancient tradition ordained a noisy scraping of feet on the stone floor to indicate the departure from the place of the judgement seat! And so we owe the central forms of Bach's Lutheran Passion-oratorios to the Roman Catholic ritual for Holy Week.

With the monodic revolution at the outset of the seventeenth century the history of oratorio as an art-form wholly controlled by composers begins. There is nothing but its religious subject to distinguish the first oratorio, Emilio del Cavaliere's *Rappresentazione di anima e di corpo*, from the first opera, Peri's *Euridice*, both produced in 1600. Differentiation was brought about primarily by the fact that oratorios without stage presentation

gave opportunity for a revival of choral music. And oratorios on
the stage discouraged, by reason of their sacred subjects, whatever vestiges of dramatic realism could survive the ascendancy
of the aria (q.v.). For lesser composers than Bach and Handel
this ubiquitous form represented almost the only possibility of
keeping music alive, or at least embalmed, until the advent of the
dramatic and sonata styles. The efforts of Carissimi (d. 1674) in
oratorio clearly show how limited a divergence from the method
of opera was possible when music was first emancipated from the
stage. Yet his art shows the corruption of Church music by a
secular style rather than the rise of Biblical music-drama to the
dignity of Church music. Normal Italian oratorio remains indistinguishable from serious Italian opera as late as *La Betulia
liberata*, which Mozart wrote at the age of 15. Handel's *La
Resurrezzione* and *Il Trionfo del Tempo* contain many pieces
simultaneously used in his operas, and they contain no chorus
beyond a perfunctory operatic final tune. *Il Trionfo del Tempo*
was a typical morality play, and it became a masque, like *Acis and
Galatea* and *Semele*, when Handel at the close of his life adapted
it to an English translation with several choral and solo interpola-
tions from other works. Yet between these two versions of the
same work lies half the history of classical oratorio. The rest lies
in the German Passion-oratorios that culminate in Bach; after
which the greatest music avoids every form of oratorio until the
two main streams, sadly silted up, and never afterwards quite
pure, unite in Mendelssohn.

Luther was so musical that, while the German Reformation
was far from conservative of ancient liturgy, it retained almost
everything which makes for musical coherence in a Church service; unlike the English Church, which, with all its insistence on
historic continuity, so rearranged the liturgy that no possible
music for an English Church service can ever form a coherent
whole. The four Passions and the *Historia der Auferstehung
Christi* of H. Schütz (who was born in 1585, exactly a century
before Bach) are as truly the descendants of Victoria's Passions
as they are the ancestors of Bach's. They are Protestant in their
use of the vulgar tongue, and narrative and dialogue are set to
free composition instead of Gregorian chant, although written in
Gregorian notation. The *Marcus Passion* is in a weaker and more
modern style and stereotyped in its recitative. It may be spurious.
But in the other Passions, and most of all in the *Auferstehung*, the
recitative is a unique and wonderful language. It may have been
accompanied by the organ, though the Passions contain no hint
of accompaniment at all. In the *Auferstehung* the Evangelist is
accompanied by four viole da gamba in preference to the organ.
The players are requested to 'execute appropriate runs or pas-

sages' during the sustained chords. A final non-scriptural short chorus on a chorale-tune is Schütz's only foreshadowing of the contemplative and hymnal element of later Passion oratorios.

The *Auferstehung*, the richest and most advanced of all Schütz's works, has one strange convention, in that single persons, other than the Evangelist, are frequently represented by more than one voice. If this were confined to the part of the Saviour, it would have shown a reverent avoidance of impersonation, as in Roman Catholic polyphonic settings of the Seven Words. But Schütz writes thus only in *Die Auferstehung* and there on no particular plan. While the three holy women and the two angels in the scene at the tomb are represented naturally by three and two imitative voices, Mary Magdalene is elsewhere always represented by two sopranos.

Shortly before Bach, Passion-oratorios were represented by several remarkable works of art, most notably by R. Keiser (1673–1739). Chorale-tunes, mostly in plain harmony, were freely interspersed in order that the congregation might take part in what was, after all, a Church service for Holy Week. The meditations of Christendom on each incident of the story were expressed in accompanied recitatives (*arioso*) leading to arias or choruses, and the scriptural narrative was sung to dramatic recitative and ejaculatory chorus on the ancient Roman plan. On slightly different lines was Graun's beautiful *Tod Jesu*, which was famous when the contemporary works of Bach were ignored.

The difference between Bach's Passions and all others is simply the measure of his greatness. Where his chorus represents the whole body of Christendom, it has as peculiar an epic power as it has dramatic where it represents tersely the *responsa turbae* of the narrative.

In the *Matthew Passion* the part of Christ has a special accompaniment of sustained strings, generally at a high pitch, though deepening at the most solemn moments. And at the words 'Eli, Eli, lama sabacthani', this musical halo has vanished. In power of declamation Bach was anticipated by Keiser; but no one approached him in sustained inspiration and architectonic greatness. The forms of Passion music may be found in many of Bach's Church cantatas; a favourite type being the Dialogue; as, for instance, a dispute between a fearing and a trusting soul with, perhaps, the voice of the Saviour heard from a distance; or a dialogue between Christ and the Church, on the lines of the Song of Solomon. The *Christmas Oratorio*, a set of six Church cantatas for performance on separate days, treats the Bible story in the same way as the Passions, with a larger proportion of non-dramatic numbers. Many of the single Church cantatas are called oratorios, a term which by Bach's time seems definitely to have implied dialogue, possibly on the strength of a false etymology. Thus Schütz inscribes a monodic sacred piece 'in stilo Oratorio', meaning 'in the style of recitative'. The further history of oratorio radiates from the heterogeneous works of Handel.

There are various types and several mixtures of style in Handelian oratorio. The German forms of Passion music evidently interested Handel, and it was after he came to England, and before his first English oratorio, that he set to music the famous poetic version of the Passion by Brockes, which had been adopted by all the German composers of the time, and which, with very necessary improvements of taste, was largely drawn upon by Bach for the text of his *Johannes-Passion*. Handel's Brockes Passion does not appear ever to have been performed, though Bach found access to it and made a careful copy; so Handel must have composed it for his own edification. He soon discovered that many kinds of oratorio were possible. The emancipation from the stage admitted of subjects ranging from semi-dramatic histories, like those of *Saul*, *Esther*, and *Belshazzar*, to cosmic schemes expressed entirely in the words of the Bible, such as *Israel in Egypt* and the *Messiah*. Between these types there is every gradation of form and subject; besides an abrupt contrast of literary merit between the mutilated Milton of *Samson* and the amazing absurdities of *Susanna*.

The very name of Handel's first English oratorio, *Esther*, and the facts of its primary purpose as a masque and the origin of its libretto in Racine, show the transition from the stage to the Church; and, on the other hand, Haman's lamentation on his downfall is scandalously adapted from the most sacred part of the Brockes Passion.

We may roughly distinguish three main types of Handelian oratorio, not always maintained singly in whole works, but always available as methods. First, there is the operatic method, in which the arias and recitatives are the utterances of characters in the story, while the chorus is a crowd of Israelites, Babylonians, or Romans (e.g. *Athalia*, *Belshazzar*, *Saul*, &c.). The second method retains the dramatic roles both in solos and in choruses, but (as, for instance, in 'Envy, eldest born of Hell', in *Saul*) also uses the chorus as the voice of universal Christendom. Handel's audience demanded plenty of arias, most of which are accounted for by futile, when not apocryphal, love affairs. The haughty Merab and the gentle Michal are characterized with fatal ease, and make parts of *Saul* almost as impossible as most of *Susanna*. The third Handelian method is a series of choruses and numbers on a subject altogether beyond the scope of drama, as, for instance, the greater part of *Solomon*, and, in the case of the *Messiah* and *Israel in Egypt*, treated entirely in the words of Scripture, and those not in narrative but in prophecy and psalm. After Bach and Handel, oratorio fell upon evil days. The rise of the sonata style, which brought life to opera, was bad for oratorio; since not only did it accentuate the fashionable dislike of that polyphony which is essential even to mere euphony in choral writing, but its dramatic power became more and more disturbing to the epic treatment that oratorio naturally demands.

Philipp Emanuel Bach's oratorios, though cloying in their softness and sweetness, achieved a true balance of style in the earlier days of the conflict; indeed, a judicious selection from *Die Israeliten in der Wüste* (1769) would perhaps bear revival almost as well as Haydn's *Tobias* (1774).

The Creation (*Die Schöpfung*) and *The Seasons* (*Die Jahreszeiten*) will always convey to unspoilt music-lovers the profound message of the veteran Haydn, who could not help 'worshipping God with a cheerful heart'. This spirit was well known to Bach, the composer of *Mein gläubiges Herze*, and it is compatible with the romantic sound-pictures and Handelian sublimity of the opening Representation of Chaos and the great chord of C major at the words 'and there was light'. The childlike gaiety of much of the rest ought not to blind us to its fundamental greatness, which brings the naïvely realistic birds and beasts of *The Creation* into line with even the wine-chorus in the mainly secular *Seasons*, and removes Haydn from the influence of the vile taste which henceforth pervaded oratorios, until Mendelssohn effected a partial improvement. Haydn strenuously resisted the persuasion to undertake *The Seasons*, which had a close connexion with Thomson's poem, as *The Creation* had a distant connexion with *Paradise Lost*. He thought the whole scheme 'Philistine' (his own word) and, both before he yielded to persuasion and after he had finished the work, said all the hard things about it that have ever been said since.

Roman Catholic oratorio was under the disadvantage that it was not permitted to take Biblical texts except in the Latin language. Jomelli's *Passione* for once had the benefit of a meditative text with some distinction of style; and in closing the first part with a dominant seventh on the word *pensaci* he achieved a stroke of genius which at the present day would still startle the listener and leave his mind in the desired frame of meditative astonishment.

But words fail to characterize the libretto of Beethoven's unfortunate *Christus am Oelberge* (*c.* 1800). The texts of Lutheran Church music had often been grotesque and even disgusting; but their barbarity was pathetic in comparison with the sleek vulgarity of a libretto in which not only is the agony of the garden of Gethsemane represented by an aria (as in Handel's lamentation of Haman), but Christ sings a brilliant duet with the ministering angel. In after years Beethoven had not a good word for this work, which, nevertheless, contains some beautiful music exquisitely scored. And justice demands praise for the idea of making a Hallelujah chorus conclude the work as soon as the betrayal of Christ has been accomplished, thus compensating for the irreverent opening by avoiding all temptation to treat the rest of the Passion story with the same crassness. A well-meant effort was made to provide *The Mount of Olives* with an inoffensive subject in English, but the stupidity of *Engedi: or David in the Wilderness* passes belief.

Schubert's interesting fragment *Lazarus* is strangely prophetic of Wagnerian continuity and has a morbid beauty that transcends its sickly text. There are signs that the despair of the Sadducee was going to be treated with some power. The results might have been a masterpiece; but fate ruled that the next advance should again be Protestant.

Bach's Passions were rediscovered by the boy Mendelssohn after a century of ignorance of their very existence; and *St. Paul* (*Paulus*) and *Elijah* (*Elias*) rose upon the early middle nineteenth century like the sunrise of a new Handel.

To-day *St. Paul* has almost sunk below the horizon; and *Elijah*, which still shares with the *Messiah* the Christmas repertoire of every British urban choral society, is in many points an easy target for criticism. Yet the ascendancy of Mendelssohn is the one redeeming feature in the history of oratorio during the first three-quarters of the nineteenth century. Let us admit the defects of *Elijah*; the all too lifelike tiresomeness of the widow (achieved after strenuous revision), the parochial softness of the double quartet, the Jewishness of the Jews (but is this a defect?), and the snorts of the trombones whose third summons causes the Almighty to capitulate: when all these unconscious profanities are discounted, there remains a vivid and coherent oratorio which, musically and dramatically, towers above later works by many accomplished composers who despise it.

Spohr is the only contemporary of Mendelssohn whose sacred music is still known. So tremendous a subject as that of *The Last Judgement* ought, indeed, to be treated with reserve; but the softness and slowness which pervades nine-tenths of Spohr's work is not reserve but self-indulgence. Spohr has moments of vision; but an almost random glance at the pages of *St. Paul* shows that even in eclipse Mendelssohn has characterization, movement, and the capacity for thrilling dramatic moments.

In England, the influence of Mendelssohn completed the devastation begun by our inveterate habit of praising the inspired literary skill of the sacred narrative, as a preface to our restatement of it in forty times as many words of our own. Deans and chapters listened in graceful official pride and imperfectly secret glee to the strains in which the cathedral organist celebrated with equal realism the destruction of Sennacherib's hosts and his own octuply-contrapuntal doctorate of music. Before 1880 our composers had, as Dr. Walker says, 'set with almost complete indiscrimination wellnigh every word of the Bible'. Had they confined themselves to the second chapter of Ezra they would have escaped dangers of unconscious humour that lurk in the opportunities for 'naturalness' in declaiming the dialogues and illustrating the wonders of scriptural narrative.

Neither Sterndale Bennett nor Macfarren improved matters; but Parry and Stanford, towards the end of the century, completely changed the situation. Stanford's *Eden* has a libretto by Robert Bridges. The disgruntled professional librettists, who were also musical critics, had the effrontery to say that this magnificent poem would be the better for extensive cuts. The real truth is that Stanford's music, especially in its orchestral introductions, is diffuse. But it has many beautiful features, and achieves a coherent scheme on exactly such lines of Wagnerian continuity as can be applied to oratorio. Parry preferred to be his own librettist; and by this means he achieved more significant results. The lapses of the amateur poet are less distressing than the clichés of the ordinary professional librettist; and the works of Parry and Stanford permanently raised English oratorio from squalor and made it once more an art-form which educated people could enjoy. Some of Parry's architectonic and dramatic ideas will never lose the power to thrill, if only the works as wholes can live in spite of a certain dryness of melody and heaviness of texture. For example, the exploit of Judith is shown with a total avoidance of the cheap and salacious opportunity for a scene between her and Holofernes. Instead, we listen to the watchmen anxiously making their circuit of the city walls in darkness. The music of their march is at a low pitch. It is reaching a normal close when, high above the tonic chord, the cry of Judith bids the watchmen open the gates to her. If this moment cannot thrill, there is no meaning in art. In *King Saul* Parry made a significant discovery as to the emancipation of dramatic oratorio from the stage conditions of time and space. The Witch of Endor prophesies the battle of Gilboa. Her tale becomes real in the telling and is immediately followed by the final dirge.

As with opera, so, but more easily, with oratorio, the method of Wagnerian continuity at last enabled composers to take extant poems and set them to music in their entirety. Thus the fragrant mysticism of Roman Catholic oratorio, dimly adumbrated in

Schubert's *Lazarus*, at last came to fruition in Elgar's wonderful setting of Newman's *Dream of Gerontius*, while the old miracle play *Everyman* was very successfully composed by Walford Davies. In his later works, *The Apostles* and *The Kingdom*, Elgar pursues a comprehensive religious design on texts arranged by himself. Oratorio on the basis of Wagnerian continuity and leitmotive is unquestionably a living art-form. Its greatest difficulty is its fatal facility. The oratorio-composer is lost who omits to transcend the limits of the stage; yet when these are transcended only the steadfastness of genius can prevent the composer from sinking to the fashion-storming eclecticism of Honegger's *Le Roi David*, which, with the aid of a reciter to read the Bible, takes up the arts of all periods from Handel to 1927 and drops each of them before anything like an art-problem arises.

Why not follow more often the method of the *Messiah* and of *Israel in Egypt*; and deal with religious subjects in terms of prophecy and psalm? Brahms's *Deutsches Requiem* is really an oratorio; and since its production (all but one later movement) in 1866 it continues year by year to tower over all other choral music since Beethoven's Mass in D. Form, disciplined form, is not the only thing needed to save future oratorios from the limbo of vanity; but it is their first need.

OVERTURE

OVERTURE (Fr. *ouverture*, opening), a detachable instrumental introduction to a dramatic or choral composition. The notion of an overture had no existence until the seventeenth century. The toccata at the beginning of Monteverdi's *Orfeo* is a barbaric flourish of every procurable instrument, alternating with a melodious section entitled 'ritornello'; and, in so far as this constitutes the first instrumental movement prefixed to an opera, it may be called an overture. As an art-form the overture began to exist in the works of J. B. Lully. His favourite, but not his only, form constitutes the typical French overture that became classical in the works of Bach and Handel. This French overture consists of a slow introduction in a marked 'dotted rhythm' (i.e., exaggerated iambic, if the first chord is disregarded), followed by a lively movement in fugato style. The slow introduction was always repeated, and sometimes the quick movement concluded by returning to the slow tempo and material, and was also repeated (*see* Bach's French Overture in the *Klavierübung*).

The operatic French overture was frequently followed by a series of dance tunes before the curtain rose. It thus naturally became used as the prelude to a suite (q.v.); and the term was then applied to the whole suite.

Bach was able to adapt the French overture to choruses, and even to the treatment of chorales. Thus the overture-movements of his Fourth Orchestral Suite became the first chorus of the Church Cantata *Unser Mund sei voll Lachens*; the choruses of the Cantatas *Preise Jerusalem den Herrn* and *Höchst erwünschtes Freudenfest* are in overture form; and, in the first of the two Cantatas entitled *Nun komm' der Heiden Heiland*, Bach has adapted the overture form to the treatment of a chorale.

Gluck could find no use for the French overture. In the epoch-making preface to *Alceste* he laid down the rule that the overture should be the musical argument of the drama. And the perfunctory overture to *Orfeo* is the only exception to the rule that in his great operas the orchestral introduction is actually interrupted by the rise of the curtain. In *Iphigénie en Tauride* it is merely the calm before the storm.

The abolition of the French overture did not, however, lead at first to any widespread adoption of Gluck's loose-knit Italian texture. The next form of overture was that of a three-movement symphony (q.v.) in sonata style. In Mozart's early opera *La Finta Giardiniera* the curtain rises upon what should have been the third movement; and in all later works the overture is distinguished from symphonic music in style as well as form. It is a single quick movement (with or without a slow introduction) in sonata form, loose in texture, without repeats, and frequently without a development section. Sometimes, in place of development, there is a melodious episode in slow time; as in Mozart's overtures to *Die Entführung* and to the fragment *Lo Sposo deluso*, in both of which cases the curtain rises at a point which throws a dramatic light upon this feature. Mozart at first intended a similar episode in the overture to *Figaro*, but struck it out as soon as he had begun it.

In Beethoven's hands the overture became more and more unlike the symphony, but it no longer remained an inferior species; and the final version of the overture to *Leonore* is the most gigantic single orchestral movement ever based on the sonata style. Weber's overtures work out prominent themes in his operas in a loose but effective sonata form, and are effective concert-pieces besides serving Gluck's purposes admirably.

Overtures to plays naturally tend to become detached from their surroundings; and hence arises the concert overture, led by Beethoven's mighty *Coriolan*, and second only to the symphony as an orchestral art-form. Its derivation implies that it is programme music (q.v.), but the programme need not impair the form, whether the form be Berlioz's or Brahms's, and the programme particular or generalized. Among overtures with a generalized programme Mendelssohn's 'Hebrides' Overture is a perfect masterpiece; and so is Brahms's 'Tragic' Overture, one of the greatest orchestral movements since Beethoven. Brahms's 'Academic Festival' Overture is a glorious working out of German student songs.

In modern opera the overture, *Prelude, Vorspiel*, or whatever else it may be called, is often nothing more definite than that portion of the music which takes place before the curtain rises. *Tannhäuser* is the last important opera in which the overture retains vestiges of a self-contained sonata form. Fifty years before Wagner's wonderful *Vorspiel* to *Lohengrin*, Méhul had achieved an equally complete departure from classical forms in his interesting overtures to *Ariodant* and *Uthal*, in the latter of which a voice is heard on the stage before the rise of the curtain. Even the most self-contained of Wagner's later preludes lose by transference to the concert-room. The glorious *Vorspiel* to *Die Meistersinger* is nobler when its long crescendo leads to the rise of the curtain and the engaging of all the listener's sense of sight and language, than when it can merely lead to a final tonic chord. Wagner himself added a page to finish the *Vorspiel* to *Tristan*, and by the richness and subtlety of that page he reveals how unready for independent existence the original *Vorspiel* was.

He also finished the *Parsifal Vorspiel* for concert use by the addition of a few extra bars, which will always sound perfunctory. The four dramas of *Der Ring* begin with introductions designed to prepare the hearer immediately for the rise of the curtain; and these works can no more be said to have overtures than Verdi's *Falstaff* and Strauss's *Salome, Electra,* and *Die Frau ohne Schatten,* in which the curtain rises at the first note of the music.

PROGRAMME MUSIC

PROGRAMME MUSIC, a nickname which is the only current term for instrumental music without words but descriptive of non-musical ideas. Musical sounds lend themselves to descriptive purposes with fatal ease. A chromatic scale may suggest the whistling of the wind or the serenades of cats. Reiterated staccato notes may suggest raindrops or the cackling of hens. Again, music is powerfully suggestive of emotion; and the emotions it calls up may fit some particular story, or may resemble those inspired by a sunset or a storm. But chromatic scales, reiterated notes, emotional contrasts and climaxes, are also normal musical resources; and nothing infuriates a musician more than the non-musical explanation of such things where the composer's aim was purely musical. Sound as it occurs in nature is too inorganic to form the raw material for art, and so there is no natural tendency in music to include, as a 'subject', any item not inherent in the art-form. Explicit programme music has thus never been a thing of cardinal importance, though it has often been prominent and always popular. But the conditions of artistic creation are not to be confounded with any correct theory of art. The doctrine of art for art's sake is correct: but it concerns results, not processes, and many of the purest works of art have been produced for ulterior purposes.

Until recent times no composer has written for the voice without words, for speech is a privilege which the human voice will not willingly renounce. No doctrine of absolute music will prevent a good composer from shaping his vocal music to the words which he sets. Good literature will inspire him to explore and express its inner meaning. Bad literature may suggest to him the truths it misrepresents; and the great composers are quicker to seize the truth than to criticize its verbal presentation or to suspect insincerity. The earliest mature musical art was, then, inevitably descriptive, since it was vocal. While programme music derives many of its characteristics from ancient times, it cannot properly be said to have existed until the rise of modern instrumental music, based upon external ideas and independent of the use of words.

A complete code of musical symbolism came to maturity in the sixteenth century. Part of it was profoundly true and characteristic of moods; part was harmlessly mechanical; and a few details were manifestly false, as when the words *atra nox* are represented by a curiously jaunty rhythm because that rhythm is indicated by black notes. When symbolism, true or false, has thus arisen in vocal music it may be expected to retain its intention in music without words. But we must not expect too much descriptive power in early instrumental music; and when a scholar tells us that a funeral piece for organ by Froberger depicts in its final rising melisma the ascent of the soul to heaven, he unwittingly accuses Froberger of sinister intentions in a precisely similar funeral piece which ends with a descent to the lowest bass.

The resources of the modern orchestra can attain a realism which at first seems less ridiculous than that of earlier descriptive music. But the expensive realism of the dozen muted brass instruments which in Strauss's *Don Quixote* accomplish in ten rehearsals what a flock of sheep achieve extempore, is not less but more childish than the thunderstorm in the *Fitzwilliam Virginal Book.*

Beethoven's Theory of Expression.—On the other hand, when superior persons object to the childishness of the birds and the thunderstorms in Beethoven's 'Pastoral' Symphony, it is they who are childish in supposing that realism is in question at all. The real cuckoo, nightingale, and quail happen to be musical birds whose themes are exactly what Beethoven wants for a break in the rhythm at a point of repose in the coda of his slow movement. Similar final digressions can be seen in slow movements with no programme at all, e.g. in the Violin Sonata, op. 24, the Pianoforte Sonata in D minor, op. 31, no. 2, and the String Quintet in C major, op. 29. Not a bar of the 'Pastoral' Symphony would be otherwise if its 'programme' had never been thought of. The 'merry meeting of country folk' is a subject that lends itself admirably to Beethoven's form of scherzo (q.v.); and the thunderstorm, which interrupts the last repetition of this scherzo and forms a tremendous introduction to the peaceful finale, is as musical as other unique features in Beethoven's pure art-forms.

Beethoven is recorded to have said that he always composed according to a 'picture' he had in his mind; and he sometimes gave his friends an explanation, jocular or evasive, of some particular composition. But the word *Bild* is much more indefinite than 'picture'; and Beethoven's dull Boswell, Schindler, often exasperated him into defending himself by saying the first nonsense that would serve to stop foolish questions. Composers who have much to express cannot spare time for translating it into other terms than those of their own art. The 'Eroica' Symphony, though inspired by Beethoven's short-lived belief in Napoleon as the liberator of mankind, is not programme music at all. The funeral march represents heroic death and a mourning world, but not the obsequies of a biographical subject; and when critics tell us that the finale is 'an inappropriate concession to sonata form', they merely show themselves unmusical without thereby becoming literary. The profound and subtle Sonata *Les Adieux, l'Absence, et le Retour* is true programme music. It represents Beethoven's feelings on parting from the Archduke Rudolph when the royal family left Vienna shortly before its bombardment. It deals only with the parting, the absence, and the rejoining of the two men. Nothing is heard of war, and the sentiment is as deep as it is manly. Beethoven's private sketch-books record that the work is 'written from the heart'; no courtly formula, even if this was shown to the Archduke. Ingenuity is misplaced in tracing external details. (The end of the first movement of *Les Adieux* has been compared to the departure of a coach.) The real emotional basis is universal and musical.

Beethoven summed up the whole theory of great programme music in his note to the 'Pastoral' Symphony; 'rather the expression of feelings than sound-painting'. Overtures to plays or operas cannot so easily dispense with story-telling; but Beethoven refuses to be drawn into a chronological series of illustrations. His Overtures to *Coriolan*, *Egmont*, and *Leonore* deal with salient emotions roused by their subjects. Wagner was able to place the substance of the *Coriolan* Overture in Shakespeare's scene between Coriolanus and his mother and wife before the gates of Rome; but Thayer found that the forgotten poet Collin's play, which was Beethoven's subject, sheds far more light on the music. The music, however, once it took shape, could do without Collin or Shakespeare. The *Leonore* Overture was at first (in the form known as No. 2) a huge prelude to the opera, with a gigantic exposition and development, and the shortest wind-up compatible with adequacy, after the trumpet-call behind the scene has relieved the tension. In the later version (*Leonore*, No. 3) Beethoven ruthlessly compresses the exposition until the trumpet-call becomes the middle point of the design, which afterwards expands in a further development, a full recapitulation, and a climax which makes this overture the first and greatest of all 'symphonic poems' (q.v.). Critics who cavil at the trumpet-call as a weakness from the point of view of absolute music only show that they cannot tell absolute music from absolute nonsense. Distance is surely too elementary a phase of sound to be excluded from absolute music, nor can the fanfares of a trumpet be separated either from the instrument or from its associations. As a piece of absolute music *Leonore*, No. 3, is a huge movement in sonata form rising steadily to a point at which the tension is relieved by the new incident of a distant trumpet-call, after which the music expands from sheer joy. Beethoven's maxim *mehr Ausdruck der Empfindung als Malerei* therefore holds here, and bridges the gulf between absolute and illustrative music.

Portrayal of Characters and Moods.—This is equally true with archaic and modern programme music; it is always characters and moods that are successfully portrayed, while chronology is useless and the illustration of incidents is apt to be ridiculous unless it contrives to be witty. Thus, the *Bible Sonatas* of J. Kuhnau (published in 1700) and their clever imitation in Bach's early *Capriccio on the Departure of a Beloved Brother* rely mainly on moods, and are successful with incidents only when these would be accompanied by music in real life or drama. If Kuhnau's music were half as vivid or inventive as his prose introductions it would be immortal. But much may be learnt from noting how his unconsciously humorous prose describes other things than the music attempts to portray and omits the very things in which the music is at its best. While Kuhnau strains himself, like a bad nurse telling bogy-stories, in his prefatory description of the size and appearance of Goliath, in the music it is the boasts (*le bravate*) of Goliath that are portrayed. The best movement in the Goliath Sonata is a figured chorale (*Aus tiefer Noth schrei' ich zu Dir*) representing the terror and prayers of the Israelites. On the other hand the cast of David's sling, with the fall of Goliath, is not nearly so sublime as the fall of a tea-tray. Kuhnau's other subjects (*Saul cured by David's music*; *The Marriage of Jacob*; *The Healing of Hezekiah*; *Gideon*; and *The Funeral of Jacob*) are all thoroughly musical; more so than he succeeds in making them. Bach's *Capriccio* describes the anxiety and sorrow of the friends of the departing brother; and his utmost realism takes the form of a lively fugue on the themes of the postilion's coach-horn and cracking whip. Buxtehude illustrated the 'nature and characters of the planets'. This is an astrological, not an astronomical subject: the planets signify temperaments and their motions are the music of the spheres. No wonder, then, that this musical subject has been adopted in one of the outstanding masterpieces of modern orchestral music, *The Planets*, by Holst.

Adaptability of Lyrical Music.—Instrumental music on the lyric scale lends itself to illustrative purposes more readily than larger forms. Nearly all the harpsichord pieces of Couperin have fantastic titles, and a few of them are descriptive music. His greater contemporary and survivor, Rameau, wrote important operas and much extremely graphic harpsichord music. *La Poule*, with its theme inscribed 'co-co-co-co-co-co-cocodai', is an excellent movement in spacious form, and is also one of the most minutely realistic compositions ever written. French composers have always contributed *con amore* to music that takes advantage of external stimulus; and already in 1801 descriptive music was considered so specially French that Haydn apologized for his imitation of frogs in *The Seasons*, saying that this *französische Quark* (rubbish) had been forced on him by a friend. But throughout the growth of the sonata style, not excepting Haydn's own early work, the tendency towards gratuitously descriptive music often appears; partly because there was no definite distinction between early symphonic music and overtures or incidental music to plays (e.g. Haydn's *Il Distratto*). Dittersdorf's Symphonies on the *Metamorphoses* of Ovid are excellent music in which the descriptive elements do not disturb the symphonic form until the metamorphosis, which is then illustrated in almost Wagnerian breadth. For instance, the first three movements of the *Change of the Lycian peasants into Frogs* show the rusticity of the peasants, the gracefulness of the goddess, and the rudeness of the peasants to the goddess; and then the Finale indicates an altercation ended, after a pause, in a low mysterious quivering sound as of frogs in a marsh.

Dittersdorf is not a great composer; but many more learned and resourceful artists have shown less than his common sense in distributing the descriptive and the formal elements of their music. It seems incredible that any composer could be so foolish as to commit himself to describing a chronological sequence in a sonata form which compels him to go through a full restatement of events which only happened once; yet many composers refused to abandon either the sonata form or the chronological sequence. Lyric forms presented no such difficulties.

Schumann and Spohr.—Schumann sometimes invented his titles after his pianoforte lyrics were finished, and sometimes wrote on the inspiration of literature. In either case, as with Beethoven, the music throws far more light on the programme than the programme throws on the music. Musical people may profitably study E. T. A. Hoffman and Jean Paul Richter in the light of Schumann's *Novelletten* and *Kreisleriana*; but if they do not already understand Schumann's music, Jean Paul and Hoffman will help them only to talk about it. In revising his early works Schumann sometimes made them more musical and sometimes destroyed grotesque touches that are musically as well as psychologically true. For instance, in the *Davidsbündlertänze* (op. 6) the hot-headed Florestan, having finished an impassioned tirade, feels that he has been making a fool of himself. His last note pauses unharmonized and he sits down awkwardly. In a later edition, with unnecessary scruple, Schumann suppressed this detail together with the prose titles and signatures. The fashion of fantastic titles affected even the most formal composers during the romantic period.

No one wrote more programme music than Spohr; and while Spohr's programme constantly conflicted with the externals of his form and ruined the latter part of his symphony *Die Weihe der Töne*, it did not broaden his style. Mendelssohn's 'Scotch' and 'Italian' Symphonies, and his 'Hebrides' Overture, are cases of generalized local colour. His 'Reformation' Symphony, which he himself regarded as a failure, and which was not published until after his death, is a descriptive work less attractive but more coherent than Spohr's *Weihe der Töne*. The Overture to the *Midsummer Night's Dream* is a marvellous musical epitome of Shakespeare's play; and the comparative slightness and conventionality of its second theme closely correspond with Shakespeare's two pairs of lovers, though it does not illustrate their quarrels under the fairy spells.

Influence of Berlioz.—Berlioz made programme music a vital issue in the nineteenth century. With an inextinguishable gift for voluminous composition he is utterly incapable of focussing his attention on either his music or his programme. The most trivial external detail may distract him at the height of his rhetoric. The moonshine and sentiment of the *Scène d'amour*, in his *Romeo and Juliet* Symphony are charming; and the agitated sighing episodes which interrupt its flow can be understood in the light of Shakespeare's balcony scene, if not by their musical sense. But when Berlioz thinks of the nurse knocking or calling at the door, he makes a realistic noise without either musical or dramatic purpose. It does not interrupt the duet, nor increase the emotional tension, nor illustrate Juliet's artifices for gaining time, nor her agitation at the interruptions of the nurse. Perhaps this was the passage on which a lady once congratulated Berlioz for his vivid representation of *Roméo arrivant dans son cabriolet*. This piece of purely orchestral music has an introduction in which real voices are heard from convivial persons returning home from the ball. Berlioz complains that the public has no imagination and that therefore certain sections which presuppose an intimate knowledge of Shakespeare's play *avec le dénouement de Garrick* should be omitted. But what the public lacks for these sections is neither imagination nor familiarity with Garrick-Shakespeare, but a capacity to take the butterfly vagaries of Berlioz's mind as their basis of reference.

With all his absurdities, Berlioz's genius for composition carried him further towards a new music than Liszt was able to advance in his symphonic poems. These, as has been said in other articles (*see* MUSIC, secs. viii–x, and SYMPHONIC POEM), are the beginnings of an instrumental music that achieves the same continuity that Wagner achieved in music-drama. But Liszt hardly even began to achieve the right sort of movement; and his conscientious plan of deriving the whole piece from transformations of a single figure was quite irrelevant even when it was effective. As a musical illustrator he is clever; but he ties himself down to chronological sequence, which, though it does not conflict with his forms, is always open to Weingartner's objection that it cannot control the pace of the listener's thoughts. The composer's first view-halloo may make one listener fancy himself in at the death of the Blatant Beast, while the mind of another will plod to the end, to learn that that event never takes place.

Strauss.—The symphonic poems of Strauss are invulnerable by this objection, even though it is often true of their details. Most listeners will probably identify Don Quixote's tilting at windmills with the passage in which Strauss uses a stage wind-machine; but this represents a later adventure in which Don Quixote and Sancho are seated blindfold on wooden horses and are persuaded that they are flying on winged steeds through the air. Strauss's music, however, does not really depend on this sort of thing at all. His earliest symphonic poems are master-pieces of new form and movement: *Don Quixote* is sectional only because its subject lends itself to an episodic treatment which Strauss has as much right as Humpty Dumpty to call variations; and in it, no less than in *Also sprach Zarathustra, Ein Heldenleben,* the *Sinfonia Domestica,* and their aftermath the *Alpensinfonie,* single designs are triumphantly accomplished in music of Wagnerian continuity. It is not necessary that the designs should be perfect. Uncles and aunts may interrupt to say that the baby is the image of its dada or mamma; and the wickedness of critics may devastate pages of the music of the hero who gave them their opportunity when he paused on a dominant chord to look round for applause; but local defects do not annihilate fundamental qualities.

Caricature.—One thread remains to be gathered into this account. Caricature is a rare and dangerous element in music, but it is as old as Orlandi di Lasso. Mozart, besides the subtleties of *Cosi fan tutte* and the comic parts of *Die Zauberflöte,* produced in his *Musikalischer Spass* a burlesque of village players and bad composers. On paper the work is a delicious study in the psychology of 'howlers', and in its finale Mozart idealizes all the nightmare stagnation of the composer whose tempo gets faster and faster while his phrasing gets slower and slower. In performance the effect is even more surprising than analysis would lead the reader to expect. But the Leipzig editors of the parts have crowned Mozart's farce by correcting the mistakes!

Caricature enters prominently into Strauss's *Till Eulenspiegel, Don Quixote,* and *Ein Heldenleben*; and also into many passages in Mahler's symphonies. Its danger is that it often lays these composers open to suspicion when they intend to be touchingly simple.

But nothing is more vexatious than the laying down of *a priori* limits to what is legitimate for artists. If sermons in the mind of the painter help him to paint, and pictures in the mind of the composer help him to compose, by all means let them get on with the work.

RHYTHM

LIKE all artistic categories musical rhythm must be studied historically, in order to avoid Philistinism towards the rhythms of early periods. But the musical rhythms of the eighteenth and nineteenth centuries are so much more familiar to us than any others, and so radically different from speech-rhythms, that we shall do well to analyse them first. Their true relation to speech-rhythms will then become much clearer, and the study of older rhythms will be greatly simplified.

Body-rhythm and Speech-rhythm.—These are two prehistoric elements in musical rhythm; and in modern music they are in equipoise, though apart from music they are incompatible. Dance-rhythm is too narrow a term for the one, and speech-rhythm is a satisfactory term for the other. We may coin the term body-rhythm as giving the necessary extension to the notion of dance-rhythm. Musical body-rhythm, even in the slowest paces, is enormously stronger than anything known to prosody. It is no exaggeration to say that it is as strong as the pace of a horse. Not even Browning could have recited 'How they brought the good news from Ghent to Aix' with comfort while riding a galloping horse; but Schubert's Characteristic Marches (op. 121) do not merely imitate that pace but go far to stimulate it if played to a body of cavalry. Gentler rhythms may be less immediately understood, but, once grasped, are not more easily changed. The music must brace itself up for any abrupt change of its fundamental rhythm. But that fundamental rhythm may be very slow and lie very deep.

In Ex. 1, below, Haydn uses an underlying rhythm of thrice two beats. The beat is a quaver, for which one second is not

Ex.1

too slow a tempo for this particular composition. Its whole group
of six beats is invariably 3÷2 and never 2÷3. In this kind of
music change from the one division to the other would be impossible without either violence or vagueness; unless it were a
permanent change of metre. So important is the notion of 3÷2
that it is not counted as 6 at all, but as 1 & 2 & 3 &. Of these
beats the first bears the chief stress, the second and third bear
less, and there is no rule to give either more stress than the
other. We are not, at present, considering the case of three beats
quick enough to mark the rhythm without subdivision. Obviously
the subdivisions (counted by '&') have no accent, except in
relation to their own further subdivisions. Musical rhythms are
measured from accent to accent; and of pairs of accents the first
is stronger than the second. In larger groups, if the rhythm is
binary, the third accent will be stronger than the second, but not
as strong as the first or fifth. At a very quick pace the difference
of strength between the first accent and the fifth may become
perceptible, but the rhythm would be inartistically stiff if such
distinctions were not soon obliterated.

Triple rhythm, whether slow and subdivided or quick and
undivided, also falls readily into larger binary periods with the
same relative strengths of accent. There is nothing to prevent it
from falling into ternary periods, but the mind ceases to apprehend a high power of three rhythmically, for we cannot know that
the third period of a slow group is not the first of a new pair.

On these data it is now possible to analyse the rhythm of Ex. 1.
It begins on the main accent, with no anacrusis. Between the
first and second quaver beats there is a group of grace-notes. In
actual time these should come on the second quaver and reduce
the length of the second main note instead of that of the first, but
they have no accent, and the second main note has its due stress
and is not noticed to have arrived late, even if the grace-notes
have been taken with some deliberation. They are like the consonants in the word 'three': it is easy to pronounce the word at a
given moment, and nobody thinks of dividing it as thr-ee, though
the consonants really take an appreciable time.

During the second bar of six beats the accompaniment (not
given here) takes its cue from the melody and divides the quaver-
beats by 3 (and the crotchets by 6). This motion thereafter pervades the whole composition, sometimes in the melody, and
always in the accompaniment, except when the whole orchestra
pauses. These triplet semiquavers become equivalent to the
average length of syllables in speech-rhythm, and the mind automatically measures all pauses by them. Besides the indeterminate
grace-notes there are definite shorter values.

No rhythm in poetry or prose ever contemplated giving one

syllable seven times the length of another, as we see in the double-dotted quavers with their complementary demisemiquavers. But in the fifth bar we have the whole six beats occupied by one sustained note, eighteen times the length of the average syllable. Yet so cogent is the body-rhythm of these long and complex bars that a deviation from the symmetry of an eight-bar period is permissible only when a change of key introduces new topics, as happens immediately after this quotation. But this will lead us to the separate topic of phrasing. Irregularities in the lengths of the bars themselves would be quite impossible, except in the case of a dramatic or final pause. Haydn has one opportunity for a dramatic pause in the course of the movement, yet he does not leave it at that, but expands it to two entire normal bars filled with organized rhythms.

Musical rhythm is not often as ornate as this, nor is this elaboration capable of much contrast or development, but the example at once carries us far away from the rhythms of poetry and includes all the musical principles so far mentioned. From it we can move a step nearer towards considering the simple relations between musical and poetic rhythm.

The technical terms of prosody are of no use here, with the solitary exception of the word anacrusis, which may be generalized to mean anything that happens before the first principal accent. When Rockstro tells us that 'the theme of Weber's Rondo brillante in E flat (op. 62) is in anapaestic tetrameter brachycatalectic, very rigidly maintained', this tells us less about the music than Weber's brilliant theme tells us about these solemn terms. A more scientific idea of Weber's theme, and of the prosodic technicalities, may be obtained from the following paradigm, to be recited prestissimo. Each dash at the end of the line represents a quarter of a beat.

Prestissimo

```
Diddle|dum diddledum diddledum diddledum diddle|dum diddledum diddledum:— —
      |1      &      2      &              |1      &      2      &
```

```
Diddle|dum diddledum diddledum  diddledum diddle|dum diddledum diddledum:— —
      |1      &      2      &                |1      &      2      &
```

After which Weber ceases to maintain his anapaestic-etcetera so rigidly, and proceeds for two lines with:

```
Diddle |diddle diddle diddle diddle diddle diddle dum dum |dum dum dum dum Dido
       |1      &      2      &                     |1      &      2
```

Such rapid rhythms at once remind us of Aristophanes or Gilbert, though they can move faster than syllables can be pronounced. If they coalesce into uniformity for a long period (e.g., *diddle-diddle* for several bars without a single *dum*) they cease to resemble speech-rhythm and subside into vibration, unless melodic interest sets up larger rhythms by illuminating a peak here and there. A common defect in second-rate music is the composer's failure to know when his quick motion has settled down into mere vibration.

Time.—The body-rhythm underlying Weber's Rondo brillante is an unchangeable binary rhythm, counted (as the paradigm shows) in a slow two or a quick four. Classical music uses only binary and ternary times, which, so long as vertebrate anatomy continues to develop with bilateral symmetry, are the only ones that yield a strong body-rhythm naturally, the elements of triple time giving just enough resistance to be overcome by a pleasant compromise.

The kinds of time, i.e., of invariable rhythmic molecules underlying each continuous piece of music, are classed not only as duple and triple but also as simple and compound. Compound time is the result of dividing simple time by three. Division by two is ignored: thus the evidently highly compound time of Ex. 1 is reckoned as simple triple time. All beats are reckoned as binary divisions and subdivisions of the modern standard note, the semibreve: the time-signature given at the beginning of a composition is a fraction, with a numerator showing the number of beats in a bar, and a denominator showing the size of the beat. Thus $\frac{3}{4}$ signifies three crotchets (quarters) in a bar. Compound time does not indicate the main beats at all, but counts the smaller beats as normal fractions of the semibreve. The main beats are written as dotted notes, in which the dot lengthens the note by one half. Accordingly $\frac{6}{8}$ is the compound time of two dotted crotchets divided by three quavers; $\frac{9}{8}$ is that of three dotted crotchets: $\frac{12}{8}$ of four. When the division by three is only local, triplets are used. Triplets are groups of three equal notes crowded into the time of two.

Binary and ternary subdivision answers every ordinary purpose of musical rhythm, being capable of expressing distinctions far more subtle than have ever been regulated in speech. It is impossible to pronounce a syllable in less than a tenth of a second; but it is easy to play sixteen notes in a second on the pianoforte. In such rapid notes a single break twice in a second would have an effect directly measured by the ear. If the broken series were levelled into an even series of fourteen notes a second, the rhythmic effect would be appreciably different, though the actual difference of pace would be only $\frac{1}{56}$ of a second.

The special sign for triplets is readily adapted to other subdivisions. In most cases such adaptation is not meant to produce abstruse rhythms, but to secure an effect of free declamation. Freedom is as necessary in music as it is in speech; but fine playing, whether in obvious tempo rubato or in apparent strictness, bases this freedom on the superlative accuracy of good rhythmic notation.

Tempo.—The time-signature tells us nothing about the pace of the music, for the choice of the denominator is determined by a tangle of historic associations, so that $\frac{3}{8}$ may mean (as in Beethoven's C minor Concerto) the slowest movement ever written, and $\frac{3}{4}$ may be a scherzo-tempo in which only one beat in a bar is countable.

The sense of tempo is a larger aspect of the body-rhythm, and in classical music it is very steady. A fundamental law of all musical rhythm is that a hurrying or slackening of tempo has no power to alter the rhythmic organization. If your phrase is too short a ritardando will not make it aesthetically any the longer; nor will an accelerando get rid of a redundant bar. On the contrary, it is crowded detail that will best profit by slackening, and loose-knit passages that have most to gain by an unobtrusive mending of the pace.

The genuine tempo rubato is, as its name implies, a rhythmic robbing of Peter to pay Paul. Chopin said that his left hand conducted in strict time while his right declaimed freely. The truth is that sound is as full of illusions as sight. One such illusion has already been illustrated by the grace-notes of Ex. 1, and other illusions are of much the same kind. The tick of the metronome measures average time-intervals; and if it is set to measure a naturally rhythmic performance it will seem to hustle the player in some passages and to drag upon him in others, however carefully we select its pace.

In the classics from Bach to Brahms a movement may give more legitimate scope for tempo rubato than some purists care to admit, but it will not drift from one tempo to a radically different tempo, unless towards the end, or as evidence of imminent break-up. The gradual drift from one tempo to another first becomes something better than a weakness when the whole nature of musical movement becomes capable of continuity over hours, as in Wagnerian opera. Then, and not before, can we view one and the same tempo from opposite directions. Thus, in *Tristan und Isolde* the last part of the love-duet in the second act is a quick movement in $\frac{2}{2}$ time. Isolde's *Liebestod* ends the opera with an exact recapitulation of this (differing only in the voice part and absolutely unaltered in the orchestra) in rather slow $\frac{4}{4}$ time. By metronome the two tempi should be identical, though the impulse in the duet is energetic and that of the *Liebestod*

reposeful. Wagner merely feels that the broader notation better
suits Isolde's dying vision; and the listener, who may know and
care nothing about the notation, agrees with Wagner. It is partly
a question of accent and comes under the heading of phrasing.

The Rhythm of Classical Music in Relation to Poetry.—We
can now return, furnished with new criteria, to the relation
between musical and poetic rhythm. Even a simple musical setting of poetry will stretch the words in ways which speech does
not normally admit. The naïve poet will unhesitatingly accept
this as in the nature of singing. Only the half-baked musical *lit-
térateur* objects, when Mozart makes Ottavio sing *Dalla sua pace
la mia dipende* (Ex. 2) five times as slowly as any speaker could
naturally utter the words, and then puts the top note and chief
accent on the unimportant *la*. The poet would be glad to sing it
that way if he could. It is quite good Italian prosody to give
a nearly equal stress to *la* and *mia*: and the climax on *la* is more
than counterbalanced by the fact that the important word *mia*
falls on a harmonically sensitive note. The grammatical sense
might have been clearer if a similar but slighter emphasis had
been given to *sua*. But Ottavio is not giving instructions to a
servant, but expressing his inmost feelings in solitude. Language
does not base its emotional accents on logical analysis. Dr. Johnson corrected a clergyman for saying 'Thou *shalt* not steal'
instead of 'Thou shalt *not* steal'. If Johnson was right, how in
the world did 'shall not' ever become 'shan't'?

Ex. 2

The sensitive note on *mia* shows one of the four main degrees
of freedom in musical accent. There is first the normal time-
accent. Many critics of musical declamation seem to know no
other forms of stress; but it can be completely eclipsed by putting the highest note of the melody elsewhere. The highest note
can in its turn be eclipsed by the longest note. And in Ex. 2,
both together are eclipsed by the most sensitive note. Moreover,
and without recourse to anything so drastic as syncopation, the
weakest note in the phrase may be given a special accent stronger
than a main beat. This is beautifully shown in the third bar of
Ex. 1, where the accented E♭, normally quite the weakest note
in the bar, could certainly bear the chief syllable in a sentence if
words for Haydn's wonderful rhythm could be found at all.
Lastly, such a displaced accent may have a double meaning, the
note retaining its original lightness in spite of its borrowed stress.

Weber has been blamed for his bad declamation in the following
famous passage:

Ex. 8   WEBER, *Der Freischütz*, Act III

Trübe Au - gen, Liebchen, tau - gen, ein - em   hol - den Bräutchen nicht

But, by your leave, this is a triumph of musical gesture. The
lively Aennchen might even point a playful finger at the anxious
Agathe with each false accent that Weber so explicitly marks.
Meanwhile the orchestra corrects the declamation in waltz-
rhythm.

By the interplay of these varieties of accent the strophic song,
with the same tune to several stanzas, condemned as lazy and
low by our prose critics of music, becomes, as Brahms always
maintained, the highest achievement of a song-writer. The interplay does not annihilate right and wrong in declamation, nor does
it prove that the classics are infallible; but it forms a musical
technique as disciplined as prosody and as unlike prose. In such
ways artistic factors reconcile their conflicts, and without such
conflicts there is neither art nor life. Wagner and Wolf are perfect masters of a musical declamation that follows the rules of
prose; but when we are told that there are no other rules, and
that the classics from Bach to Brahms merely blundered insensi-
tively, it is time to point out that musical rhythm cannot be learnt
from a bell-metronome nor poetry from a pronouncing dictionary.

Let us now try a few experiments in setting blank verse to
music. The first step will be to find a constant musical rhythm
to represent the average line. This average rhythm will horrify
the poetic ear if it is put forward as a specimen of blank verse,
and probably if a line could be found that fitted it exactly, that
line would be a very ugly one. Still, the fact remains that the
musician's average idea of blank verse is accurately represented
by the following scheme, which represents two lines:

Ex. 8a

etc.

Now read the first paragraph of *Paradise Lost* rigidly to this
scheme at the rate of two syllables to a metronome-beat of 80
to the minute. You will not satisfy the poet's ear; but you will
find that the lines accommodate themselves better to this than
to any other uniformity; that extra syllables can be managed by

grace-notes, and that the interval of two quavers between each line is a natural part of the scheme. We can proceed thus for eight lines, with rheumatic pains but not complete disaster. The imperative 'Sing' is a heavy word to put into anacrusis, even of double length, and our three main beats must override many accents in lines that so often have four. Also the interlinear pause of two beats is irksome when the sense runs on. In the ninth line we must alter the scheme, for no anacrusis can digest any part of 'In the beginning'. So we must 'invert' the first foot thus:

Ex. 3b

In   the be - gin - ning, how   the Heav'ns and Earth

But before we condemn the scheme let us see how far the torture is mitigated by merely adding musical rise and fall:

Ex. 4

Blank verse has been worse recited than this. The rigid musical timing proves unexpectedly flexible already; and the rubato of a good singer can go far to improve it without becoming vulgar.

Now let us legalize the singer's rubato, and, without altering the two-quaver intervals between the lines, help the *enjambement*

by a pianoforte accompaniment that makes the ear expect the
resolution of a discord. Sensitive harmonies will further aid the
rhythmic sense. The ³⁄₂ notation is now becoming troublesome;
so that bars are divided into three and the lengths of the notes
doubled. But the original ³⁄₂ scheme is nowhere violated.

After this point any attempt to continue this literal interpretation of the metre would make the music drag hopelessly. Already
the first two lines would be the better for running over the pause
and doubling the pace of 'that forbidden tree'. But this would
mean using two time-scales and would take us into free composition. The object of this illustration is not to show how these
words ought to be set, nor to prove the very doubtful proposition
that they are singable to any kind of music; but simply to bring
out the most elementary relations between music and verse.

Phrasing.—The higher art of phrasing is chiefly observable in
groups of very much simpler bars than those of our illustrations
so far. Two facts, often ignored, must be realized before we
can understand phrasing at all. First, music, being in time and
not in space, is never apprehended in a *coup d'œil*, but always in
a momentary present connecting a remembered past with an
imperfectly anticipated future. Consequently we miss half the
aesthetic values of rhythm if we insist on knowing all about it

Ex. 5

from the first note. Rhythms have as much right to change their meaning while we listen to them as the cats of Wonderland have to grin; and 'they all can and most of them do'.

The second point is that the bar represents no fundamental rhythmic fact. It did not come into existence so long as music was printed only in parts. When music began to be printed with all the parts ranged legibly on one page, it was necessary to score the pile of parts with vertical strokes to range them in partitions and guide the eye. Hence the word *score*, and the French *partition* and German *Partitur*. The nascent body-rhythm grew stronger and gradually made it convenient that the bars should coincide with the groups indicated by the time-signature, and this gave rise (but only in recent times) to the delusion that the bar was the permanent unit. It is often obviously not so. When Mozart writes in moderate common time his phrasing is sure to make an odd number of half-bars somewhere so that a theme that originally lay on 1, 2, 3, 4 now lies on 3, 4, 1, 2. In such a case it is pedantic to say that the accent has changed and still more pedantic to blame Mozart for not either taking shorter bars throughout or changing to them according to the rhythm. If the half-bar displacement is really awkward Mozart will put it right, as when he rebarred the duet 'Bei Männern welche Liebe fühlen' in *Die Zauberflöte*. But long bars imply delicate accents and these accents become no harder when the phrasing contracts.

Beethoven writes his scherzos, and some very powerful other movements, in the shortest possible bars, and it is often difficult to tell whether the first of such bars is a main accent or an anacrusis. In the first movement of the C minor Sonata (op. 10, no. 1), when we reach bar 22 it becomes manifest that bar 9 must have been an anacrusis; but we cannot have noticed that at the time, for when theorists go back to bar 1 and say that that initial bump was an anacrusis we can only smile. In three late works Beethoven helps the players by the words *Ritmo di tre battute* and *Ritmo di quattro battute*. The most famous of these passages is in the scherzo of the Ninth Symphony. Why did Beethoven not use there $\frac{6}{4}$ or $\frac{12}{4}$ bars so that his *ritmo di tre battute* became self-evident as a change to $\frac{9}{4}$? Because if you wish to ride this Pegasus you must please to rise on your stirrups once in Beethoven's bar, and not only once in three or four. The change to three-bar rhythm is obvious enough; but the return to four-bar is not, as Grove said, effected by the drums, but comes where nobody can possibly detect it. And Beethoven, having helped the conductor at this point, is quite content, as in earlier works *passim*, that the listeners should gradually become aware that the three-bar swing is no longer in being. In the trio, Beethoven wishing to indicate that two of its crotchets correspond to three of the scherzo, first wrote in $\frac{2}{4}$ time. But this made the lilt as unrecognizable as the true proportions of Iceland at the top of a map on Mercator's projection. So he changed it to alla breve bars $\frac{2}{2}$.

The common sense of the whole matter is that hard accents and soft accents are equally liable in the long run to obliterate the distinction between the first and the third of four beats, and may go far to weaken that between the first and the second. We shall never find that Beethoven's short bars will fit any one interpretation throughout a piece, nor shall we often be able to fix the point at which the rhythmic angle is shifted. And when we have fixed everything some overlap will upset us or some extra bar make us hold our breath. Four-bar rhythm is more important to music than limericks are to literature, but the limerick is hardly more adequate or historically qualified to be taken as the fundamental basis for rhythm. And we must not take a lofty timeless view of rhythmic inequalities and changes. Farmer Giles is mistaken in the idea that the lady he finds sketching in the woods where you cannot see round the corner would find a better subject on the top of a hill where you can see six counties.

Older Musical Rhythms.—In measuring the distance between the musical rhythms, the most familiar to us and those of the sixteenth and earlier centuries, the first thing we must dismiss is our strong body-rhythms. Only the lightest ballets and fa-las of our great madrigalists have any such element. The greater part of the sixteenth-century polyphony is held together by a time-system which merely counts semibreves and settles whether the semibreve is to be perfect and equal to three minims or imperfect and equal to two, and also whether three or only two semibreves are to go to a breve. The law of accent holds with pairs of minims about as strongly as in modern music, but it is already very much weakened with pairs of semibreves. Examine the first two lines of Palestrina's *Stabat Mater*, which is as wonderful in rhythm as it is in harmony.

Ex. 6

Sta-bat Ma-ter do - lo - ro - sa   Jux - ta cru-cem la - cry - mo - sa

The music of the second line is identical with that of the first, and both lines are an exact quantitative rendering of the verses, with longs twice the size of shorts. The time signature tells us that the breve contains two semibreves and the semibreve two minims. Accordingly the modern editor draws bar-strokes at regular breve-distances throughout the score. Then comes the modern choirmaster, warm from a rehearsal of 'Be not afraid' in *Elijah*, and beats four in a bar, down, left, right, up, while the dutiful double choir sings:

Sta-bat	Ma-ter do	(sniff) lo ro	Sa jux
1 2 3 4	12 3 4	1 2 34	12 3 4

Ta cru	Cem la (sniff) cry	Mo sa
12 34	1 2 3 4	12 34

But now let each singer, at a starting signal from the conductor, merely move one finger regularly up and down in minims, downwards for accented beats and upwards for unaccented. It will then be found perfectly easy to override these gentle accents whenever the sense dictates, and the choir will find itself declaiming the words beautifully.

Ex. 6a

If bars must be drawn let them come only where there is a normal accent. We must not put a bar-line after *mater*, because this would come in the middle of a semibreve, or, as Morley calls it, a stroke. The examples of Victoria and Josquin given in the articles MASS, MOTET, and MUSIC are barred freely by these rules, but no such single scoring is adequate for an elaborate polyphony. Ex. 7 gives a passage from Victoria's *O quam gloriosum* in full score barred so as to display what cannot be shown in the short score given with MOTET.

From this we can see Victoria's Miltonic art of finishing a big paragraph. The lower voices enjoy their own rhythms until the slow swing of the soprano draws the bass along with it. Then the alto joins, and the tenor is compelled to regard his own rhythm as a syncopation against this majority.

Little has been said so far about syncopation, and little now remains to be said. Its main point, even in the sixteenth century, as Ex. 7 shows, is that it requires a strong body-rhythm to contradict. A common fallacy of self-centred composers is to write syncopations that never encounter opposition at all. We must not confuse this with the legitimate case of a rhythm the meaning of which first appears later in the course of the music, nor with the case of an intentional vagueness. Nor, to return to the sixteenth century, must we put the unanimous speech-rhythm syncopations of Ex. 6 into the same category as those of the tenor at the end of Ex. 7.

Ex. 7   VICTORIA, *O quam gloriosum*

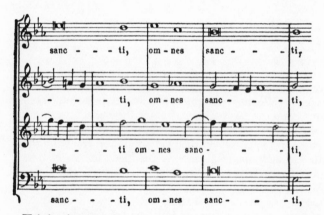

Triple time in the sixteenth century was very different from what it is in music with a strong body-rhythm. For one thing, it continually obliterates the difference between 2÷3 and 3÷2, as in Example 8 by Lasso.

Ex. 8

2nd Choir

This swing from 3 to a 3 twice as slow is called *hemiole* and survives as late as Bach and Handel. Thus, in the first chorus of the *Messiah* the hemiole which Handel always uses in triple-time closes gives the cadential accentuation:

Ex. 8a

the |Lord shall be re - veal - | ed

The opposite swing from $\frac{3}{2}$ to $\frac{6}{4}$ with a curious bump in the last ($\frac{6}{4}$) bar, characterizes the French courantes of Couperin and Bach.

Before Palestrina we find in England a fairly steady slow triple time (3 divided by 2 or 4) in Tallis; but a little earlier we find Obrecht writing music which abounded in amazing complexities, such as three depths of triple rhythm:

Ex. 8b

$\frac{3}{4}$ ♩ ♩ | ♩ ♩ over $\frac{3}{2}$ ○ ♩ | ○ ♩ and again over $\frac{9}{1}$ |○| ○ | |○| ○ |

The complexity is illusory, for the ear makes nothing of it, and the same is the case with the capacity of the ancient time-system of mode, time, and prolation to multiply triple rhythms up to twenty-seven beats. The fact that the process was by multiplication shows at once that no real rhythmic effects are concerned, and that the system is only a device by which the long-suffering tenors may count out the enormous notes of some unrecognizable canto fermo. If we want genuine highly compound times we must leave these multiplication tables and study the last movement of Beethoven's Sonata, op. 111, where the theme and first variation are in triple time divided by 3 ($\frac{9}{16}$); the second variation divides the half-beat by 3, producing $\frac{18}{32}$ (which Beethoven misnames $\frac{6}{16}$); the third variation divides the quarter-beats, producing $\frac{36}{64}$ (misnamed $\frac{12}{32}$); and the fourth variation returns to $\frac{9}{16}$ time and divides it by a uniform triplet vibration of twenty-seven notes to a bar, afterwards surmounted by the unmeasured vibration of a trill. All this is sublime in its cogent clearness.

Genuine complexity was achieved by Palestrina in the second Kyrie of his Mass '*L'homme armé*', a work as beautiful as it is ingenious. But Mozart achieved something unsurpassed in the ballroom scene in *Don Giovanni*, putting his vigorous body-rhythms to the supreme test of making the characters actually dance and pass remarks in them. (See Ex. 9, overleaf.)

Recent Rhythmic Developments.—Rhythms other than binary and ternary cannot develop a very strong ictus, though Holst manages in the ballet of *The Perfect Fool* to make some good

Ex. 9   MOZART, *Don Giovanni*

dance-rhythms of ⅞. But they tend to flow like speech-rhythms,
and they are very reluctant to change their pattern. A rhythm
of 5 falls into either 3+2 or 2+3. The famous 5-time movement in Tchaikovsky's 'Pathetic' Symphony is 2+3 and is in
absolutely square eight-bar rhythm throughout. Again 7-time
will be some form of 4 and 3, or will suggest 8 with a beat
clipped. Ravel in his Pianoforte Trio, showed that it is possible
to divide 8 into 3+2+3 so inveterately that no listener can possibly hear it as 4+4. The effect is excellent, and other versions
of it are used in a much quicker tempo and with more variety by
Holst in his *Fugal Overture*. But we must call things by their
right names and not say that a thing is complex when it clings
like grim death to its one pattern and falls into phrases of 2+2.
for pages together. The *Pantoum* of Ravel's Trio blends an
impish ¾ with a sanctimonious 4/4 very amusingly. An early pianoforte sonata by Cyril Scott attempts to get away from all regu-

larities. Its thirteens and threes do not always succeed in avoiding straightening out into plain $16 = 4 \times 4$; and when successful are conscientious rather than impulsive. The rhythms of Greek tragedy, interpreted syllabically, are suggestive, and so are many oriental rhythms. But they are not body-rhythms; and it may be doubted whether any great increase in variety of strong body-rhythms is imminent at present.

RONDO

RONDO, a musical form originally derived from the rondel in verse; as may be seen, long before the development of instrumental forms, in some of the *chansons* of Orlando di Lasso. The *rondeau en couplets* of Couperin and his contemporaries shows the same connexion with verse. It consists of a single neatly rounded phrase alternating with several episodes (the *couplets*) without any important change of key. Ex. 1 shows Bach's handling of this early form. The later rondo is an important member of the sonata forms (q.v.), chiefly found in finales; but rondo form sometimes occurs in slow movements. Ex. 2 is not more elaborate than the Adagio of Beethoven's Fourth Symphony. Philipp Emanuel Bach invented an extraordinary kind of rondo, not part of a sonata, but on a voluminous scale with wildly incoherent episodes and modulations. (See pp. 194-9.)

The later sonata-style rondo forms may be divided into two main classes:

1. *Sectional rondo*, i.e. with little or no development or transition between the episodes and the main theme; very characteristic of Haydn, who, however, may run away with it in unexpected developments. The name rondo implies at least two episodes, and a sectional rondo may have more. Beethoven in his early works shows the influence of Haydn in this type of rondo; e.g. the finales of Sonatas, opp. 10, no. 3, and 14, nos. 1 and 2; and the slow movements of the Sonatas, opp. 2, no. 2, and 13 (*Pathétique*). The sectional rondo last appears on a gigantic scale in the finale of Brahms's G minor Pianoforte Quartet, op. 25; and it lends itself, like the cognate idea of a dance with several 'trios', to Schumann's pianoforte pieces and to some of his finales.

2. *Rondos influenced by the form of a first movement* (for which *see* SONATA FORMS). In the normal scheme for this, which is Mozart's favourite rondo form, the rondo-theme (which may contain several clauses) is followed by a well-organized transition to the key of the first episode, which key is chosen as if for the 'complementary key' of a first movement. The return to the rondo-theme may be elaborate or abrupt, and the theme itself may be reduced to its first complete clause (but not to a mere fragment, without loss of the rondo effect). The second episode will be in a new key and may be followed by wide modulations, or itself be widely modulatory, or it may even be entirely a development of the previous material, as in the rondo of Beethoven's Sonata, op. 90, given on p. 196. When the rondo-theme

returns again it is followed by a recapitulation of the first episode (perhaps preceded by the transitional passage suitably modified) in the tonic; after which the coda may contain a final return of the rondo-theme. When the second episode is concentrated on development the only difference between the rondo and a first movement is the slender fact that the whole first theme returns immediately after the first episode. Yet the rondo style can be recognized from the outset by the tunelike character of the main theme, and also by the fact that, unlike the most tuneful openings of first movements, it comes to a definite close instead of swinging continuously into the transition passage. A rondo with a development in its middle episode may return to the tonic with an immediate recapitulation of the first episode, omitting the expected second return of the main theme, thus: A, B (new key), A, C (development), B (tonic), A, Coda (where A is the rondo-theme and B and C the episodes). Mozart, Schubert, and Brahms have a form, always worked on a very large scale, which consists only of A, B (new key), A, B (tonic), Coda; where a certain amount of development is edged in apropos of the transition-passage on its recapitulation. Only the style of the main theme can distinguish this from a first movement that omits its normal development-section.

In the rondos of classical concertos (q.v.) the orchestra (especially in Mozart) finds its opportunity in a series of accessory themes announced as soon as the solo instrument has given out the rondo-theme. These accessories are then held in reserve for the coda.

Two examples of rondo forms are given on the following pages.

Ex.1   *Gavotte en Rondeau* (Rondeau en Couplets) from Bach's Sixth Violin Solo

Couplet III

Dal 𝄋 e poi

Couplet IV

Dal 𝄋 e Fine

Ex.2 Outline of Sonata-form Rondo with developing middle episode.

and indicate prevalent movement of accompaniment. Blank bars indicate prevalence of the same chord.

Nicht zu geschwind und sehr singbar vorzutragen

SCHERZO

SCHERZO (Italian for 'a joke'); a quick movement evolved from the minuet and used in the position thereof in the sonata forms (q.v.). The term is also used as a mere character name. Haydn first used it, and its adverb scherzando, for the middle movement of an early sonata in C sharp minor, and afterwards in place of the minuet in the set of six quartets known sometimes as 'Gli Scherzi', and sometimes as the 'Russian Quartets' (op. 33). He never used the term again, though his later minuets are often in a very rapid tempo and sometimes on a larger scale than any of the earlier scherzos of Beethoven. Haydn wished to see the minuet made more worthy of its position in large sonata works; but he did not live to appreciate (though he might possibly have heard) the fully-developed scherzos of his pupil, Beethoven.

The formal essence of the minuet and trio lies in their combination of melodic forms with an exact da capo of the minuet after the trio. No other movement in the sonata has leisure for so purely decorative a symmetry. Beethoven's typical scherzos purposely exaggerate this quality. He does not follow Mozart's example of minuets with two trios, for the style of his mature scherzos is so continuous that a second trio would give it an elaborate rondo character unlike that of a dance-movement. But after Beethoven's scherzo has run through the stages of scherzo, trio, and scherzo da capo, it goes through the same trio and da capo again; and then tries to do so a third time, as if it could not find a way out, so that it has to be abruptly stopped. Modern players and listeners are impatient of these grotesque repetitions; but the art-form is true to its own nature, and we should be the better for leisure to understand it. Apart from the wonderful little A flat *Bagatelle*—No. 7 of the set written at the age of 15 and published (presumably with extensive revision) as op. 33— Beethoven first used the double repetition in his Fourth Symphony (with a shortening of the last da capo); and his last example is in the C sharp minor Quartet (op. 131). An outline of the Scherzo of Beethoven's Seventh Symphony is given on pp. 202–6.

The scherzo of the Ninth Symphony is so enormous that its main body differs from a complete first movement of a sonata only in its uniformity of texture and its incessant onrush, which not even the startling measured pauses and the changes from four-bar to three-bar rhythm can really interrupt. Beethoven directs as many repetitions of its subsections as possible, and his coda consists of an attempt to begin the trio again, dramatically cut short. The scherzo of the C minor Symphony was originally meant to go twice round; and a certain pair of superfluous bars, which caused controversy for thirty years after Beethoven's death, were due simply to traces of the difference between the *prima volta* and *seconda volta* being left in the score.

Beethoven does not use the title of scherzo unless the music is humorous. Thus in the Sonata in E flat (op. 31, no. 3) it is applied to a lively sonata-form movement which is technically the slow movement, while the following slow minuet is the dance-movement. The second movement of the F major Quartet (op. 59, no. 1) is a unique example of scherzo style in a most elaborate sonata form.

Perhaps this gigantic movement may have been the inspiring source of the Mendelssohnian scherzo, one of the most distinct new types of movement since Beethoven, and quite independent of the notion of an alternating trio. The scherzos in Mendelssohn's *Midsummer Night's Dream* music, in the 'Scotch' Symphony, and in the String Quartets in E minor and E flat major (op. 44, nos. 2 and 3) are splendid examples. Even Berlioz shows their influence in the 'Queen Mab' Scherzo of his *Roméo et Juliette*.

Of Brahms's scherzos there are several distinct types, ranging from a quiet allegretto and trio in melodic forms to the sonata-form *Presto giocoso* of the Fourth Symphony, which within seven minutes accomplishes the most powerful scherzo since Beethoven. Every degree of lyric beauty and dramatic passion is comprised in the various movements that Brahms puts into the position of scherzo in his sonata works.

Chopin produced a new type of independent scherzo; obviously inspired by Beethoven, but with a slightly macabre tendency of his own, except in the very diffuse and light Fourth Scherzo. The majority of classical scherzos are in a quick triple time with only one countable beat to a bar; and this custom is the last vestige of the derivation of the scherzo from the minuet.

Of modern scherzos there is nothing specific to be said; the term still applies to lively intermediate movements in cyclic instrumental works, and is otherwise a mere character-name.

Outline of SCHERZO of Beethoven's Seventh Symphony

(The phrasing given here is the most natural; but any phrasing whatever will prove that the themes change their accents in the course of the movement.)

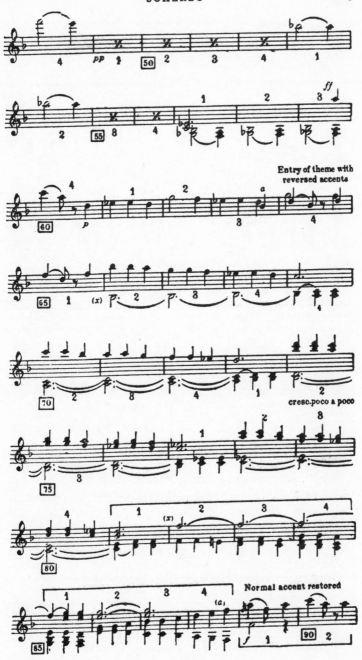

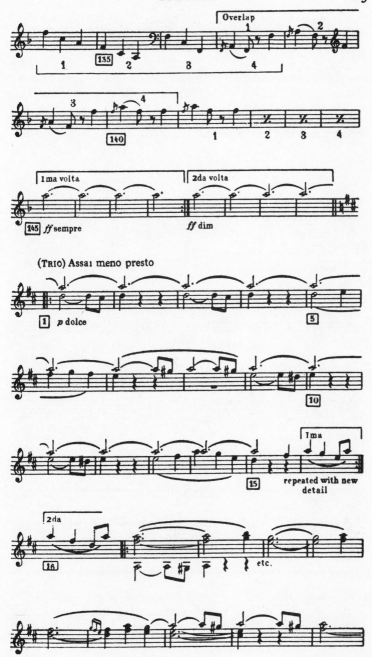

Scherzo Da Capo.
The first part (bars 1-24)
repeated *pp*, and the *pp* maintained till the *cresc.* at bar 74. Trio Da Capo also: then Scherzo Da Capo again leading once more to trio, which is cut short in the following Coda.

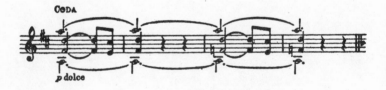

SONATA

SONATA, originally a piece 'played', as opposed to 'cantata', a piece 'sung'. By the time of Corelli the term had come to mean a group of instrumental movements. (A movement is a piece of music forming, or starting as if to form, a complete musical design.) The sonatas of Corelli are classified as *sonata da chiesa* (Church sonata) and *sonata da camera* (chamber sonata). Both kinds were usually for one or two violins with continuo bass (*see* CHAMBER MUSIC and INSTRUMENTATION). Handel, when a boy, wrote six for two oboes, and in later years several for flute, and also for one oboe.

The *sonata da chiesa* consists typically of a slow introduction, a loosely fugal allegro, a cantabile slow movement, and a lively finale in melodic 'binary' form (*see* SONATA FORMS). The *sonata da camera* consists mainly of dance-tunes (*see* SUITE). Bach, who uses neither title, keeps the two kinds unmixed in his six sonatas for violin alone, the first, third, and fifth being *sonate da chiesa* and the others *partitas*. A fusion of the two styles persisted in Italian violin music almost to the end of the eighteenth century.

The sonatas of Domenico Scarlatti are small harpsichord pieces of which the best known are extremely brilliant single movements in binary form. The complete collection of five hundred and forty-five, published by Longo, shows that Scarlatti experimented audaciously in remote modulations; that he also wrote some orthodox violin sonatas; and that he sometimes followed a lively movement by a slow cantabile, as Paradies did in his sonatas. Clementi's early sonatas are at their best when they resemble a sober and heavy-handed Scarlatti in a first movement which maintains a uniform rush of rapid motion; and Mozart has left a fine example of the kind in the first movement of his F major Violin Sonata (K.377).

The main classical sense of the term indicates a work for not more than two instruments, containing at least two and in the complete scheme four well-contrasted movements, of which the first and last are on the same tonic, and the others in demonstrably related keys (*see* HARMONY, sec. v); the forms being those dealt with in the following article.

SONATA FORMS

SONATA FORMS cover the whole ground of instrumental music from C. P. E. Bach to the advent of Schumann's pianoforte lyrics and Liszt's symphonic poems, and are still living forms. Their rise made Gluck's reform of opera possible; for they represent a general change in the language of music which made it a truly dramatic medium. They comprise the largest and most central problems of pure music; and the outward forms must be studied in constant connexion with instrumentation, harmony, melody, counterpoint, and rhythm (qq.v.).

Elements of Form.—Two types of form are externally common to the true dramatic sonata style and the earlier melodic forms used in the suite (q.v.). The terms 'binary' and 'ternary' have been chosen for these; and, as we shall see, badly chosen. A binary melody falls into two portions, of which the first ends away from tonic, and the second ends on the tonic. *Barbara Allen*, quoted in the article MELODY, is an exquisite example on the smallest possible scale. A ternary melody, such as 'The Bluebell of Scotland', has a complete first clause, a second clause not as complete, and a third clause consisting of the first over again; a form conveniently symbolized as ABA.

No view of music can be correct that neglects the fact that it moves in time; though a composer may develop Mozart's capacity for seeing music spatially, i.e. like a picture, all at once. Now, when do we know that a melody is going to be 'ternary'? Obviously when its first clause has shown itself to be complete. If the sequel refuses to divide itself according to a 'ternary' rule, the ear is not going to reverse its judgements merely because we have chosen a bad term of classification. After the first clause, anything may happen. The rest of the tune may be no longer than the first clause. All that we can expect of it is that it will cover a wider ground than the first clause, even if in fewer notes or in less time. But this is not all. Every tune of several clauses lends itself to repeating its sections. Binary tunes repeat their two sections. Does a ternary tune repeat its three sections? Try the experiment on the very typical ternary theme of the variations in Beethoven's 'Kreutzer' Sonata. Play the first clause with its repeat and try repeating the second clause before returning to the first. You will hardly have the patience to finish the experiment. It will at once reveal that under the test of repeats our 'ternary' melody is not ABA, but A, BA.

Thus, while both these forms divide only into two repeatable portions, the one named 'binary' has an incomplete first part

Ex.1

Andante   BEETHOVEN, 'Kreutzer' Sonata

while the first part of the other is complete. Our pundits would make musical terminology less misleading if they would kindly find Greek or Latin names, not longer than the forms themselves, that should express 'form-with-an-incomplete-first-part' on the one hand, and 'form-with-a-complete-first-part' on the other. Clearly the distinction is that between higher organizations and lower, or sectional, forms. From the so-called binary form originates the sonata form *par excellence*, that of the first movement of a sonata. From the so-called ternary form originate all those sectional forms of music that begin with a complete symmetrical melody, however many sections the form may eventually develop. Thus the 'ternary' type underlies the rondo (q.v.).

The Sonata Style.—Sonata form represents a style that is evident in every bar from the outset, however its themes may be distributed. We are told that the binary form of a dance-movement in a suite has a polyphonic texture and a single theme; and that Philipp Emanuel Bach created the true sonata form by inventing the 'second subject'. Good teachers make sure that their pupils understand that the 'subject' of a sonata is not a single theme, like the subject of a fugue; but in spite of all precautions a host of bad musical forms and crooked musical doctrines have grown up from the provincial fact that English musicians have fastened on the terms 'first subject' and 'second subject' instead of translating the excellent German terms *Hauptsatz* (principal member) and *Seitensatz* (subordinate member).

Some of Sebastian Bach's most typical gigues have at least two distinct themes, while more than one of Haydn's ripest sonata movements derive everything from their first themes. Accordingly we may illustrate the true distinction of style by examples which refute superficial doctrines.

The two following examples are almost exactly the same length, yet Haydn is beyond Bach's scope in the first eight bars. If Bach could have accepted so trite a theme as Haydn's, he would have postulated that it did not end with a bump: and bars 5-8 would have horrified him, for he would have supposed that a movement that began so vulgarly was condemned to continue in the same style. Bar 8, however, enters on matters that Bach had never known. In it the first bar of a new period overlaps with the last bar of the old; and therewith we are plunged into a polyphony quite lively enough for Bach, and quite unpredictable in rhythm and key, its fourth bar overlapping with the answer in A minor, and the viola and violoncello entering in F major at intervals of two bars. Then, arising from bar 18, there are four bars on the dominant of F, with that merely jingling figure (c). We need not set limits to Bach's intelligence, and we may suppose that such a composition would have convinced him that here was no trivial *divertissement*, as he called the non-polyphonic sonatas that were becoming fashionable in 1745, but a new art with enormous possibilities.

Bars 23-26 transform the two notes of (a) into rich sustained harmonies. Then figure (b) bursts out in a new type of phrase, built up in three-bar periods, which the ear need not trouble to recognize as such in the general bustle. The third of these periods abandons the figure and makes a melodious close into five bars of cadence on figure (b) with upper notes that merge into (c), nicely phrased. It is idle to say that all this has more than one theme, and worse than idle to deny that Bach's gigue has at least two distinct themes. But Bach's relatively uniform texture will tolerate neither interruption nor irregularity of rhythm.

Haydn's exposition groups itself clearly into bars 1-8, the first group (*Hauptsatz*), asserting the tonic and overlapping with bars 8-22, which effect the transition (plus the sustained chords 23-26) to the second group (*Seitensatz*) in F major, bars 27-40, with its cadence-phrase (*Schlussgruppe*) in bars 36-40. These sections could not be more distinct with any number of themes.

There are no rules whatever for the number or distribution of themes in sonata form. When critics tell us that Mendelssohn is weak 'in second subjects, where the human element is required', they disqualify themselves by a terminology as useless as that of the friend who did not see where the painter was going

Ex.2 Bach. Gigue from 3rd Suite for Violoncello

Ex.3 Exposition in sonata style

Finale
Presto

HAYDN. *String Quartet*, Op.42

to put his brown tree. Any generalized criticism of sonata themes
is bound to be nonsense; for themes stand in endless variety of
relation to the whole. They are details, which give pleasure in
themselves as well as in their relation to the scheme. But it is
foolish and vexatious to lay down rules as to what pleasure the
details shall give. If you examine frescoes with a microscope or
miniatures with a telescope you will not enjoy them; and if you
expect Beethoven's 'Harp' Quartet to show you the purport of
its first movement in its themes you might as well try to study
foreign poetry through a traveller's phrase-book.

So much, then, for the vital element of drama in the sonata
Historically it originates wholly with Haydn and Mozart; and
Philipp Emanuel Bach contributed to it nothing but a romantic
rhetoric. His chief pride was in his invention of *Sonaten mit
veränderten Reprisen*; that is to say sonatas in which the repeats
were written out in full in order to control the fashion of altering
and amplifying the ornaments on repetition. Now, could anything more clearly betray a non-dramatic style? The survival of
repeats in the most dramatic works of Beethoven and Brahms
shows how powerfully an architectural symmetry can dominate

a series of emotional tensions: but imagination boggles at the thought of using these repeats to display a new set of ornaments.

Haydn saw that the only place for C. P. E. Bach's device was in purely lyric slow movements. Even there he never had the patience to plod and pose (as C. P. E. Bach did to the bitter end) through a repetition of both parts. When his second part comes to recapitulate the second group it combines both versions. This form appears for the last time in history in one of Haydn's 'London' Symphonies, in the wonderful movement of which the theme is quoted in RHYTHM, Ex. 1. Though 'binary', it is manifestly lyric, and could no more be applied to active movements than the Spenserian stanza could be applied to drama.

A more important step toward the true sonata style was made by Philipp Emanuel's less romantic brother, Johann Christian, who settled in London, founded the Bach and Abel Concerts, and had a great influence on the boy Mozart. J. C. Bach is the first composer to lay a dramatic emphasis on the transition between his first and his second group. In crude or deliberately formal examples this has been wittily described as 'presenting arms' to the new key. Its point is not that there is any difficulty in apprehending the new key, but that the move into it is dramatic and not decorative. Whether the move be made with intellectual music or with common forms makes no difference. Beethoven preferred, in his most characteristic early works, to disguise it cleverly. In later works he acquired the grand formal breadth of Mozart's chamber music in this transition.

First-movement Form.—The general scheme of the first-movement form or, *par excellence*, sonata form is as follows. There is a first group in the tonic, followed by a transition to another key, where there is a second group that usually ends with a neat little cadence-theme. These groups constitute the exposition, which may be repeated. Then follows the development, the function of which is to put the previous materials into new lights, regrouping the figures into new types of phrase, modulating freely, and settling, if at all, only in new keys. Eventually a return is made to the tonic, and so to the recapitulation. This recapitulates the exposition, but it gives the second group in the Ionic, and so completes the design. The development and recapitulation may be repeated; a coda may follow the recapitulation.

This account has required so many words that the illusion is apt to arise that it conveys more information than, say, the statement that the plan of a cathedral is cruciform, and that the arms of the cross are called transepts, and so on. It gives us no means of distinguishing an ambling decorative movement by

Boccherini from the first movement of a Beethoven symphony; and the description of the development is the only point which would rule out the sequel of our second example as a specimen of sonata form. Haydn, Mozart, and Beethoven differ widely in their handling of every part of the scheme.

The most regular form is to be found in Mozart, whose transitions are always broad and smooth. The effect of 'presenting arms' is evident only in small or perfunctory works; and if it is found at all in larger works it is on such a scale and with such a purpose as Beethoven would give it. The second group contains at least one definite new theme and a number of cadence-phrases in various rhythms. The development is short, consisting of one broad sequential process that leads through a wide range of keys back to the tonic. Sometimes it contains an entirely new theme. Such an episode, which is generally placed at the beginning, by no means always indicates a lighter style and texture. It may be a relief from unusually concentrated figure-work in the exposition; and the developments of two of Mozart's most serious works (the C minor Serenade for eight wind instruments, better known as a string quintet, and the G minor Pianoforte Quartet) are episodic. The return to the tonic always has the effect of being accurately timed after a delightful period of anticipation.

The recapitulation is full and has a deceptive appearance of regularity. In reality it is anything but mechanical. It has just that kind of difference by which stereoscopic pictures produce the effect of binocular vision. In the light of the recapitulation the listener finds that those points which were superficial in the exposition have now become solid. The composer instinctively conceives his exposition in relation to the question 'How will this sound when it returns?' The minimum change happens automatically with the transition to the second group, for this transition must no longer lead to the complementary key of the exposition. One quaint primitive device in the transition is that of making it not leave the tonic at all but simply come to a pause *on* (but not *in*) the dominant. This dominant is then taken literally as a key. In such a case the recapitulation need alter nothing; the second group merely follows in the tonic instead of in the dominant. Even this automatic device makes the recapitulation give a more solid impression than the exposition; for the pause on the dominant, treated paradoxically in the exposition, is now treated rationally.

We need not deny that formal devices are apt to become mechanical; but we have no right to the *a priori* opinion that Mozart is writing unimaginatively every time that he decides that the most familiar course is the wittiest. It is much wiser to

regard the most exact recapitulation as the extreme case of delicate balance, and even in the most exact the crucial detail will
appear. Here is a case in a difference of a single bar; Mozart's
String Quartet in E flat (K.428) has the following clause in the
first theme:

Ex.4

In the recapitulation you have this:

Ex.5

The little comment of the second violin is expanded and made
to turn the following 'added sixth' chord into a momentarily
solid supertonic key. Similar points make the recapitulation of
the second group also stand out in higher relief. Most interesting
of all are the ways in which Mozart in a minor movement trans-
lates the second group from the major into the minor mode. It
is worth while trying the experiment of literal translation (not
always an easy task) and then seeing what Mozart has done in
such cases. For codas Mozart either finds a slight expansion in
the recapitulation of his second group adequate, or else he adds
a neat final paragraph. If the development contained an episode
Mozart's coda may allude to it. In the finale of the so-called

'Jupiter' Symphony he uses the coda for his quintuple counter-point on all the five themes of the movement. (*See* COUNTER-POINT.)

Haydn's practice in his later works differs from Mozart's in almost every particular. His second group often contains no new theme until the cadence-group at the end; his development is long and divisible into several stages, often including an illusory early return to the main theme in the tonic followed by a new excursion into remote regions; and as to recapitulation, the term is seldom applicable at all. The first theme, indeed, returns, but it is followed by a brilliant peroration full of new developments and giving the repose of recapitulation only in the fact that it remains firmly in the tonic. If after such a peroration Haydn chooses to end quietly and abruptly with his cadence-theme, the effect is witty. But it does not make him a formalist. He is a master not only of form but of spaciousness in the smallest pos-sible compass. One main theme for both groups gives him more room for expansion than two; and instead of saying that his recapitulations are free we ought to say that he invented the most brilliant type of Beethoven's coda. And these features of his form are not, as has sometimes been alleged, primitive. They are only partially visible in quartets before op. 50. Then they appear in full vigour, and Haydn's admiration for Mozart only confirms him in his independence.

Mozart's more symmetrical form is a function of two things, a more polyphonic style and a larger scale. We may sum up the relation between Mozart's form and Haydn's thus: that in Haydn we are aware of an expansive freedom which proves, on scrutiny, to have an all-pervading sense of proportion; while in Mozart we are aware of beautiful and symmetrical proportions which prove on scrutiny to be handled with an all-pervading freedom.

Beethoven combined the forms of Haydn and Mozart, writing on a scale large enough to contain Mozart's regular recapitula-tions together with Haydn's free perorations, and developing a tragic power all his own. Such new power was not to be obtained without a new technique. A passage from Haydn and one from Beethoven may be chosen to show how Beethoven set to work. In the first movement of Haydn's A major Quartet (op. 20, no. 6) the second group has been duly ushered in by a highly-organized transition passage and has already started a new theme. This, however, comes to a pause on the dominant, and then we have the following modulating themes—Ex. 6.

Ex.6   HAYDN. *String Quartet*, op. 20, No.2

The harmonic colour of these keys is delightful, and their mutual relations are of direct importance. The passage is improvisatorial and ruminating. Its modulations are within the local range of its start in E minor, and its windings only confirm the drift towards E major. Without them the passage would lose its freedom: with wider modulations it would lose coherence.

Now take the opening of the second group in the first movement of Beethoven's Sonata, op. 2, no. 2. Here is its skeleton outline:

Ex.7

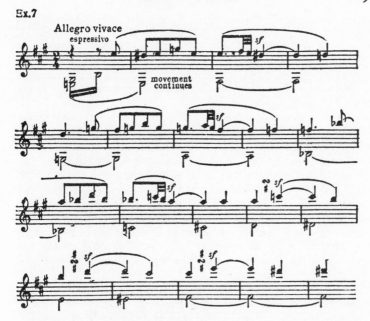

To analyse the enharmonic modulations and keys of this
passage is, in Kingsley's admirable parable, like making an
exhaustive chemical analysis of a plum-pudding and omitting
to ascertain that the cook had boiled it in a cloth. The gist of
the matter is the steadily rising bass, with its accelerated later
steps, and the profound psychology of its pause for eight bars
(after the quotation) before plunging into the final cadential
steps G♯, A, and B, in widely different octaves. This is one of
the epoch-making passages in musical history. Its importance
does not lie in its wonderful enharmonic modulations. These
could not in themselves have achieved more than had been
already achieved by C. P. E. Bach: for without the rising bass
their purpose would be merely to astonish and not to construct.
But with the rising bass and similar resources the whole art of
tonality expands. This soon enabled Beethoven to choose
remoter keys for his second group. (*See* HARMONY, sec. v.)

Ex. 8 gives the outline of the first movement of Beethoven's
'Eroica' Symphony. Blank bars indicate the continuance of a
harmony. They are often without theme, and are the lungs of
the organism. Quaver-bars or other rhythmic indications above
the line indicate the prevalent movement in accessory parts,
whether contrapuntal or homophonic. Fine detail is not indicated, and short passages marked as repeated may be assumed to
be rescored often beyond recognition. The outline, however,

gives a comprehensive summary of the structure of this highly significant movement, and by means of it the reader will be enabled to apprehend, almost at a glance, the inexhaustible expansive and contractile power of Beethoven's phrase-rhythm. Nine conductors out of ten overlook the first theme of the second group entirely, but it is the one constant element in all Beethoven's dozens of sketches.

Freedom in a recognizable recapitulation can go no further than the marvellous modulations with which Beethoven transforms the first group; and anybody inclined to cavil at the exact recapitulation of no less than one hundred bars comprising the transition and second group may be surprised to learn that this is, by the clock, precisely the same length as Isolde's *Liebestod* (*see* RHYTHM), and that in the *Liebestod* Wagner exactly recapitulates, without transposition, the last movement of the love-duet in a previous act. Recapitulation is as inveterate in musical form as symmetry is in architecture; and nobody understood this better than the first and most uncompromising realist in the application of music to drama.

Other Movements.—A thorough understanding of the style and methods of first movements makes all the rest easy. As to slow movements, the first thing that must be realized is that if a theme conceived in an average quick tempo be played four times as slow it will take four times as long. Some composers, and even some teachers, do not seem to have learnt this remarkable fact. In the music of a master slowness means bigness. The first sixteen bars of the slow movement of Beethoven's D minor Sonata (op. 31, no. 2) look like, and are, a single binary sentence closing into the seventeenth bar. But the all-seeing eye that takes this in at a glance may miss the important fact that that binary sentence takes a whole minute by the clock. 'Quavers at 96' is a very good metronome-tempo for this movement, and it gives exactly 16 of those bars to a minute. The metronome at 72 to a bar gives a good, moderate tempo for the finale. Now, see how far one minute takes us in the finale. The simple binary first sentence of the adagio takes as long as the two closely-printed pages from the beginning of the finale to the middle of its cadence-theme! Thus in the slow movement of Beethoven's Fourth Symphony (another case of sixteen bars to the minute) the fifteen bars beginning in E flat minor and dwelling in G flat (bars 50–64) are a very spacious development; and so are the seven bars in the middle of the slow movement of the Trio in D major, op. 70, no. 1. Such passages are ample developments if they modulate widely and contain important changes of rhythm, instead of merely dwelling on the dominant before the return of the main theme, as in the slow movement of the D minor Sonata.

Ex.8

BEETHOVEN,
'Eroica' Symphony, 1st Movement

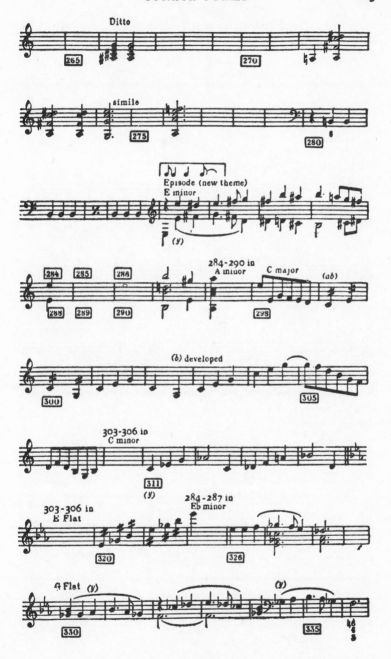

continued for 28 bars 340

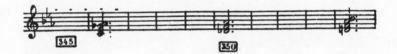

345   350

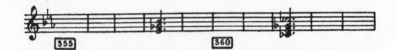

355   360

no movement

365   370

(b)

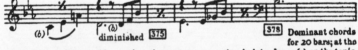

(b)   (b)
       diminished 375   378 Dominant chords
                                            for 20 bars; at the
17th of which the horn, unable to endure the suspense, prematurely introduces (a) on the tonic

RECAPITULATION
First Group
Bars 3-7 -   C♯ = D♭
                                        till   F major

398   400   7   405

(ab)

5   410
4   ♭3
                                    (b)   gva

D♭, the swing of the pendulum

415   420

Transition theme on dominant of Eb, followed by whole 2nd group; in all a transposition of 45-148. Details are changed at bars 127-134, but the framework is untouched.

(c) as in bars 332 foll: but without superstructure

* The allusion is probably intentional as Beethoven had great difficulty with those introductory bars At all events he found that their proper shape was that of final bars.

No wonder that in any movement slower than andante the full sonata form is unusual and of gigantic effect. The full-sized rondo-form (*see* RONDO), as in the case of the Fourth Symphony just mentioned, is still more voluminous in a slow tempo. Movements of more normal size may be in A, B, A form, or sonata form without development (Mozart's favourite form); or may consist of a theme with five or six variations and a short coda. Haydn's form of variations on two alternating major and minor themes is sometimes used by him in slow movements, and sometimes (in small works) as the first movement or as finale. (*See* VARIATIONS.)

The finale is often in first-movement form, but will, in such cases, have a much simpler texture. The last part of a work that moves in time will always relieve the strain on the attention. Hence the large number and importance of rondo-finales; and hence the paradox that both Haydn and Beethoven found the fugue an excellent form for a finale. For the fugue, while continually stimulating and exercising the mind by means of details, makes no claim on the listener's memory over long stretches in a major composition.

The first movement, slow movement, and finale have thus an unlimited dramatic scope. A purely lyric or dance movement added to such a scheme would in itself be dramatic by contrast, as a song may be a dramatic element in a play. This justifies the dance-form of the Mozart–Haydn minuet and trio, of which Beethoven accentuated the dance-character when he expanded it to the scherzo (q.v.). Haydn's very earliest minuets show an inveterate irregularity of rhythm which stamps them even sooner than his other movements as dramatic. Mozart's minuets are smoother, but he can pack operas into them without bursting the bounds of melodic form. The minuet of his E flat Quartet (K.428), for example, has five distinctly expressed themes; and its trio, which in contrast has only one theme, moves, however, in four distinct new keys.

The Sonata as a Whole.—The full scheme of a sonata consists, then, of these four movements, the minuet or scherzo being either second or third. Two movements, suitably contrasted, will make a sonata, even if (as in Beethoven's op. 54) neither of them is in full first-movement form. But it is exceptional for a mature work to claim the title of sonata on merely lyric forms. And in the case of quartets, the feeling of the classical masters is that when so many as four players are assembled it is a waste of opportunity to give them less than a four-movement work to play.

Why do the classical sonatas maintain this scheme of self-centred movements with no community of theme? The answer to this lies in the relation between their time-scale and their emotional content. In its early forms the sonata is a new kind of suite, complete in its contrasts. In its later developments the individual movements, while complete as designs, raise emotional issues which each movement is unable to satisfy without the others. The first movement of Beethoven's not inaptly named *Appassionata* Sonata (op. 57) whirls us through an immense tragedy in eight minutes. The movement is irrevocably completed; but our emotional reactions have not more than begun. We need the unutterable calm of the slow movement with its theme rooted to its tonic chord, and its simple and solemn variations in the ancient form of *doubles*. A foreign chord replaces that of its cadence; the vision is broken and the finale rushes headlong to the end of a tragic fate. The whole emotional scheme is perfect; but for one movement to take up the themes of another would be to tell a twice-told tale. Hence the classics, including Brahms, are not only cautious but cryptic in the few cases where they allow one movement to allude to another. The only occasion for clearness in such allusions is with introductions, which may well foreshadow the following movement, and, in the case of introductions to finales, may dramatically recall the past.

The emotional unity of the sonata is already significant in Mozart and Haydn. Their artistic hypotheses are those of comedy; and even so tragic a note as the last page of Haydn's F sharp minor Quartet (op. 50, no. 4) can be sounded only in the severe form of fugue. One of the most significant gestures in all the history of music is that of the introduction to the finale of Mozart's G minor Quintet. The slow movement is one of the profoundest things possible before Beethoven. One is inclined to resent the notion that such music can have limitations. Being perfect it is infinite, and you cannot compare infinities. But you can be clear as to their elements; and the terms of its art forbid this pathetic music to handle tragic action. For tragedy, music needs such resources as are shown in Ex. 7, and these would shatter Mozart's aesthetic system. But after that slow movement even the finale of Mozart's own G minor Symphony would sound peevish. So Mozart writes a solemn slow introduction which bids the art of music run away and play, for the rest is too sad for it. And so the bright rondo-finale is another story. Mozart would neither violate his aesthetic system nor anticipate Mendelssohn's naïve way of striking a religious note with a complete unconsciousness of its blasphemy.

The Sonata Since Beethoven.—The sonata style belongs to the sonata time-scale and to the classical key-system. Music in the Wagnerian time-scale, or in 'atonal' or other new harmonic systems, has no more to do with it than Greek prose. Nor do changes in the general outlines of the form mean much in themselves. The classical forms are, even externally, far more varied than those of later sonata works; and the essentials of the sonata lie much deeper.

Schubert achieved wonderful things in his sonata works, but died before he had perfected his forms. His expositions digress into developments, his developments subside into long twice-repeated lyric episodes, and his recapitulations reveal that re-capitulating is the very thing his expositions are not designed to bear. Nevertheless Schubert was on the high road towards genuine new forms.

What these forms were to be was best revealed by Brahms. It is fashionable to deny that Brahms invented new forms; and this is like Humpty-Dumpty's complaint that Alice's features were arranged so exactly like other people's that he could not be expected to recognize her. Forms must be studied in detail from phrase to phrase, and classified afterwards: not classified by guesswork and warped to fit the guess. Brahms has many new ways of phrasing and of developing themes (*see* MELODY, Ex. 11); and no two of his forms are alike. Least of all composers does he resemble Schumann, whom he was at first accused of imitating.

Schumann's sonata works show an interesting artificial system. His ideas were lyric and epigrammatic; and they shaped themselves squarely and with a Macaulayesque habit of antithesis. With this style he contrived to build important sonata works as one might construct a landscape in mosaic. He knew what he was doing, and the result is often delightful. In his D minor Symphony he achieved a new continuity of form and theme, retaining the classical group of four main movements, but running them together without break and using transformations of the same themes in all four. Schumann's hard outlines and square rhythms have been copied without his wit in countless later sonata works, especially by those Russian composers who, led by Nicolas Rubinstein, danced upon his grave in derision of these very features.

Mendelssohn handled all sonata forms with an often dangerous facility, but sometimes with genius. The opening of his D minor Trio is the prototype of those innumerable allegros which are really andantes riding an ambling horse or running up a descending escalator.

The masterly scheme (there is only one) of Spohr is (as Schumann remarked) not so easy to imitate as it looks; but it is the prototype of most pseudo-classical works up to the present day; and many teachers believe it to be the only orthodox form. Against such teaching young artists do well to revolt, but why call it classical?

The quality most conspicuously absent in sonata work since Brahms is movement. The fundamental mistake of Bruckner was in associating his Wagnerian style with sonata forms at all. Sibelius solves Bruckner's problem, and takes and leaves the sonata style as he pleases, and always with clear purpose, whether convincingly or not. Reger's meticulously regular forms are hard to accept as the really proper vessel for his strong chromatic brew; and as for imitating him, one might as well try to write a Meredith novel from one metaphor to the next. The art of movement is the crux of the sonata problem; and the classical solutions of it from Haydn to Brahms are the greatest things in pure music.

SUITE (*Suite de pièces, Ordre, Partita*), a group of dance tunes in melodic forms (*see* SONATA FORMS). It consists essentially of four principal movements with the insertion of one or more lighter movements between the third and the last.

The first movement is the *allemande*, in slow common time and rich flowing rhythm, beginning with one or three short notes before the first full bar.

The second movement is the *courante*, of which there are two kinds. The French *courante* begins with one or three notes before the main beat, and is in a triple time ($\frac{3}{2}$) which, invariably at the cadences and sometimes elsewhere, drops into a crossing triple rhythm of twice the pace ($\frac{6}{4}$). In homage to Couperin, Bach often uses the French *courante*, but he is happier with the Italian type of *corrente*, a brilliant continuously running piece in quick triple time ($\frac{3}{4}$ or $\frac{3}{8}$).

The *sarabande* is a slow movement in triple time beginning on the full bar, and with at least a tendency to the rhythm

of which Handel's aria *Lascia ch'io pianga* is a familiar example. Bach's *sarabandes* are among the most simply eloquent and characteristic of his smaller compositions.

Then come the *galanteries*, from one to three in number. These are the only suite-movements (except some of Couperin's *courantes*) which can have an alternative section and a da capo. The commonest *galanteries* are: (1) the *minuet*, often with a second minuet, which is called 'trio' only when it is in real three-part writing; it is a little faster than the stately minuet in Mozart's *Don Giovanni*, and it always begins on the full bar. (2) The *gavotte*, a lively dance in a not too rapid alla breve time; the gavotte always begins on the half-bar. A second alternating gavotte is frequently founded on a pedal or drone-bass, and is then called *musette*. (3) The *bourrée*, which is not unlike the gavotte, but quicker and beginning on the last quarter of the bar. (4) The *passepied*, a lively dance in quick triple time, beginning on the third beat. These dances are not always cast in binary form, and there are famous examples of gavottes and passepieds *en rondeau*. Other less common *galanteries* are: (5) the *loure*, a slow dance in $\frac{6}{4}$ time and dotted rhythm; (6) the *polonaise*, a leisurely triple-time piece, with cadences on the second instead of (as in later polonaises) the third beat of the bar; (7) the *air*, a short movement, quietly flowing, in a more florid style than its name would suggest. It sometimes precedes the sarabande.

The suite concludes with a *gigue*, in the finest examples of which the melodic binary form is combined with a light fugue style. The gigue is generally in some triplet rhythm, e.g. $\frac{3}{8}$, $\frac{6}{8}$, $\frac{9}{8}$, $\frac{12}{8}$; but examples in a graver style may be found in slow square time with dotted rhythms, as in Bach's first French Suite and the sixth Partita of the *Clavierübung*. In Couperin's first volume of *Ordres*, the *gigue* is followed by an enormous number of pieces which cannot have been intended to be all played on the same occasion, though they were all in the same key.

Examples illustrating the Suite:

For another type of Gigue see 'Sonata Forms', Ex. 2, and for a Gavotte see 'Roudo,' Ex. 1.

Suites on a large scale begin with a prelude in some larger form. Bach's French Suites have no preludes; his English Suites all have a great first movement which, except in the first suite, is in full da capo concerto form. His Partitas cover a wider range both in their preludes and their other contents. Some large suites have finales after the gigue, the great Chaconne for violin solo being the finale of a partita (*see* VARIATIONS).

The later uses of the word 'suite' comprise almost all sets of pieces mainly in forms smaller than those of the sonata, especially such pieces as have been selected from ballets or from incidental music to plays.

SYMPHONIC POEM

SYMPHONIC POEM (*Symphonische Dichtung, Tondichtung, Poème symphonique*, &c.), as a term, was first used by Liszt in his twelve *Symphonische Dichtungen*. It implies a large orchestral composition which, whatever its length and changes of tempo, is not broken up into separate movements, and which, moreover, gratuitously illustrates a train of thought external to the music and to its conditions of performance. The form of the symphonic poem is dictated by its written or unwritten programme; and so it is not every piece of 'programme music' that can be called a symphonic poem. Beethoven's Sonata *Les Adieux* and his 'Pastoral' Symphony are, for instance, works in which the poetic idea does not interfere with the normal development of sonata style.

Great disturbances in musical art have always been accompanied by appeals to external ideas. New art-forms are not born mature, and in their infancy their parent arts naturally invite other arts to stand godfather. It is certain, first, that no theorizing can long prevent musical ideas from growing where and how they please; secondly, that musical ideas are just as likely to be inspired by literature and other arts as by any other kind of experience; and lastly, that, as musicians gain in mastery, their music outstrips their literary analysis. Hence the frequent ability of great composers to set inferior words to music which is not only great, but evidently based upon those words. Hence the disgust of great composers at unauthorized literary interpretations of their works. Hence, on the other hand, the absence of any strain on the classical composer's conscience as to making his music gratuitously illustrative. Accordingly, the importance of the symphonic poem lies, not in its illustrative capacity, but in its tendency towards a new instrumental art of tomorrow.

The symphonic poem has been described elsewhere (*see* MUSIC, ix, and PROGRAMME MUSIC) as the application of the Wagnerian time-scale to symphonic music. Liszt is successful only where he is writing on a hardly more than lyric scale, as in *Orpheus*, or, at the utmost, on a scale less than that of the earliest and best of all symphonic poems, Schubert's *Wanderer Fantasia* (op. 15). Schubert had not the slightest idea that he was writing a symphonic poem; but in that piece he achieved everything that Liszt attempted, even to the metamorphosis of whole sections. Listz's efforts on a larger time-scale do not even begin to solve the problem; they achieve no sense of movement at all, and the device of deriving all their themes from a single figure

236

is totally irrelevant. Saint-Saëns and César Franck are incapable of such failure, and their symphonic poems flow very convincingly, though not on a very large scale. They also illustrate their subjects amusingly enough. The first achievement of real Wagnerian symphonic art belongs to Richard Strauss. The power of composition in his *Also sprach Zarathustra*, *Ein Heldenleben*, the ostentatiously but deceptively patchy *Don Quixote*, and the *Symphonia Domestica* will carry conviction long after we have forgotten all about their programmes.

SYMPHONY

SYMPHONY. The term συμφωνία was used by the Greeks, first, to denote concord in general, whether in successive or simultaneous sounds; secondly, in the special sense of concordant pairs of successive sounds (i.e., the 'perfect' interval of modern music; the fourth, fifth, and octave); and thirdly, as dealing with ἀντίφωνον, the concord of the octave, thus meaning the art of singing in octaves, or magadizing, as opposed to ὁμοφωνία, or singing and playing in unison. In Roman times the word appears in the general sense, which still survives in poetry, viz., as a harmonious concourse of voices and instruments. It also appears to mean a concert. In St. Luke xv. 25, it is distinguished from χόροι and translated as signifying 'musick and dancing'. Polybius and others seem to use it as the name of a musical instrument.

In the seventeenth century the term is used, like 'concerto', for certain vocal compositions accompanied by instruments, e.g., the *Symphoniae sacrae* of Schütz. The modern use of the word symphony for the instrumental ritornello of a song is also found in Schütz's *Kleine geistliche Concerte*.

The principal modern meaning of the word is a sonata for orchestra (*see* SONATA FORMS). The orchestral symphony originated in the operatic overture (q.v.), which in the middle of the eighteenth century began to assimilate the essentials of the sonata, style. Mozart's overture to his early opera, *La Finta Giardiniera*, marks the breaking-point between three-movement symphony and operatic overture, since it contains the usual first movement and slow movement, and the curtain rises with what sounds like the beginning of its third movement.

Though the sonata style is dramatic, the stiffness of its early forms did not help Gluck towards his ideal of an overture that should prepare the listener for the drama. Hence the overtures of Gluck are based on the contrast of loosely knit passages of various textures in vague forms which he learned from San Martini. These are no less evident in the symphonies of Philipp Emanuel Bach.

The differentiation between symphony and overture raised the dignity of the symphony; but the style was more essential than the form; and in Mozart's and Haydn's mature works we find the sonata form as firmly established in the overture as in the symphony, while the styles are quite distinct. Mozart's most elaborate overture, that of *Die Zauberflöte*, could not possibly be the first movement of one of his later symphonies; nor could the finale of his 'Jupiter' Symphony be taken for a prelude to an opera.

See also MUSIC, SONATA FORMS, INSTRUMENTATION, OVERTURE, SCHERZO, VARIATIONS.

VARIATIONS

VARIATIONS, the term given in music to groups of progressively developed versions of a complete self-contained theme, retaining the form of that theme though not necessarily its melody. This is the classical sense of the term, but there are modern developments of the variation form to which this definition is at once too broad and too precise to apply. The aesthetic principle of variations appeared at very early stages of music. During the sixteenth century an artistically mature variation-form automatically rose in the polyphonic treatment of Gregorian hymns verse by verse. Accordingly, the hymns and Magnificats of Palestrina might be described as contrapuntal sets of variations on ecclesiastical tunes, like rich and free examples on the simple plan shown later by Haydn's variations on his Austrian national anthem in the 'Emperor' Quartet (op. 76, no. 3). Already in the sixteenth century instrumental music was climbing up the trellis of a primitive variation-form. A favourite plan (*see* the *Fitzwilliam Virginal Book, passim*) was to put together several popular or original tunes, with an ornamental variation sandwiched between. Sometimes sets of variations on a single tune were produced, with excellent effect, as in Byrd's variations on 'The Carman's Whistle'. Such variations were naturally grouped in order of increasing brilliance, and they often include passages that would catch the greatest pianoforte players.

In the seventeenth century a highly artistic form of variation solved with great simplicity the problem of expanding instrumental pieces to a length admitting of growth to a big climax. This was the ground bass, a single phrase placed in the bass and repeating itself *ad infinitum*. It originated in the dance forms of the passacaglia and the chaconne. Both were in slow triple time, the chaconne having a strong accent on the second beat, while the passacaglia, by some chance, developed the liberty to transfer its theme to other parts than the bass. The genius of Purcell was cruelly hampered by the non-existence of large musical forms in his time, and he seized upon the ground bass with avidity. By the time of Bach and Handel lighter sets of variations, consisting essentially of embroidery on a melody, had come into vogue. Bach's *Aria variata alla maniera Italiana* tells us where this fashion began; and in France the *air et doubles* was taken over from early English virginal music. *Doubles* are variations each of which divides the rhythm into quicker notes than the one before. The most familiar example is that known as 'The Harmonious Blacksmith' in Handel's E major Suite. Some-

times the air itself was stated in a tangle of ornamentation, while
the *doubles* simplified the melody and varied the accompaniment. But Bach had meanwhile applied the principle of the
ground-bass to variations on a complete symmetrical movement
in binary form. His Aria with thirty Variations, commonly
known as the 'Goldberg' Variations, is (with the exception of
Beethoven's Thirty-three *Veränderungen* on a waltz by Diabelli)
the most gigantic set of variations in the world. A melodically
interesting ground bass could not be maintained on so large a
scale; but the thirty-two bars of Bach's theme are so many clear
harmonic steps which can be represented by many analogous
progressions, without loss of identity. (Ex. 1a and 1b.) There
is no question of retaining or varying the melody of the aria,
which is a tissue of ornaments that will bear neither development
nor simplification.

Ex. 1a Harmonic Theme   BACH, 'Goldberg' Variations

Ex. 1b
Var. 25

The rise of the sonata style again brought the melodic-em-
broidery variation into prominence; for in sonata forms we identify themes entirely by their melodies. Now, with not more than
three or four exceptions, the best sets of variations by Mozart
and Haydn are movements in their sonata works; and their
independent sets are either early or perfunctory exercises and
encore-pieces. Two common mistakes of professional and amateur criticism are, first, the judging of Haydn's and Mozart's
variations by these *parerga*, and secondly, the much graver error
of despising the embroidery variation on principle. It is either
vulgar or sublime. And it is handled lovingly by precisely the
greatest masters of deep harmonic and rhythmic variation,
Beethoven and Brahms. Haydn is fond of a special form first
known in Philipp Emanuel Bach. It consists of alternating

variations on two themes, alternately major and minor; the first a rich and complete binary melody, and the other a shorter binary melody, often beginning with the same figure as the first. The first theme usually returns as if it were going to be unvaried, but its first repeat is an ornamental variation. The form is rarely worked out far enough to include more than one variation of the second theme; and sometimes (as in the famous 'Gypsy' Trio) there are new episodes instead of variations of the second theme, so that the form becomes a sectional rondo. The only strict example of Haydn's type of alternating variations in later music is the first allegretto of Beethoven's Pianoforte Trio in E flat (op. 70, no. 2); but a magnificent application of it, without change of mode, though with a wide range of key, is shown in the slow movement of his C minor Symphony.

Beethoven, in his last works, invented another variation-form on two themes, of which the second is in a different key and time. The examples of this are the slow movement of the Ninth Symphony and the Lydian figured chorale in the A minor Quartet. In the slow movement of Brahms's F major String Quintet (op. 88), the alternation of the two keys gives rise, in the last line of the movement, to one of the most astonishing dramatic strokes in all music. Beethoven uses embroidery variations as means of obtaining extraordinary repose in slow movements. The extreme case of this is the slow movement of the Sonata op. 57 (commonly called *Appassionata*), which is described in the article on SONATA FORMS. In this, and in many other instances, his method is that of the *air et doubles*, which grows to a natural climax which can subside into the rhythm of the plain theme. Until his latest works, such sets of variations are never finished. Their dramatic intent is that of a repose which is too unearthly to last; and at the first sign of dramatic motion or change of key the sublime vision 'fades into the light of common day', a light which Beethoven is far too great an idealist to despise. See the Andante of the B flat Trio (op. 97); and the slow movement of the Violin Concerto, which contains two episodic themes in the same key. In his later works Beethoven found means, by striking out into foreign keys, of organizing a coda which finally spins down in fragmentary new variations, or even returns to the plain theme. Thus he was able to end his Sonatas, opp. 109 and 111, with solemn slow movements.

Beethoven also found other applications of the variation forms. Thus the finale of the 'Eroica' Symphony has not only the theme but many other ideas in common with the brilliant set of Variations and Fugue for pianoforte on a theme from *Prometheus* (op. 35); and the Fantasia for pianoforte, chorus, and orchestra, and the choral finale of the Ninth Symphony, are sets of melo-

dic variations with freely-developed connecting links and episodes. In the case of the Ninth Symphony, a second thematic
idea eventually combines with the figures of the first theme in
double fugue.

But Beethoven's highest art in variation-form is independent
of the sonata. From his earliest display of pianoforte playing,
the wonderful twenty-four Variations on a theme by Righini, to
his supreme variation-work, the thirty-three on Diabelli's waltz,
he uses and transcends every older means of variation and adds
his own discoveries. Before Beethoven the basis of variations
might be a ground bass, a melody, or a harmonic scheme.
Beethoven discovered that rhythm and form can, with a suitable
theme, be a solid basis for variations. The aria of Bach's 'Goldberg' Variations is in its phrasing as uniform as a chess-board;
and if its harmonies had not a one-to-one correspondence with
each variation the form would be lost. But there are themes, such
as Haydn's Corale St. Antonii, which Brahms varied, where the
phrasing is interesting in itself. A similar example is the theme
by Paganini (Ex. 2a) which inspired Brahms to compose two
complete sets on it.

Ex. 2a   Formal theme by PAGANINI

Ex. 2b   Outline of Variation by Brahms

The climax in the history of variations dates from the moment when Beethoven was just about to begin his Ninth Symphony, and received from A. Diabelli a waltz which that publisher was sending round to all the musicians in Austria, so that each might contribute a variation to be published for the benefit of the sufferers in the late Napoleonic wars. Diabelli's theme was absurdly prosaic, but it happened to be, perhaps, the sturdiest piece of musical anatomy that Beethoven (or any composer since) ever saw; and in it moved Beethoven to defer his work on the Ninth Symphony! The shape of Diabelli's waltz may be illustrated by a diagram which represents its first sixteen bars; the upright strokes (not the spaces) being the bars, and the brackets and dots (together with the names underneath) indicating the rhythmic groups. The second part also consists of sixteen bars, moving

Tonic	Dominant	Rising sequence	Close in dominant

harmonically back from the dominant to the tonic, and rhythmically the same as the first part. This plan is astonishingly elastic. The alternation of tonic and dominant in the first eight bars may be represented by another familiar form in which three bars of tonic and a fourth of dominant are answered by three bars of dominant and a fourth of tonic; as in Variation 14 (which must be reckoned in half-bars). Again, when the theme answers the tonic by the dominant it raises the first melodic figure by one step, and this may be translated by the answer on the supertonic harmony. In the course of fifty minutes a few of these thirty-three variations become vague as to more than the beginnings and cadences of the theme; and there are three simple variations in which one would like to ask Beethoven whether he had not inadvertently omitted a bar; but the momentum of the theme is never lost; and after a group of three slow and rather free variations this momentum breaks into an entirely free fugue (Variation 32) on a salient feature of what must by courtesy be called Diabelli's melody. A free fugue is a favourite solution of the problem of the coda in a set of variations. The momentum produced by the revolution of true variations in the orbit of the theme gives the key to the whole problem. A fugue solves it by flying off at a tangent. Very sublime is the way in which Beethoven, after letting his fugue run its torrential course, returns to the orbit of his theme in an ethereal little minuet with a short coda of its own which, sixteen bars before the end, shows signs of beginning to revolve again.

Again, let us regard the period of the theme not as an orbit but as diurnal rotation. We can then describe the codas of

Brahms's Paganini Variations as produced by accelerating the spin till it breaks away for a while and then resumes for a few final catastrophic whirls; exactly like a dying top (though this, of course, does not accelerate its spin). Without acceleration Beethoven ended his wonderful C minor Variations (most perfect of passacaglias) in this way. Brahms found in Haydn's Corale St. Antonii the opportunity for another method. He took the first five bars as a ground-bass, within which narrow orbit the finale moves until its climax broadens out into the rest of the glorious theme, and so rounds off the whole work.

Bach poised the contrasts and climaxes of the 'Goldberg' Variations so accurately that the ending of the whole by a simple da capo of the theme is astonishingly effective. It is as if a charming old ancestress of a living line of great folk were to step from the frame of her Holbein portrait and bow to her assembled posterity.

To speak of the progress in variation-form since Beethoven is like speaking of the progress in reinforced concrete since the Parthenon. The classical variation-form is limited only by the composer's imagination and technique; and the removal of its foundations does not enlarge it at all. There is no reason to condemn other kinds of variation; and many great and beautiful works in non-classical variation-form exist, from Schumann's *Études Symphoniques* to Elgar's 'Enigma' Variations and Dohnányi's Variations on a Nursery Song. But no 'free' variation that breaks down the phrasing of its theme and follows its own discursive ways will ever achieve anything externally so unlike the theme as a strict harmonic and rhythmic variation on classical lines. (*See* Ex. 2b.) Nor will a series of such variations acquire anything like the classical momentum. On the contrary, in clumsy hands the free variation becomes apologetic in the way in which it offers raw chunks of the original melody as evidence that it has not forgotten its duty, like Lewis Carroll's poetic *Tema con Variazioni*, the preface to which is an unconscious epitome of modern misunderstandings of the form.

Variation writers may be scientifically classified into those who know their theme and those who do not. There is no reasonable doubt that many very clever composers, from Mendelssohn onwards, have completely misunderstood the nature of the deeper classical variations, and have thought that anything so unlike the original tune must be quite independent of it. Mendelssohn's *Variations sérieuses* have a beautiful theme with a structure that might have given rise to splendid features; but Mendelssohn simply ignores this structure and replaces it by weaker things in almost every variation. Schumann shows more insight. He has no great grip of his theme, but he tries to distinguish by titles those variations which are true from those which are episodic; thus in the *Études Symphoniques* the études are numbered separately from the variations; the Andante of the F major Quartet is called *quasi variazioni*; and the strictest set he ever wrote (on a theme by Clara Wieck) is called Impromptus.

Brahms stands alone in his grip of his theme. Reger is no nearer the classical form in his variations than in his other works. The present state of the form seems to indicate that if the composer does not aim at strict variations his most vital results will be on the line of melodic development, as in the above-mentioned works of Elgar and Dohnányi, the Symphonic Variations of Dvořák, and those variations of Reger which are closest to this type.

INDEX

REPRINTED LITHOGRAPHICALLY
BY JARROLD AND SONS LTD
NORWICH